A WALK WITH A WHITE BUSHMAN

A WALK
WITH A WHITE
BUSHMAN

LAURENS VAN DER POST

in conversation with

JEAN-MARC POTTIEZ

William Morrow and Company, Inc.
New York

Originally published by Chatto & Windus Ltd., England, 1986.

Library of Congress Cataloging-in-Publication Data

Van der Post, Laurens.
A walk with a white Bushman.
1. Van der Post, Laurens—Interviews, 2. Authors, South African —20th century—Interviews. 3. Africa—Description and travel—1977–   . I. Pottiez, Jean-Marc. II. Title.
PR9369.3.V33Z478   1986   808'.0092'4   87-1622
ISBN 0-688-07264-X

Printed in the United States of America

First U.S. Edition

1   2   3   4   5   6   7   8   9   10

We owe a great deal to
JANE BREWSTER
for preparing the transcriptions of
these discussions for publication
and to
INGARET GIFFARD
for a unique and characteristic
contribution

CONTENTS

Grateful acknowledgements are due to the following for their kind permission to reproduce copyright material:
Faber & Faber Ltd and Harcourt Brace Jovanovich, Inc., Orlando, Florida, for an extract from 'Little Gidding' in *Four Quartets* by T. S. Eliot; The Bodley Head Ltd, Francisco Campbell Custódio and Ad. Donker (Pty) Ltd, Johannesburg, for extracts from *Collected Poems*, Vol. I, by Roy Campbell; Routledge & Kegan Paul Ltd and Princeton University Press, Princeton, New Jersey, for an extract from *Letters*, Vol. 2, by C. G. Jung, edited by G. Adler in collaboration with Aniela Jaffé, translated by R. F. C. Hull; William Collins Sons & Co. Ltd and Pantheon Books, a Division of Random House, Inc., New York, for an extract from *Memories, Dreams, Reflections* by C. G. Jung, recorded and edited by Aniela Jaffé, translated by Richard and Clara Winston.

The spirit of man is nomad, his blood bedouin, and love is
the aboriginal tracker on the faded desert spoor of his lost self;
and so I came to live my life not by conscious plan or
prearranged design but as someone following the flight of a bird.

LAURENS VAN DER POST

A WORD AT THE BEGINNING

LAURENS VAN DER POST

A word about Jean-Marc Pottiez and the discussions recorded in this book; and perhaps it is best to start with the words themselves as they need some explanation. As they are my own, I know how inadequate they are, but to improve and correct them with hindsight and deliberation, and to the measure of the changes which inevitably have taken place in ourselves and the life of our time since Jean-Marc and I first began these conversations, would destroy a subtle, living substance which could be of special value. When Jean-Marc abandoned his original idea of making a programme for French television or radio, of which he has been such a distinguished representative in Japan and the Far East for many years, no other incentive for our talks remained except the natural desire of two friends to converse with each other whenever possible. There was no thought of publication in Jean-Marc's mind or mine, and, thanks to the genius of the Japanese for inventing significant instruments out of the small or, as it seems to me at times, the invisible, no conspicuous technological device intruded during our talks to remind us that the reason for its being there had not always been so innocent.

So the only changes made are corrections of idiom, the removal of some of the repetition which is inevitable in protracted conversation, and some amplification, where needed for clarification. The result, I believe, is therefore not only words caught on the wing of recollection startled into flight by the quick and probing interest of a friend, but also the imprint of the time which enfolded us. There is, I feel, woven into the texture of these spontaneous questions and answers, a presence of time, which out of its own character adds to all we think and do an immediacy that could be more valuable, however subtle and intangible its traces, than a solemn revision checked against any archival material. That would certainly have made our conversations more substantial but would have killed stone dead this living thing of time which reveals itself only in the spontaneous word.

Evidence of this respect for the conversations as they happened will not be hard to find, as, for instance, in matters we talked about during and immediately after the Falklands war; in the discussions of government and democracy, statesmen, politicians and their policies like those of our own Prime Minister and her opponents. All these have been left unrevised and free to run the risk of being outdated. Nor have any value judgments been altered after they were made. As far as international events are concerned, South Africa obviously intruded in a major way. There too no attempt has been made to reassess what was said some time back, in the light of what is happening now. Here, even more than in all other discussions, we were concerned with the abiding rather than either the temporal character of events or any political medication for the symptoms of the sicknesses of the world of which they are a part, and which the aberration and delusion of a slanted era would pass off as instant relief and lasting cure.

Nonetheless, there is one drawback in this approach, which I regret. Jean-Marc, who made these recordings and transcriptions so faithfully, did not do justice to himself. His contribution was crucial and far greater than it appears. Without his kind of questioning, his experience and wide-ranging interest in life and history and his sense of the future, none of these answers would have been what they are, and whether he likes it or not, and in spite of the precaution of rationing himself so severely, he is woven and interwoven in the material and just as responsible for any meaning it might possess as I am. In fact, if it had not been for him, most of these thoughts and their reference to events and people would never have been recorded, so full and exacting is the pattern of the life I am otherwise compelled to observe.

Above all, I hope that the nature of this happening between us will remove any semblance of presumption on our part. We talked freely over the years of whatever came to our minds, from insects, flowers and birds to God and man and his sorry affairs, and we may seem to have taken a lot upon ourselves in the process. If we did, it was not as persons who wanted to preach and convert and who knew all the answers. Born as we were in the great natural context of Africa, we share a feeling of intuitive commitment to life, naturally wanting to know and search for more, confident that we would be aware as much of what the words were trying to say as of the literal facts in themselves. Neither of us could ever have sat down solemnly at a desk in cold blood and written consciously with wilful concentration about some of the things we discussed. There was present always this unusual sense of freedom to express and speculate on whatever floated naturally into our minds, and this freedom, I believe, had a great deal to do with our origins and some strange synchronicities of life and experience.

Jean-Marc Pottiez was born in Africa. Africa claimed him almost before birth, nourished and held him for his first vital nine years of life as profoundly and firmly as it did me. Yet he was also indelibly of France, of the ancient Celtic Breton heart of France. So, like me, he started as it were with two hearts, a European one and an African one. After the anguish of the Second World War, translation to France and a university education in Paris, where he took a degree in philosophy, then Algeria and the misery of it, he went to Japan as I had done, settled there and married a beautiful Japanese lady who has given him a beautiful daughter. So he found, as I had done earlier, by a very different, longer and more roundabout way, that he possessed a Japanese heart as well. So there we were, two similar sorts of three-hearts individuals, destined to meet almost as if to a preconceived design, since there must be added to these singular synchronicities also the fact of the preponderance of French blood in my own line of descent.

It was not surprising that, when we met, we recognized instantly a kinship not only of temperament and ideas but, as it were, of time and space. The fact that we first met in the mountains of Switzerland in this place where seven valleys meet (where I am writing these words), seems too strangely appropriate to be misunderstood. Ever since I came back from the last war – which lasted longer for me than for most – Switzerland has played an increasingly important role in my life. It was here, while still a soldier in the British army, that almost on my first day in Zürich I met Carl Gustav Jung and a momentous friendship began for me which lasted until his death. It was here that the European part of myself rediscovered its history and, in this small but focused country where our lines of communication with our classical European beginnings in a world of city states are still intact, repaired its strained sense of continuity – something which figures in these conversations and therefore requires no elaboration. Most important of all, I found again my contact with nature among these white, time-wise old mountains, and profound valleys, with the beauty of grass, flowers and plants embroidered in the earth spread like a cloak about them; a contact which I had lost after my bonds with the bush, the veld of the gold and blue uplands, the deserts of my native continent, and the urgent sea, had been broken.

So, as soon as the charge of exploration of the last known-unknowns in my native continent had been fulfilled on behalf of an Africa that is not yet, I began to come to Switzerland at the beginning of every year to resume my writing and breathe again the air of spirit and earth that was natural to me. The effect of this regular contact has been magical, and neither habit nor repetition has staled or rendered contemptible this growth of familiarity with the scene. I seem to see this place where the seven valleys meet always as for the first time, and I know that their beauty and power to evoke will not fade but remain infinitely renewable. Only this morning I saw the head of the wild, white horn of the mountain at the end of the valley wear the dawn like a halo around it, and now at sunset it is there standing up to the night with a star on its brow. In between, the light in the valley has been like an ecumenical transubstantiation of honey and trembling with a pentecostal flicker. And immediately I and all about me felt bonded in a covenant of heaven and earth. So I could not imagine a setting which the two of us, cut off from our African selves, would have found more evocative. Here we were together for the first time and we talked almost without stop through the nights and days.

We met again and again in London in my wife Ingaret's and my home which he calls our 'space ship'. Twice I have been to Japan to see him, there were other meetings in London, and now we are once more in Switzerland. And from the beginning I was puzzled by an element in our meeting, a strange 'I have been there before' feeling which all people of sensitivity feel at least once at some inscrutable moment in their lives, which became stronger at every subsequent meeting until, despite all separation, changes of location and divergence of occasion, I felt convinced, irrational as the feeling was, that we were always meeting at the same place. Then one night by a fire in the mountains I recognized it. It was something I had experienced when I first met Jung on that cold afternoon in the autumn by the Limmat in the ancient city of Zürich, and he took me to his home and we talked far into the night. All the time it was snowing, and I knew that I was in Switzerland and experiencing something that could only happen in Switzerland, in the presence of a great person whom Switzerland and Swiss culture alone could have brought forth. Yet I had an overpowering feeling that I was also back in Africa, around a camp fire lit, as it were, by the first man to receive the gift in a star-loud, Kalahari night. Similarly with Jean-Marc: no matter where we met or where we talked, we seemed to be talking around such a fire in the vast natural world of Africa.

The significance of this for me is that, when talking around a fire in Africa, no matter how varied and strange the company grouped by it one talks the kind of talk you never talk anywhere else, except perhaps in the dark on the deck of a ship pitching in to the long blue South Atlantic rollers, with the Southern Cross standing straighter, higher and brighter over all with every thrust of the ship's bow. In these circumstances one talks about things that do not even occur to one in towns. For instance, one talks naturally about God, of God and to God; one talks about mystery and wonder and one's own experience of these things. One talks about everything in life in a way which shows there is really nothing ordinary or mean on earth but all is extraordinary, and that the discovery of the extraordinary in the ordinary is more exciting than talking of the extraordinary which since it is extraordinary in the first place suffers a certain tautological demotion in the flicker and flame of African fire-light. Moreover, one talks of these things, so sanctified with wonder, with a natural humility and awe, and in voices that are low rather than loud, and with laughter which does not shatter but harmonizes with the silences in between the sounds of the night. So, what might seem presumptuous as the printed word is in fact no presumption, because the living word used by such fire is not so much the speaker's own as something lent to him for the occasion.

I remember once coming back from a long expedition into the desert which had been full of nights of camp fires and such conversations, and the habit acquired in those long months, after the confusion and brutalization of war still had hold of my imagination. As a result, after dinner with a dear English friend in his club, I found myself talking to him about God and a controversy raging in the religious world at the time. At once he looked embarrassed and, after a while, he came as near as a spirit full of *politesse de cœur* could come to voice a protest to a friend, 'Please, Laurens, must you call Him that? Could you please not refer to Him as the Deity?' I felt rebuked, as if I had broken the unwritten rule of English clubs, that you did not discuss business in them, perhaps especially not the business of the universe.

And then there came the moment at the end of our talking, of the discovery that Jean-Marc and I held a fourth heart in common, a heart that is perhaps the greatest as it is the most enigmatic of all, the 'heart of darkness' of which Conrad writes so magisterially in that vast translucent story of his which goes under that name, and which he too had to discover in Africa. It is something which Jean-Marc and I surprisingly did not talk about although it is everywhere by implication. One of the most terrifying questions asked of me was his blunt: 'Is God's heart black?' Insofar as there is an answer accessible to words at my own disposal, it is to be found in what follows. But there could have been more, had the question been framed rather differently: 'Is God also in the heart of darkness?' And we both would have known the answer.

Jean-Marc was born within the sight and sound of the Congo, perhaps the most remorseless and awesome of the many great rivers of the world I have crossed. It was the only river, I believe, which could have led the seeker in Conrad so unerringly to the heart of darkness that is within as it is without us. I know this with some certainty because I have often seen the Congo come out of the dawn like a gulf-stream in the sea of the urgent night, its water profound with brown as if still stained with the indelible ink of the darkness of the continental heart in which it has its source. I have watched it at the end of an inexorable day of sun vanish undiminished in a cataract of gleaming black over the last fast fall of the night, and felt as uplifted as I was afraid. For this was an image one had to obey: a symbol of the moment of the truth of knowing why Conrad's story had to draw near to its end with that cry of: 'The horror! The horror!' Following the stream of life, he had come at last to the point of no return in his seeking, where he faced his own reckoning with the horror of what man in the culture of his civilizations has made of the primitive in himself and imposed on others. It is a moment of truth from which most people shy away and, as a result, imperil themselves and the life of our time.

D. H. Lawrence, for instance, rejected the Africa which carries this charge with a sea-lawyer's justification that it was 'the continent of dark negation', and promptly proceeded to find darker gods elsewhere. But we know that it is not just a heart of negation. We know it is a heart full of riches and untapped energies, that it is, in its heart of hearts, a heart also of other light. It is the aboriginal matter of God the Alchemist, the primal stuff out of which the resurgent dawn of another day of creation is made. Despite all the brutal manifestations of man in command of the black earth and all other contradictions that would end with the horror, we found ourselves at one above all else in going with the ancient Chinese, who, when the season of their great troubles after their long summer of wisdom was inevitably upon them, spoke of this heart of darkness as 'the midnight when noon is born'.

In this conclusion there is for me a private reassurance and personal confirmation that has some objective meaning. I have found increasingly as my own life rounds that my nearest neighbours no longer live next door but often far away. On my beat around the world, which is larger than most, I find more and more men and women who are not in touch with one another but nonetheless already belong to a community that is still to come and has as yet no institutions to express and serve it. They are our true neighbours, and they make the new and greater neighbour-hood inevitable. And it is as such a neighbour, in his being and doing, such a 'citizen' in Dante's purgatorial sense, that I would above all salute and introduce Jean-Marc, who, in his receiving and listening, gave more than I could in the giving.

BEFORE SETTING OUT

JEAN-MARC POTTIEZ

Before setting out, I should explain that the following 'conversations' (in fact, all I did was listen and ask some simple questions) were recorded between 1982 and 1985. Originally they were intended to lead to a programme on French television or radio, but one morning I woke up and decided they should be published instead. Fortunately Laurens van der Post and his publisher were kind enough to accept this sudden change of course, and the challenge it entailed.

Why publish this sort of journal de route, *this travel diary? Above all, I thought that it could be useful to others who, like me, are groping their way out of the beaten tracks and the beaten words. Laurens van der Post's spoken words contain not just fire, water, music and silence, but also a form of spiritual vitamins. They not only sustain and charm, they also heal. I have met many people in different countries who have said that a particular book or film by van der Post happened to change or transform their outlook, or even the whole of their lives. Why? Because a man like van der Post, who has travelled on many roads and crossed many deserts with death as a constant companion, who narrowly escaped being beheaded and for years suffered hunger and disease at the hands of the Japanese (against whom he bears no malice but whom, on the contrary, he sincerely loves), cannot help but throw himself completely in to his works. The man and the writer are cast in one piece. You cannot dissociate them. Hence the sincerity, hence the fire of his words, which reach for your heart and your mind.*

I cannot say how much Laurens van der Post and his books have brought and meant to me. One thing is sure: Laurens helped pull me out from the quicksand I was sinking into at one point in my life. But first I should mention how I came across his books. It was Nagisa Oshima, the Japanese film director, who was then working on the screenplay of his film Merry Christmas, Mr Lawrence, *who passed me the flame. Very kindly he lent me the book on which it was based,* The Seed and the Sower. *Many words and sentences had been underlined, and it was covered with feverish annotations in Oshima's hand. I devoured it, as he had. Afterwards, Boris Biancheri, the then Italian Ambassador to Japan, teased me because I had not read more books by the same author; he spoke so enthusiastically of* The Lost World of the Kalahari *that I pounced on it and devoured it, savouring it as I have since every book written by van der Post. For the first time in my life I dared to write to an author, and said in my letter that if he could dive so deeply into the abyss of the Japanese mind and come up with the essential, it was because he was an African. Only an African could have noticed, as Laurens did in his prison camp in Java, how the moon had a strange and powerful influence on the Japanese, particularly the new moon, the black moon. I added that a man of all continents like him had to play the vital role of a bridge between individuals and nations torn apart by indifference, intolerance, war, hatred, ideologies, racism, nationalism, the black tide of all 'isms'. We began to correspond, and suddenly I received a postcard from Gstaad, Switzerland: he was inviting me to stop by. It just so happened that I was bailing out of the French radio and television, and at the same time breaking an emotional tie that had bound me for too long. The landing was rough, precisely in the quicksand. Stuck and bleeding, I found this invitation and the call from the snow high above my head more than I could resist. I accepted and left Paris to meet this 'Eurafricasian' who was already so close to me.*

I knew that van der Post was in the habit of going to Switzerland every year to start a new book. Was it because he wanted to be closer to the sky and the mountains he loved, or closer to the spirit of his friend C. G. Jung, another explorer of another dark abyss, the abyss of the unconscious? Now that I know him better, I think all those reasons are valid. In any event, I left Paris just after Christmas and, after a quick flight to Geneva, switched to the slow approach by train, the earthy approach, the Swiss approach. Our little train, full of skiers, tourists, commuters and students, began climbing giant mountains and zigzagging between earth and sky. Three seats to my right, in front of me, a beautiful Swiss girl sat with a wicker basket on her lap from which she took an apple and a book. Crunch! Crunch! Crunch! She chomped upon the apple as she read, and you could measure her interest in the book by the intensity of each bite and crunch. It seemed that for her too a book could be devoured and the words could be food. In the background, through the windows, there were the columns, the lace, the festoons, the arches, the towers of the snow, the cathedral of the snow, the Christmas snow, the miracle snow, the snow which, jumping with joy, I ate flake by flake when I saw it for the first time in France, while my school mates jeered at this new extravagance of 'le négro', my nickname. Time became a crystal ball. Bleeding was cauterized by ice and beauty.

Finally the little train arrived at Gstaad. Among the crowd, strangely

*enough, I instantly recognized Laurens van der Post waiting on the platform –
although I had never seen a photograph of him at that time. Together we started
to walk in the festive snow, the fertile snow, a walk which has lasted until today
– a walk with a white Bushman lighting fires in the desert, around which we
can huddle and listen to stories, and dream and hope and be born again.*

*Listening to Laurens, listening to his stories about Bushmen, frogs, lions,
praying mantises, elephants, mambas, owls, rhinoceroses and baboons (only my
brothers, the gorillas of my native Congo, were missing from the feast), suddenly
the person in me who had been gagged and thrown into the pit and had somehow
survived – the little boy I once was, who had listened so often to the stories of his
African companions in the thickest and darkest part of the heart of Africa, in the
bush of Ebinzo – sprang to life again. I could hear – was it my heart or was it the
tom-tom in my memory? – a frantic beat. I felt good again, warm again, hungry
and thirsty again, whole again. And then I knew. I knew what I had missed and
longed for during all those years of repression and slow death. I knew that once
again I had to use the sun, my own sun, the equatorial sun, as the dial and
measure of all things, and that I would have to go back to where I came from if I
was to progress on the road. Ultimately, through this walk with Laurens, I
confirmed what I knew from the beginning but had tried to forget: that homes,
orchards and gardens cannot offer shelter to those who have been born with
tom-toms in their hearts.*

Tokyo, 8 January 1986

A WALK
WITH A WHITE BUSHMAN

JEAN-MARC POTTIEZ: *Laurens, I cannot help identifying you with the Bushmen. Your life, your deeds, the tracks you are following, your way of thinking, of feeling, of talking, your dialogue with the sun and the moon as well as the infinitely small or the invisible – all that is Bushman. You are no longer looking at the mirror, you are already on the other side, looking at us.*

LAURENS VAN DER POST: My own story began with the Bushman stories. I had a nurse, Klara, who was a Bushman woman, a Stone Age person. Hers was the first human face I can remember. I remember being fascinated by the light of an African sun playing on some blue object. And gradually this blue object became a necklace of blue glass beads – the most beautiful colour – and with it came the most wonderful apricot skin, and then the slightly Mongol face of Klara. She had a beautiful face with those very ancient eyes of the Bushman. I looked into her eyes and it was always as if I looked at the first dawn of the first day. It is one of the dearest faces. Even as I talk about it I am filled with the most incredible emotion.

This is in a sense my story. I mean, everything in life is a story. And the story of mankind is history: without history we have no meaning. The story of man, and of life made flesh in man, is in the soul and its own perceptions. It provides us with our sense of wonder. It provides us with the sense of living mystery in life. And it helps to heighten our sensitivities, our perceptions, our awarenesses. And it carries us on. With a story you go on a journey in time and space, in life and creation, always travelling. I'm thinking about this particularly because people always laughed at the Bushman stories and said they had no meaning. And I suddenly realized, they only had no meaning because we had lost the key and the code – we had lost the meaning of the stories. So I decoded them, and they immediately began making sense all over the world to people. I started in 1952 because I was still rather war-shattered. My story was moving into a new phase, and I had to begin it again. And it almost seems to me as if in this there's a parable for all of us, for mankind. All of us who are discouraged, who sit back and say,

3

'What's the use – look what we're doing, it has no effect, it has no consequences. What's the use of doing anything? Why, look, we're trying to cure poverty. Nothing is happening. Look at South Africa – they can't get rid of their bloody apartheid. What's the point of trying?' Well, this is heresy to me, because the story is timeless. Life is timeless. If we play our role in it we redeem it from time. And I remember the particular feeling of this sort of world destruction I'd come from, that there was something timeless in this wartime story that I'd lived.

Then something happened when I was in America. I was in a small place in Texas with friends, who knew that I knew Jung, and they asked me to talk about Jung one evening. And at this meeting there was an American college boy, who was just going from school to university. After I had spoken, he told me about a recurrent dream that was worrying him, and I said, 'Well, I'm not a psychologist. But curiously enough your dream makes me think of a *Bushman story* . . .' And I told him this Bushman story. The story made an enormous impression on him, as it had on me too. But then, I did not see him again. Yet barely two and a half months ago I suddenly got a letter from him, recalling this incident and asking me if I remembered the story on that occasion. He said that story changed his whole life. It made a different man of him. The story still lived in him. And he was still feeling that every day was a revelation to him. He said that after that occasion, like everybody round him, he had gone into oil as they do in Texas. And he said he had made money, more than he needed in life. And he wanted me to know that he'd just endowed the University of Texas with a faculty of Jungian psychology. The first university in the world to have a faculty of Jungian psychology. And he asked me if I would like to come out and be the first professor. I very sadly wrote and told him that, much as I would love it, I couldn't because I didn't know enough; I still had a long way to go. But I was tremendously moved by the living force of that Bushman's story.

Sometimes I'm tempted to think the Bushmen lived in vain, because their culture's been destroyed, they vanished, and one thinks they vanished in vain. But think: five, six hundred years ago, in southern Africa, a Bushman imagination conceived a story that created a faculty of Jungian psychology in Texas. That Bushman is the founder of the faculty, not I or the generous, imaginative American. We were merely the messengers. To me, this is life. Nothing which is truly done, nothing which is truly conceived, nothing which is matched to the living word and the true word is ever vain. May I add, too, that this is both a good Bushman and a very American story. It could only have happened first in America and I must stress it because it ought to take some of the arrogance out of us and give us a glimpse of the true America of the heart and why I like it so.

You are really, I feel, a white Bushman . . . You do not mind my calling you that?

Well, to me in a sense it is a compliment, but it is not a surprise because my nickname in my own family was 'Bushman' as a child, so I am very happy with it. And there is something more I would like to say about the Bushmen.

Not only do I find it inconceivable that lovable people like Klara could be extinguished and would be lost for ever, but I believe also in repentance . . . I believe in repentance for the evil we have done to the Bushmen. I felt that I should in a way try and redeem it. This is what I have felt all my life, that the individual must not wait for governments and he must not wait for groups and powerful people to do something. He must take care of what is on his doorstep; that is the material that he has in life and he must work with that. I think, in a way, one of the links I had with the Zen Buddhists in Japan was the shared sense that you do what is necessary at a given moment with all your heart and all your soul. You do not wait and say, well, there will be something better tomorrow. You do it, you accept it . . . And I think this is how my life has been, so that if you ask me to define what I've done and so on, I think, 'Well, I've just tried.'

Later on in my life I felt sure there would be war in Europe and nobody in London would listen. Well, I thought, the only thing to do is to go and write a book about it. I had to do everything I could. And even now sometimes something happens in the world, and it occurs to me that we are all responsible. So I do what I can about it and pick up the telephone or write a letter. Because I happen to have friends now all over the world who tend to be in positions of power, and I don't hesitate to use those friendships even if something is happening at the other end of the world. If I feel something is important I ring them up and say, 'Look,

about so and so, this is your old friend speaking, may I suggest . . .'
That's all.

This is the direct and friendly approach or strategy. But you favour the indirect way, the way of the sower and the seed. Those are key words and key concepts in your works.

Yes, this is a very profound parable and somewhere in *The Seed and the Sower* I say that a human being who achieves his own truth through the act and the quality of his doing and his being becomes the seed of new growth.

I think that instinctively in my own life, throughout the experience of my own darkness which seemed to me so horrible, I came to realize that darkness, if properly approached, could be the source of the increase of light for me. I think this is the great mystery of life: that if evil is seen steadily in relationship with the whole of one's being, then it can lead to an increase of good. Good comes through the challenge.

I can see a strange black stone on your table. Could you tell me what it is?

Well, I love this stone very much because it represents perhaps the beginning of matter as we know it. This is the oldest, geologically the oldest, rock there is in the world. This tends to prove what I've always believed, that Africa is the oldest and the first country in the world. It was the first country to rise out of the waters in the beginning . . . Just feel how warm and soft it is too. It's got a marvellous surface and it comes from 15,000 feet down in the earth of Africa. It was sent to me by a great friend, with a very moving letter, saying, 'This is a symbol of what you and I have tried to build on all our lives.'

So this stone suggests it – Africa's heart is black, and the heart of our Mother Earth is black. Do you think God's heart is black too?

How could I possibly answer for God? I cannot think or feel about a Creator like that. You know the ancient word for God is 'that which cannot be named'. From the beginning it is axiomatic that even the word which was His cannot define him. And what of the commandment not to have graven images of him? Jealousy is the least of many explanations, I believe. It is simply impossible to contain what God is in a single image. If we try we err, we fail and we go astray. For some mystics he is a white radiance, a light of lights, but the alchemists who tried so devoutly and

6

humbly to carry on the Christian revelation from where the churches, with their take-over by dogma, tried to arrest it, would have recoiled from thinking of the heart of God as black. Black for them was the devil. But a God in whom the opposites in the universe are seen as contained and transcended, would be nearer to what they sought and sometimes experienced. All I know is that not the whole of the art, the music, the poetry and the discoveries of science and truth I have met, could express what I believe is the experience we have of God. And when I say that, I want to cross myself and pray because I fear what God may do to me, through what he could ask of me alone; all because, through the precious gift of consciousness, he has passed on to us the awesome responsibility of how we respond to his asking and to the business in which it involves us of choosing between good and evil, truth and error, not only for our own but also for creation's sake. All I believe I know is an experience, a mystery that is not mysteriousness but a life-giving wonder, a something which alone gives food to the greatest of all natural hungers, a hunger which is a fact even for the atheist, no matter how much he denies it the food that it demands.

Everything that one tries to do beyond that diminishes, but I think what one should work at is one's relationship with God, this overwhelming 'is-ness'. What is the impact of God on me or the thought and feeling of God to me? What does it mean for my life, what does it mean for the life of my time? Once I start groping in that way great energies begin to flow into me. And this is a fact. All civilizations, from the oldest to the newest, they could not do without this. One of the strangest ideas ever conceived is the idea that religion is the opium of the people, because religion is the call to battle: it's a call to fight in life as you've never fought before. The idea of God is very uncomfortable because again it increases your responsibility. If there is no God, there is no point in being responsible – it's just chaos and eternal night. But if there is one, it is harder and yet more bearable because in Him is the dimension really where it all begins. C. J. Jung talks about the 'I' and the 'thou'. He talks about an area in the human being which He calls 'the self', and that is the area where the 'I' and the 'thou's' have a dialogue with one another. But even there, where man and god-image meet, and we are most whole, there yet is more.

You were born in the interior of Africa and still now you quite often go back to that continent. I believe that in your life and your books Africa has always played a magnetic role. But how was it at the beginning? What impact did Africa make on you?

Long before I went to school I had a kind of African schooling. First of all I had Klara, who was a most important person in my life, and from her I got the education a young Bushman has through her telling me the stories and the myths and the legends of her people. Then, on our farm, we had Bantu and Hottentot people; I got their myths and legends as a boy because I was always playing among them. And we had Cape Coloured and Malay people, who told me stories about Malaya as well as their myths and legends. All this was in my ears and head before I went to school, and to me this was my real teacher – until my father gave me, I remember, a simplified version of the Tale of Troy, the *Iliad*, and of course we read the Bible. The Bible interested me enormously because the Old Testament stories were not far removed from the African stories; on the contrary, they were very close. So these things were all mixed up together until I went to school. And my mother was a marvellous story-teller. So my real education came from stories … which makes an enormous difference.

Do you remember, the first time I wrote to you, I said that only an African like you could understand the Japanese? Because of their special relationship with nature, and their special kind of sensitivity. You give a good example of this in The Night of the New Moon *when you show how strangely the Japanese behaved with the new moon. How do you explain such behaviour?*

Of course, I had known from my reading and from my visit to Japan the role that the moon and the moonrise play in the Japanese character. But here suddenly I was in this prison where the whole of life was under a microscope – it was super life-sized. Everything was enlarged, really. And it seemed to me that, unconsciously, their link with the moon was far greater and far more immediate, more accessible, in terms of mood and feeling than it was to us. It was a little more remote to us, more in our background, whereas, because I was an African, what was a very important part of my life was the sunset. The Japanese would go to certain places to celebrate the moonrise, they would go to Arashiyama

8

and watch the moon come up – and you know how lovely it is to see the full moon come up there. But we would say in Africa, 'It's going to be a lovely sunset now – I think we'll go there, that will be the best place to watch it from . . .' We were very much sunset-conscious. And our moods were influenced by it.

So I was predisposed to notice in prison a strange kind of longing among the Japanese for the moon; and out of this longing a kind of frustration and a kind of rage over the frustration which added to the power of this very deep longing. It was just like a tide in the sea being pulled up in their characters. And this seemed always to be most evident as the moon swelled and became more and more full. And one became quite frightened of them. There were certain Japanese who seemed to be more influenced by this phenomenon than others. There was one, for instance, whom the troops called 'Mad Harry', because you know that the Latin for madness is 'lunatic' – touched by the moon. He ran amok sometimes, hitting and beating anyone in his way and generally acting so strangely.

I've seen the phenomenon in Africa. I have heard lions roar at the moon just as dogs bay at the moon. I heard a lion one night start as the moon came up at 8 o'clock and, so obsessed was he with it that he was still roaring at it in full daylight after it had set the next day. But this phenomenon I watched so closely and anxiously, seemed to wane with the moon, and a very pure, almost resolved kind of excitement and expectation built up within the Japanese. They were almost joyful and suddenly, when the new moon appeared in our sky, there was a feeling of catharsis, of having been cleansed, among them, as if somehow they had done the night journey themselves. You know, they had grown with the moon, they had waxed and they had gone back into the darkness and were emerging into the light again.

I can't express it in any other way, because it was so mysterious. Most of the really bad excesses we encountered occurred really about the time when the moon started waning, when it started going back into the darkness. You see, this tide of longing was drawn absolutely to the full, and then suddenly what was there but the night again? Just as if they all participated, this became a terrifying feeling, and I often wondered if there were a rearrangement, a reversal, of the poles in the Japanese spirit, with the moon a sort of implied masculine, and their sun a great feminine. You know, for the Germans too the moon is masculine and the sun is feminine and these things are signposts of the spirit; they and we should perhaps not think, so much as wonder, aloud about such things.

There is a big difference between Africa and Japan in terms of ghosts. I mean, you told me that ghosts walk at noon in Africa in the full sun. In Japan, or at least in the western world, ghosts are free to roam more in the night.

Yes. In my part of Africa the haunted hour was between noon and three to four in the afternoon.

Is it peculiar to South Africa, or does it happen in the rest of Africa too?

Well, I can only say it is so for all the Africans with whom I've been in the bush at that hour of the day. I mean, all the animals go into the shade to have a siesta – to sleep, perchance to dream. Africans get out of the sun, make for the shade. It is as if all living things turn then to some sort of darkness and shade, as a protection against excesses of sun. And they call it the 'dead' hour of the day. It is strange, because if you think of it, when you have this immense ferocity of the sun at its highest, it's almost as if nature takes a dagger and plunges it into the sun. At that moment, midnight is born. This is where the night begins. And the poles are reversed at night as the sun goes down in Africa.

When night falls and the moon comes up in Africa, the release from the tyranny of the sun, the coolness, the beauty of the night takes place and the noises of a new and utterly different sort of life come out of the night. So for Africans the classical symbolism is reversed. They are renewed in the night, and this sense of renewal takes over, whatever happens to the sun on its journey into night on the other side of the world. Perhaps that is why sunset means so much for us Africans. Sunset is for us like a form of moonrise, you see. It's as if all that has been too much and excessive in the day dies in the sunset hour.

Have you ever experienced ghosts in your life?

I've never had an experience of ghosts anywhere in the world. But I feel that you can only encounter ghosts in your native country. I think you must be in your country if you are to have any chance of witnessing this phenomenon. But I have been in the bush, in this 'dead' hour, when I've sometimes been inexplicably afraid, without any reason, but looking round as if about to encounter something, without shape or name.

10

Although I have not actually seen a ghost I have had this fear of some great unknown terror without shape or name. And suddenly, it seemed to correspond to a general overall dread. The birds, fast asleep, would suddenly wake up frightened, and cry, and odd animals yelp with fear, just as I felt it at its keenest, as if the whole bush were experiencing it. It was a collective experience of a dread, which did not need my evidence, and yet the bush alarmed me more because the noises would be different, and more orchestrated with warning, if they were noises at all. And very often a funny little wind would stir – spin about itself with demonic fury and leave, crackling like a fire. These subtle things would happen all around. And I myself could never sleep at that hour of the day. I could only fall asleep briefly, once the shadows began to lengthen. But I have always felt, since I was a boy, that this was the hour of the day when I had to be most alert, when caught between noon and afternoon.

You told me once a very interesting story – a case of possession – was it in the Kalahari Desert? One of the African members of your expedition was possessed by the spirit of a tree . . .

Yes, I do remember. It was in central Africa – almost the last journey which I ever made with what were called 'porters' – people who used to carry travellers' luggage for a living. It was already most unusual then. But it was in a part of central Africa where there had always been a very heavy and barbarous traffic in slaves, right into this century, which explains perhaps why the system still persisted.

When I was travelling in Africa I always tried to make camp an hour or so before dark. Since there is no electric light or lamp in the bush, you had to choose a likely place for firewood in good time. You could then get the fires and the food going. And everybody arranged their place of rest before sunset. But on this particular day we were going through dreadful country. And I pushed us all very hard, but in the end I had to choose a camp in a hurry, in country as bad as ever. There was a sort of large copse of very strange trees – I recognized them as a species of acacia but I can't tell you the specific name. I didn't like the look of them. Trees have personalities and characters, and these trees definitely made one feel uncomfortable. I had to say, 'We'll go and camp there – we'll get good firewood there.' My bearers begged me not to, but I pointed out that we could not go on in the dark.

Also, it was a part of Africa where you found man-eating lions. They were common in that part because it had many over-populated areas. Elsewhere in Africa you get troublesome lions, but they don't normally eat people. We were a surly, unhappy camp from the start, and in the middle of the night there was a terrible howl. . . . I jumped up and grabbed my gun because I did not know what was going on. I rushed out and there was a very bright moon. Already the fire was flaring up from my camp. A man was hanging from a tree and the others were cutting him free. And they said to me, very angrily, 'You see, we told you there would be trouble if you camped with these trees.' They managed to bring the man round and revive him. He was a bearer whom I liked very much, and I said to him, 'Mtumna, for God's sake, what have you been up to? Have we treated you so badly that you want to leave us like that?'

And he said, 'Oh, bwana, it's not like that at all. But all night long the tree has been telling me to go and do that. How could I . . . the spirit in the tree . . . This is a tree of the mamba.'

Mamba, the snake?

Yes, perhaps the most poisonous snake in the world. He said this again and again, 'The snake spoke and said he wanted me . . . I had to obey. It's stronger than I am.'

How was it possible? How could he know?

He said the snake knew the spirit and language of the ancestors, could know his mind for him and order him even to kill himself. But actually Africans have a very different relationship with snakes from ours. For many, like the Zulus, a particular snake is an ancestor returning to his people. And I've seen occasions when the snake would go into a hut while the people were working out in the fields, and they would find it there at night, and say, 'Oh, great grandfather has come to visit us – we must not disturb him.' And they put milk and food out for the snake and wait until he leaves of his own accord. You must remember that the mamba is a versatile snake – he swims, walks and yet is also a tree snake. I had a great friend – a born naturalist – who lived by the junction of the Limpopo and Pafuri Rivers, near Crooks Corner, in what was then deep, remote bush. He had made a wonderful garden where he grew tropical fruit. He lived surrounded by the animals, birds and trees. He doctored them when they were wounded. He had one great tree, which was hollow. Every May, always the first of May, a mamba would appear out of the hollow onto the branch beside it, and curl up in the sun. As it got colder the mamba would appear for fewer and shorter hours each day, until it vanished totally into the hollow. But on the first of October every year the mamba would reappear – and my friend knew spring was on its way. He would explain, 'Now, that is my calendar!' He added, 'It's also the guardian of all in my garden.' I saw the mamba and my friend over a period of many years until the appearance of the *Frelimo*, the freedom fighters, across the border in Mozambique. All that time the mamba came every year to guard the tree and garden. Every November, when it was really hot, the mamba would disappear into the bush like a salmon into the sea.

All these things have an enormous bearing on the imagination of the Africans, and also on mine. Somehow, these things fertilize the human spirit and urge it not towards superstition but, through wonderment and reverence, into new directions of thought and spirit. Through one's capacity for reverence, perception of life is heightened immeasurably by a thousand and one such things. One sees life in a way one couldn't otherwise have seen it. And they all play an enormously creative role as a result. They have been created in their own right and light, and even snakes are ladders to a greater awareness. Just through seeing creation in their archaic script and rhythm of living action, they stimulate a movement and intimation of something creative in others.

And it gives you a set of values?

Oh, they are the inspiration of great values, because as people look upon nature so they in a sense become. You know Tennyson wrote about nature as 'red in tooth and claw'. But the only part of nature that is truly red in tooth and claw is man. There are certain groups of animals who are exceptions and as such will remain nameless – they are in a way the outcasts of the natural world. But in nature 'the tooth and claw' pattern is only there if animals have to kill for survival. And all nature accepts that. There is no complaint about that in nature. The complaint is against man, because he is the only one who kills for profit or for fun. He has this great, awesome corrupting power to kill unnecessarily, against the law of the bush. We are really the red in the tooth and claw of nature. But if you live in partnership with nature you will realize how lawless we have been and, alas, are still.

To which animal do you feel most attracted?

I don't really know because I love them all.

Do you have a totem?

I know so many Africans who have totems. For instance, the Sotho people of Botswana have animals who keep the spirit, the soul of the nation – you have the Men of the Crocodile, the Men of the Lion, the Men of the Elephant, and the Buffalo, the Baboon, even. They are whole tribes. One of the greatest tribes of all are the Men of the Duiker. The duiker is a very beautiful little antelope, dove-grey and very fast. It's name comes from the Dutch word for diving. When it rains, and you go out into bush country, you will see it going about in this continuous diving motion, up-down, down-up, over the bushes and tasselled grass.

Like a dolphin.

Like a dolphin. It has a rational and historical explanation that is most unusual. One of the great chiefs of the tribe, Khama the Great, when young, was pursued by his enemies who were out to murder him. He was badly wounded and, exhausted, crept into a place of dense bushes. When enemies appeared, hard on his heels, making a great noise, just there where he had gone into the bushes, a duiker jumped out and set off running for his life. So the enemy said, 'Oh well, obviously he hasn't gone that way, because otherwise the duiker would have come out before.' So the chief was saved by the duiker, and the people who prospered under him naturally became the Men of the Duiker. But if you think of the Men of the Crocodile, for instance, you have to go down in time and spirit, and there are very many deep, symbolic associations to be considered, such as the fact that the crocodile was a great symbol in Egyptian mythology – the sacred crocodile. So, that one is unusual.

You have not been associated, by one of your African friends, with an animal?

No, perhaps because I have been adopted into a small African clan, a tribal offshoot of the Ama-Xhosa, the Fingo who have a first spirit but no totems. The Ama-Xhosa and the Zulus are the two great nations of southern Africa. The Fingo were more a very bright and intelligent part of it and, because of their particular history, not always popular. All I can say is that I feel I understand this identification with animals because I myself am very moved by animals, and have had experiences with animals that are very special to me. For instance, I am very moved by the rhinoceros which is, to me, one of the most beautiful animals in Africa. I know that in comparison to the antelope it looks ungainly –

Or even to an elephant . . .

Even compared to an elephant – and I love the elephant. But the rhinoceros is a prehistoric animal, one which has been pushed to live on the edge of its environmental capacity. If it is pushed much further it will not survive, for it really goes back to the age of the dinosaur and the pterodactyl. The hippopotamus also belongs to that age, and both animals, in that perspective as well as in what they are, I find extraordinarily moving.

They must have a long memory incorporated in their being.

They have that and more – a something which is an antique response to what is oldest in animal life. They represent a kind of continuity, a living continuity in flesh and blood against incredible odds of life and time and chance, which is miraculous.

But tell me, how can a rhinoceros be beautiful? Do you have an illustration?

I remember, it came when I was in Africa making a film with a rhinoceros. I had noticed that in Africa many animals, when they get really old, go away on their own. I know that the common theory is that it is an evolutionary design to make quite certain that the herd is kept and bred by what is young, strong and brave. And the young bulls come and throw the old people out. Well, of course, there is rivalry among all animals in the mating season. They fight for the female, because there are more men around than are necessary. The bull has to fight for the right to procreate; and of course the older they become, the fewer their chances. But they are never more than pushed away from the women. They do not get chased out of the herd altogether.

So you sometimes see an elephant or a rhinoceros on its own who is kept away – miles from anyone. You might see a wildebeest or a buffalo, or a hartebeest or lion on his own. And lions do not grow quite as old as they could sometimes, because they have such problems in finding food in old age. For me, it's almost a religious pattern. It is almost as if when an animal has lived its life, has done his duty as a young animal and bull in protecting the herd, there comes a moment when he feels he must do something in nature that he has to seek, find and experience on his own. They are what I call *'Sanyassin'*, after the name conferred in India on the men who renounce the world and all their possessions and take to the road on a great walkabout in search of resolution and holiness.

You pause as if you have something else in your mind.

As I came to the word *Sanyassin* I had a recollection, bright and electric as if it were lightning, of an old Kalahari lion I had once known over a period of days. There were, perhaps, somewhere over the horizon, other lions. It was lion country but I never saw any for days except this one, still great in his old age, a thick Titian red mane thrown almost nonchalantly over his tawny shoulder and every reason to walk in pride. And yet his bearing was without arrogance and his carriage of a certain dignity of profound meditation, and the last time I saw him was as he went over a yellow sand-dune and down behind it, and so into the heart of one of those deep mythological African sunsets we have talked about. Somehow he was heraldic for *Sanyassin*. Then in another place and another time I also met the rhinoceros *Sanyassin*.

When you were working on the film . . . ?

Yes, the film had a theme that has always been very close to me – the way in which the natural world of Africa seemed to be strangely and significantly also inside one. The film had developed naturally in terms of its own pattern as we progressed. I remember how it naturally moved to its close in a *Sanyassin* theme and at the right moment we found just the right rhinoceros actor to represent it – so appropriate was the actor that he reminded me of a particular *Sanyassin* I had met on the road in India, with the sunlight like a pollen of dust over him. He had been rich and powerful with a large family around him but one day suddenly had renounced all for ever, and now, obedient to this urgent call for a reckoning of his own with life, was walking all over his great mother earth of India.

And then this actor, this rhinoceros, who with the hippopotamus and the crocodile still belonged to a vanished world and expressed its

16

forgotten idiom of life; they were charged with a solemnity and almost a sadness that is their profound nostalgia for their original home. For days I had this one rhinoceros in mind, and followed him around on and off. Almost on the last day, in the early morning, I came across him in a clearing that was full of dew-drops and slanted sun. He was standing there, looking at me. I stopped my truck and said to the people with me, 'Now, whatever happens, do not interfere. I've got an appointment with this fellow and it's between him and me.'

I laughed in the way one does when it is not at all a laughing matter, and then began to walk very slowly towards him, before I could change my mind. At once he heard me and pointed his nose at me as he lowered it almost to the ground. I had the oddest of feelings that there was something in him that wanted a meeting too. I came to within a few feet of him. And then something in me said, 'Far enough, more will be a violation of dignity. You will stand there. It is near enough to communicate.'

I stood there for about two or three minutes looking at him and wondering about him. I thought with great emotion how beautiful he was, how lovely was his marble head and so, quickening all over, I explored for the first time every idiom of his antique being. I found nothing that, in the context of its own time and the language of life, was not dignified, honourable and exceedingly lovely. I have not often been so moved by such a sense of discovery as he gave and this new capacity of response he evoked within myself; this resolution that once you break through into the rhinoceros's idiom, discover what a rhinoceros mother would find beautiful in a rhinoceros son, the impression animal beauty makes on you is blinding. All these emotions went through me while looking at him, until there came a moment when he turned sideways. He said a sort of 'goodbye' and I too turned away.

But when I returned to the truck, everyone was in great agitation because a game ranger who was travelling with us had been violently sick. He explained how he had been tossed by a rhinoceros once and spent nine months in hospital. I had been between him and the animal and if the rhino had charged he would not have been able to shoot it. Yet I assured him there never was any question of the rhinoceros charging or I would not have gone so close. There was just a great overdue settlement of peace after war, between us and all the protection of life in that.

Perhaps all this will help to explain why the rhinoceros is such an important symbol to me and to life. Much of its meaning as a living image has to do with a highly developed sense of smell. The rhino's eyesight is weak. According to Adolf Poortman, a distinguished Swiss zoologist who was a friend of mine, the sense of smell in animals was the first of the senses to be specially developed. So the sense of smell in the animal is what intuition is to the human spirit. It tells you of the invisible, of what cannot be detected by other means. It tells you things that are not there, yet are coming. You see into the blind opaque past and round the corner of time.

Therefore it requires a memory and brains to decode what is detected by this complex sense of smell.

Yes, but it is this smell of things to come, of intuition, on which man's capacity for creation depends. And I think myself, you see, that the act of creation is very sudden – it may be building up there in the dark. But when it happens, it happens like a flash of lightning. Life has taken a leap forward. But intuition is the 'vision' in creation and the human spirit that leaps into the dark and, through the dark, into unknown areas of itself and life. There is an old saying, look before you leap. Wait until you can see, and then leap. But then perhaps you never leap at all. Intuition is the leap forward to creation when all other senses fail and would arrest it. So that intuition is the most vital element, I think, of all the instincts we have inherited. This impels man to leap into the unknown, into new areas of awareness that he has not discovered before. Looking at this rhinoceros, it occurred to me that this intuition is not unarmed. It has a horn, the sword, as it were. In the animal world the rhinoceros is Arthur and his horn Excalibur. I felt happy in the imagery of this conclusion.

And so we ended the film with the rhinoceros walking down a winding road with that amazing resilient and nimble step that is his, carrying his great weight as if it were no more than a feather.

The elephant, the hippopotamus and the rhinoceros were the great road-builders of Africa. They made roads from one water to another, from east to west, south to north, all over Africa. Our own roads, until we started taking out the curves and the feeling for contour in them with our passion for the straight arrogant Roman way, were based on the paths they made. Watching the old rhino from behind, walking out of sight, it was as if he were still making a path for us to follow.

Special as this rhinoceros was, I can remember a rush of other examples, for the numbers of species in which this Sanyassin pattern applies is, I believe, great.

Take the elephant. I have seen elephant walking about on their own, and it is marvellous when you see a great lone elephant in wide open country which is not really elephant country, with the grass perhaps only up to his ankles. And, though walking slowly, with monumental dignity, it is amazing how fast he looms up because he takes such long strides. Black, vast basalt, he dominates the day and darkens the blue as he approaches with this deliberate tread, picking up and putting down his feet with an easy resilience as if to correspond to the drumbeat deep down in the heart of the earth. All about his movement is point and counterpoint of a vast orchestration of life with this drumbeat and pulse of the blood-red earth. He is almost upon one before one realizes how much his senses are not focused on the scene but on something inapprehensible ahead, almost as if he were a great somnambulist following a dream in his sleep. Trance-like he passes, leaving one with a keen sense of ritual, as if he were pledged at the head of a procession of pilgrims of life. And the mystery, the act following on below the burning horizon of faith and trust implicit in his going, is all the greater because one cannot remotely guess at any physical object of his search, there, some hundred miles from the nearest known water. One knows only that he comes in the world already armed with great instinctive foreknowledge, an unusual intelligence, formidable memory made more formidable by a long life. For myself, I can only vouch that I have never watched him and his kind come up, go by and down the blue horizons, and even now cannot remember them, without being moved, knowing only that in their last long range they seek no ordinary food or water, but a round-up of their ancient spirit.

Perhaps one encounter with such an elephant stands out above all. I was in the Kalahari Desert after the rains had fallen. I knew that elephant in that part of the world on such occasions would be drawn to the desert but that the main herd would be hundreds of miles away. One evening at sundown, hard by our camp, there was one tall elephant bull. How he appeared there so silently was almost frightening. At one moment there was nothing, and the next he stood there, tall and black with shadow. But there was no aggression in him. His skin was covered with dust of a long journey and his air of arrival was total. He stood there as if he had been summoned, looking at us, quite unafraid. We felt there was something there – such a sense of peace came from him, such a sense of resolution, that in the end we did not bother about him, but just let him stand there. When it was quite dark, every time the fire was replenished and a flame shot out sideways, the light caught his flank. I lay under my mosquito net quietly, thinking he might have gone. But no, he was there, and I felt strangely at peace and comforted that the fire, and our presence, had meant something to him. Then, by morning, he had gone on his road again, none of us having heard him go. Our guide, who was born in the desert and received his total education from it, felt convinced he had been there to tell us something. But what?

In your meeting with the whaler, Thor Kaspersen,* you immediately recognized each other, because he was a hunter of whales, and you were a hunter of elephants. But have you been pursued by nightmares and dreams like he was by his dreams of a singing whale?

No, but may I add I was never a hunter of elephants. I have had to shoot a few but always with great regret and sadness afterwards because of so much of life extracted in the process: at one moment there was so much of life looming so large in one's sights and then just nothing, and beyond, the blue, as if a black hole had been made in it.

No nightmares, no particularly meaningful dreams about other animals?

I have only once had a gorgeous nightmare. And I think that had a rational cause. It was about a lion. Long before the dream, the story began in the Kalahari – I was travelling across it with a man named Ben who was born in the desert, and a man who was also a Bushman who had grown up with him. They were roughly of the same age and spoke alternatively Afrikaans or Bushman to each other. I was looking for an important legendary place, and my guide and the Bushman said that though they had only been there once, they were certain they could take

---

* *Yet Being Someone Other* and *The Hunter and the Whale.*

me there. It was an evening when the rains had broken – when there was always a sense of the miraculous and all was very beautiful. We made camp while it was still raining. Our guide, Ben, said to me, 'You know, Colonel, I came through here once, at the age of seven; the rains had broken, we were driving cattle across the central Kalahari to the markets in the Transvaal. I am certain we camped just down there. And the Bushman agrees with me. If you'll come with us, we'll show you a small pan, certain to be full of water now, and we will perhaps find some wild duck.'

It sounded irresistible. I took my gun and my little kit for collecting grasses. We walked about two miles and there, some distance below, there was the pan and the water, as he said, full of a sunset in reverse. Unfortunately there were no duck. So when we came to the edge of the pan, Ben said, 'You know, I would just like to walk around the pan because under that tree over there, that's where we camped.'

Now when you've camped in the wilderness of Africa, you have a very strong feeling about your camp, much more than you ever have about a home. As the old hunters used to say, wherever you've camped, you've left something of yourself behind. Besides, a camp expresses something also in the human mind. It's one of the most evocative images of all the institutions we create; not arrivals but more stages of life. Ben felt compelled, almost religiously, to go and visit his old camp and pay his respects to it. Even I could see that there had been a camp there because when you have 2,000 cattle by water for two or three days, round trees at night to protect them from lions, they fertilize the sands and change its ecology for good. So there new grass had grown to form a keen green ring round the tree, although it was more than thirty years since they had camped there. And, of course, I said, 'No, you go, Ben, but I'll stay to look at the grasses here.' I put my gun down after breaking it and reloading it with heavy buckshot. It was just a drill.

Instinctively?

Yes, I was trained to do it as a child, in certain parts of the bush. I took some blotting-paper from my satchel and started working on the grass. There were some plants I didn't know, and I began digging round the grass; suddenly I felt uneasy, and at the centre of my unease, I smelt lion. I picked up my gun, stood up and swung round. About 50 yards away, just by a bush on the slight incline towards the pan, there was the lion, very angry. As it saw me, for no apparent reason it came at me fast – and the sprint of a lion out to kill is almost supernaturally fast. And though I would like to say I held my fire until it was almost upon me, actually I had to shoot as quickly as I could. I got both shots off at him and threw myself to one side. There was a great snarling roar from the lion and it went over in a sort of somersault – for the speed at which everything happened at once was bewildering in the extreme. Then the lion disappeared in a streak of dust that exploded in a cloud out of which he emerged to come at me again. I shot once more as his head loomed out of the dust and he went over again. I had time to reload. Just then Ben and the Bushman started shooting from the other side and nearly shot me. In the end they had to put twenty-seven bullets into that lion before it was dead.

A lion can be that resistant!

The life in the lion, the power, the will to live, are unbelievable. It was a marvellous illustration of how life may leave the animal, but the animal never abandons life. Then six months later I was travelling back to England in a ship, during a very bad storm in the Bay of Biscay. I woke up at night in my cabin screaming because the lion was coming at me again, in my sleep. I suddenly realized that the fear which I experienced at that time was so great that, for the efficiency of my reactions, it had to be deeply suppressed. Only now that I was safe at sea, was it allowed to come out. I kept on saying to myself, it's just a dream – you're asleep in the cabin of a fine ship in a great storm – there can't be any lion. But the fear I experienced was so great, the atmosphere it created so momen-tous, that I got up and put on my overcoat and although it was a bad storm I went to join the captain, whom I knew well, on the bridge and drank cocoa with him for about two hours before I could face my cabin again.

That is the only real nightmare I've ever had about animals, and I've not had it since. But it had a sequel in Zürich, of all places. I had told my story to Dr Jung and to James Hillman, the director of studies who was then at the Jung Institute, who also told it later to a great friend of Jung's, Fowler McCormick, an American millionaire who was a very generous supporter. It happened one afternoon when Hillman took

Fowler McCormick up to the remarkable zoo in Zürich – have you seen it?

No...

Well, there's a wonderful place where they keep the lions. When Hillman and McCormick arrived there was one lion on a small mound, lying in the sun, and they paused to watch it. This made Hillman ask Fowler McCormick, 'Did you hear what happened to Laurens?' and began to tell him the story.

Hillman told me that the moment he started, this lion stood up on his little hill. When he came to the point in the story where the lion charged me, this lion in the zoo suddenly charged towards them as far as he could get. Now, what do you make of that?

How strange indeed . . . Of all the animal stories you know, which one has meant the most to you?

It will have to be about elephants – one of many, and I shall have to abbreviate it or I could be about it all day. It begins with the appearance on the rim of a blue day in Kenya of some bull elephants walking in single file across a great plain, not as elephants usually do but indifferent to all about them, as if something invisible ahead were drawing them. They did so for some three hours and there was nothing to explain their strange compulsive march, until a clump of trees and bushes appeared like an oasis in that waste of land. Then came an inkling of what it was all about. A ring of lions was slowly tightening round that circle of bush, but a tall manly bull, in the lead, walked straight through the pride of lion, vanished into the bush and some time later walked out of the bush with an elephant cow and her newly born calf, between them.

Oh . . .

Yes, the bulls took the cow and the calf into their keeping and they went off, without a backward glance. Now, how had they known?

Some kind of invisible tom-tom?

I do not know – for me it remains a tremendously moving illustration of the caringness and the provision that is in nature, and in the animal species, to make the survival of life possible; the in-built protection of life. It is one of the most tender and caring episodes I know. I could tell you so many stories about elephants I have known. But this, somehow, is one of the most beautiful.

We'll come back later to these special relationships, not only with the animals but with wilderness in general. It's strange how people tend to standardize, to stereotype their judgements and opinions about animals, when animals are all as different as are humans. For instance, very often one confuses African elephants with Asian elephants. In fact they are very different, aren't they?

Oh, totally different.

In what points?

Well, first of all, the African elephant is much bigger. He stands much higher in the shoulder. He's much darker. He's much stronger. And then, his character is different. He's much more independent: he doesn't domesticate. The Belgians in the Congo were trying very hard to tame elephants and make them work. And up to a point they were beginning to have results, but only up to a point. In India, they had the Indian elephant to act as a sort of super-horse. But then the African elephant has too complex and immediate a temperament. He can be as fierce and formidable as he is loving and caring, and occasionally his loneliness makes him aggressive to man, as if the Greek saying that loneliness makes men either gods or mad applies also to his species. He becomes what we call a rogue elephant – but a rogue to whom? And what price our projection? And who are the intruders?

Yes – I understand; but to return to the Indian elephants. They are tamed and work for their owners. Therefore it seems that something of their nature and identity is lost for ever. They are too close to man.

Yes, but the African elephant – it's not in the culture of the bush, specially not in the elephant culture. It's a tremendously independent animal. But he's got huge potential – it's not that he would be incapable. Because you have great bonds between the African elephant and the people that he has known. An elephant is very, very intelligent. I had a friend with a vast ranch of 120,000 acres in Kenya but who always came with me on many of my expeditions just for the love of bush and wilderness. And every year the elephants came and trod his fences down and trampled all over his land. And he thought, well, this is a nonsense and must stop. So just about the time before the elephants would reappear, he took his fences down, at their usual place of entry. The elephants very quickly spotted this. So from then on and every year they wouldn't just push through anywhere as they could easily have done. They followed the fence along until they came to the gap and then went through. He said, they were 'great and intelligent gentlemen!' Other animals would trample and charge and repeatedly damage his fences but the elephants just knew instinctively what was demanded of them and obliged. Of course they are also tremendously aware.

I have been very struck by the fact that long before scientists discovered that dolphins were talking – not only talking but singing and joking – you were writing about a singing whale. Long before them. It seems that for you, animals are not only talking, but singing. They help you, they carry you on their backs to another world and they are really on the trail, guiding you, opening the way.

They do so even through the dreams of contemporary man. You would be amazed at the numbers of persons who have never even seen an elephant who have come to me to talk about elephants that recur again and again at the centre of their dreams.

I like what Jung said about the plants being 'thoughts of God' and the animals 'priests of God'. They are still in the Garden of Eden. They have not been chased away like us. And they have the key to Eden.

They have in a sense not been expelled from the garden by God, though man in his exile does his best. For Jung they were 'priests of God' because they did not follow their own will but did only God's will. 'In the beginning was the Word –' Well, to me, every insect and animal somehow is part of the Word made life, made flesh, made real. It is the word in action. Everyone and everything carries this charge. It carries, as it were, a signature of creation. Nothing is unsigned in life; a great seal is stamped on great and small. And it is not a meaning that is capable always of articulation. But it is amazing how they can give one the companionship nothing else can. Their living companionships – their presence and daily acknowledgement of their validity – their own particular kind of dignity, create a wonderful, naturally ecumenical sort of atmosphere. And this is the most valuable part of the animal life. They give a companionship of life and create an atmosphere in which the processes of creation are more likely to be continued than not. It's the most indefinable thing to talk about, the atmosphere, yet it is decisive because in the end it is that which makes the rain fall.

25

Is this the sort of thing Jung meant when he talked about 'participation mystique'? You see why I called you a white Bushman, and expect you to have the answer.

Yes. He, of course, had this sort of thing in mind and I could not have been so aware of these things if I had not always had the Bushman as a guide. It started almost before I could speak, from the moment the sunset inflamed the necklace of beads round the throat of Klara and I would see her antique face as she put me to sleep. I was committed, from that moment on, to a very special and profound interest in the Bushman and his fate. I could not have come to an understanding of the role of the animal in my own and human imagination, for instance, if it had not been for this commitment. Indeed, there is almost nothing of importance in my life which does not owe something to this commitment.

I see now the meaning of what you wrote in your diary when you were about eleven years old: 'One day I will go and seek the Bushmen and beg their pardon for what we have done to them.' Your feeling for them has never diminished, but the Bushmen are vanishing. What can be done to save them from total extinction?

Well, that was the problem which exercised me from the beginning, because the Bushman's whole life is founded on a principle which is utterly alien to all cultures in the world – not only the European ones but all other cultures except the hunter cultures, which are Stone Age, prehistoric cultures, and totally incomprehensible to us now. And here the Bushman finds himself in the power of a very highly conscious, highly organized civilization which finds everything that he represents totally unimportant, totally discredited. So the problem is, what does one do about this? Well, I thought the only way that I personally, as a human being, could tackle it would be to translate this Stone Age idiom into a contemporary one and to try and show that it is important to us who have all the power that these values should not disappear; that in fact they should be honoured in a contemporary way in our own spirit and society. The Bushman was a walking pilot scheme of how the European man could find his way back to values he had lost and he needed for his own renewal.

So I tried to interpret these things, and the only way I could think of doing it was through mythology and legend and story. I tried to present their stories – people laughed at them. Only yesterday I was looking at a book written by a man who poses as the greatest expert on rock art in South Africa; that is, Bushman art – they were great painters. As a child I knew these paintings were all over the country. In fact, when my family landed in Africa some three centuries ago, the whole of the interior of Africa was like a great, open-air Louvre because wherever there was a cave or a rock it was painted with great loving care. It was a staggering cultural phenomenon, this rock art. But now the Bushmen are being eliminated; they are just a tiny little group left in the Kalahari Desert where there are no rocks for them to paint on even if they wanted to . . . they do a little painting on ostrich-egg shells but the great art has vanished from the land. Well, this man who is supposed to be a great expert on them mentions what I consider a very great Bushman story, an exceedingly tragic story, in which in mythological terms the Bushman faces up to the fact that his whole culture and he himself have to be destroyed. And he calls it one of the funniest stories ever written, because it depicts such an incongruous assembly of animals, insects, natural and imagined elements. How could you trust the interpretation of the art and life of the Bushman by a man like that?

Anyway, my approach was to tell the Bushman's story in terms of animals, just as the Red Indians did. One of the greatest Red Indian myths I know is a story called the Jumping Mouse; it is a most moving story. It is told entirely in terms of animals – who, deep down, evoke a response in spite of our human inhibitions – and illustrates the quest of man's spirit, using the insignificant image of a little mouse: the mouse sets out in search of the truth and by the end of the journey it has lost the perspective of a mouse, has acquired the vision of an eagle and indeed is finally itself transformed into an eagle.

I found the Bushmen had no rights at all in the Kalahari Desert. All the others, the black people, the white people, had some rights, but the Bushmen had none, although they were dependent on their hunting in order to survive. If they hunted certain animals that were called 'royal game' which had preservation orders on them and a police patrol found them eating one of those animals, they were immediately snatched away and put into prison in a town where they had never been. These sorts of things were going on, and they were being suppressed and they were losing their heart to live. I thought, I must save these people.

So I made these films of mine, I wrote my books; and the films had a tremendous impact in Great Britain. There were questions asked in Parliament and I was able to get the Commonwealth Office to appoint a person to go and live with the Bushmen to look after them. So for the first time they had a person to protect them. Three years after that happened – that was in 1956 – the greatest Bushman territory, which then was called Bechuanaland, was made into an independent African state, Botswana. The man who was in charge of the Bushmen resigned and the Bushmen were surrendered into the hands of their old enemies, people who tended to regard them as, at best, animals.

How can that be? Why are the Bushmen hunted down by their neighbours?

They were once hunted down by white and black people who killed the older Bushmen and took the young women and the children as slaves. They created at one time, not long ago, a kind of slave community. They would take the wives because they were attracted by the light colour of their skins – they took them as concubines.

But can't we reverse the situation for the few left by trying to reason with their masters and inform the world?

Well, I have tried to. We have reported their plight to the United Nations, but they do not really want to know; they are content in the excuse that the new world says it is making 'good citizens' of them. It is the same sort of attitude that UNO had towards the Falklands; they seemed to feel, 'Well, there are only a few thousand, so what does it matter?' I do not see any solution and I am afraid that this precious Stone Age culture, which is a pilot scheme of the original pattern of creation, where man and nature lived in harmony together, will vanish.

In this world we will not do anything about Cambodia, we will not do anything about the boat refugees, we will not do anything about anything small and special and unique (except perhaps a few rare plants and animals) – so how can we hope to save the Bushmen? I have concentrated on gathering their stories and their myths, I have made a film record of their lives so somehow, although their society may disappear, their spirit will never disappear. But it is very tragic and I feel this is a typical example of how the quality of life in this technological society of ours has deteriorated, where quantity is increasingly playing a more important role than quality.

Look at our concept of democracy today. It was Voltaire who said, 'I disapprove of what you say, but I will defend to the death your right to say it.' In other words, it is this respect for the differences between people which is the essence of democracy; and this is being allowed to disappear by default all over the world. This is really what the Falkland Islands issue was about, as far as we were concerned. But in a sense the Bushmen are both black and white, so I tell the Bushmen's story over and over again because I want both black and white to see how power corrupted them both.

If 'power corrupts', nationalism can intoxicate and drive people crazy. How can we get rid of nationalism at a time when everyone knows that interdependence is an absolute necessity to solve our problems?

I think it must be done by doing what you and I are trying to do – by speaking as individuals, by getting as many individuals as possible to become aware of the horror of what we are doing. We must never forget that the greatest damage we are doing to the Bushmen is to the Bushmen inside ourselves. Because what you do to another human being you do to yourself. If we could only get this message through. Again, this requires a new awareness, a quickening of the human imagination, getting European man once again to think ultimately, to think religiously, to recover reverence for all forms of created life, and to see that the whole message of creation is unity of variety. Not unity in the modern sense which is feeble, lethal conformity. It is conformity, not unity, that is a source of weakness. But the unity of differences enclosed in a transcendent value, this is what creation is about.

In your book on Jung, you quote him as saying, 'Two thousand years of Christianity had to be replaced by something equivalent.' But what, and how?

Only religion can replace religion. It must be a religious renewal that

* *Jung and the Story of Our Time*, p. 141.

29

we are after. What was very profoundly interesting to me was that I really only began to understand people once I had come to terms with and absorbed and understood the mythology which came out of the earth of Africa – that is, the mythology and stories of the Bushmen. Until I had absorbed that and seen the meaning of it, Christianity did not come alive for me. But I suddenly discovered that here in the beginning was the same sort of religious seeking that I had pursued throughout my Christian culture. It all set me on course again and made me understand more about the meaning of birth and sacrifice, the resurrection, death, immortality. The Bushmen talk of all these things in terms of animals, the animal heroes of their stories. The deep inner meanings the psychologists talk about, they are all there. It is almost as if the Bushmen represent something which we now only find in our dreams. I shall never forget when I was questioning a Bushman very deeply about the meaning of a story and he said to me, 'It is very difficult, because there is a dream dreaming us . . .' Well, he was saying what Shakespeare said at the end of *The Tempest*, which was the last play he ever wrote:

> 'We are such stuff
> As dreams are made on, and our little life
> Is rounded with a sleep.'

It is surprising that Shakespeare, who never left England, was nevertheless able to describe animals unknown to him, such as dolphins.

Oh, it is marvellous. I always say to people that we have a Bushman in ourselves; we have a first man in ourselves, and it is by making what is first and oldest new and contemporary that we become creative. We work through this and once we are in touch with this area, as I find that Shakespeare continually was, then there is nothing ordinary left under the sun or the moon, and you get the same kind of accuracy, the same kind of understanding, no matter what form of life you encounter. It is not so much a conscious understanding as an act of man's living participation in his own being, of observing and recognizing that although a thing is outside, it also represents something inside himself. So he 'knew' in a way which is the greatest possible way of knowing. It is by using this consciousness that the artist creates.

The Bushmen had this ability to an extraordinary degree. The reason it was so difficult for us to understand him was because he, as I knew him in the desert, felt known wherever he went. The stars knew him. He believed that when he died a star would fall from the sky to go and tell life everywhere else that something which was once upright had fallen down. So he felt known, he felt known by the sun and the moon. Wherever he went he felt he belonged. But modern man has lost this feeling of being known. Look at what we call the crisis of identity in modern society. Modern societies – European and American societies – are crammed full of human beings who feel they are not known in this sense of the word. They hunger for the act of recognition at this level. This is what St Paul was referring to in that great statement of his in Corinthians – on a Shakespearean level – which means so much to me, when he says, 'Then shall I know, even as also I am known.' He had this feeling of being known and as soon as he had this feeling of being known, he could make that great trumpet call of his in Corinthians.

I think they are both an example to us of what we should recover in our own spirit. And they are also a warning to us, that if we do not recover this sense nature will turn on us one day, and we will be eliminated as the Bushmen were eliminated – because you cannot eliminate something precious in life without killing something in your own soul. We modern people think we can just trample on something in our way as you trample on an ant, and it will not make the slightest difference to the universe; but it is not true. Somewhere it has an impact, and it does affect us, no matter how small or insignificant. In meaning there is no quantity, only quality; size and amount and distance do not apply, position and direction of spirit is all. That is why it is important that we recover this sense of belonging and the responsibility as individuals of being a good neighbour to all forms of life.

So, I am interested in the Bushman for many profound reasons, but there is one reason which is particularly relevant to the world today, and particularly to South Africa. I tell the people there who say to me I romanticize about the Bushman – and I do not, there are the stories and the paintings to establish what I am saying: 'There is one reason why I have told the Bushman story over and over again and have never stopped telling it to you. I must repeat it as it is all-important; it is the one historical mirror we possess in Africa wherein both black and white can look and see their fallible human faces and see how, when they had another human being absolutely in their power, they were corrupted by their power and eliminated him. This is the great lesson we can look at in it, and we will see that neither of us is better than the other.'

Jung was very interested in Africa. Why did he call Africa 'God's country'? Did he suggest that the African type of sensitivity and relationship with nature and with other people is the best way to approach God?

When Jung talked about 'Africa' it was not the Africa you know. He went to Africa in 1925–6. At that time it was the greatest fortress of natural life left on earth, and this natural life to him was profoundly religious. Remember how he held that the animals were the priests of God because they do God's will, not their own. Only the human being with his consciousness, with his discovery of fire, has a certain freedom of choice; it would seem as if consciousness and the freedom to choose, the awesome responsibility of choice, all arose at once. But the animal does God's will – he is an acolyte of God. He said he felt in Africa almost like Adam in the garden, when everything was new. There he was in touch with the original pattern of creation. Man was not in charge in Africa. Nature – that is, God's nature – was in charge. Therefore it was God's country still, with a soul. Humanly unpredictable things were happening all the time: things over which man had no control. One arrived at a river in flood and there was no bridge by which to cross. You just had to sit there, and it was no good looking at your watch. You had to wait for the water to go down before you could cross it. This gave Jung immense pleasure: after a European life where man seemed to be entirely in command, he was in a place where God and his creation were in control. That is some intimation of what he meant by Africa being 'God's country'. In his *Memories, Dreams, Reflections*, there is a wonderful description of his first glimpse of the interior of East Africa at dawn, one I can vouch for, and in a sense measure, because I too saw it at dawn for the first time in 1926 – the year when, unknown to me, he was there. Only a fear of disproportion, of inflation, prevents or forbids me from thinking of it in terms of synchronicity.

And there's a very revealing scene in your book on Jung when he told you that he almost went African when he attended a dance, but he resisted at the last moment.

Yes, that happened on Mount Elgon, which is a very strange mountain in Africa. It has a mysterious people called the Elgonyi living on it, as on an island, and Jung went to live with them for a time. One night towards the end of his stay, as he watched them dancing, he found himself intoxicated by the heat and gathering pace of the seductive rhythm. The whole thing was in danger of escalating and getting out of control, sweeping him along as well. So he felt he had to disperse the dancers lest they and he started up something which no one would be able to control. He felt this wild spirit of Africa in him. But it was there, you see, and more food for the research which led to his theory of a 'collective unconscious' in man. This theory is to the spirit what the theory of relativity can be to physics. The collective unconscious is a great area of unknown spirit and awareness in man which remains the same for all, regardless of race or creed. In all human beings there is such an area in which the whole of life participates, as it were, mystically. And Jung was very impressed by how much people in Africa were in touch with it and how much they realized that the meaning of their lives depended on their not losing touch with the collective unconscious. It is from this collective unconscious that all our greatest energies come, all the patterns that give life meaning. The Africans had ceremonies and dances, music and stories to express this, and ritual to contain it.

He had found it was the same among the American Indians, Chinese and Tibetans as well as the people of India. This to him was the area where all men are one, where the brotherhood of man already existed. This collective unconscious spoke to the conscious mind of people everywhere in dreams and symbols, and a dream to him was charged with the truth in symbolism. Of course for Jung a dream was the original gateway, a door into this collective unconscious, whose key was Freud's greatest discovery.

There is a very moving story where he is talking to an Elgonyi witch-doctor, or seer, about dreams, and the Elgonyi man told him, 'Yes, of course, there are what we call little dreams and great dreams. Little dreams are the dreams that people have about their own particular lives. Great dreams are the dreams that affect the lives of all men.' Jung then asked him, 'Can you tell me a great dream that you've had?' And the witch-doctor answered sadly, 'I'm afraid we don't have great dreams any more now – the District Commissioner has them for us instead.'

How can you come in touch with God through the collective unconscious?

If you enter the collective unconscious with all your awareness and modesty you come, as it were, to a mirror of God, and again you can have what is nowadays called a dialogue with God. What Jung has called the 'I' and the 'thou' in the human being can confront each other and renew their total meaning in each other.

What Jung said about the Elgonyi witch-doctor and the District Commissioner could be said of the individual and all groups and all societies who live by proxy. It is so easy to let other people decide and dream for you! I think Jung touched upon that subject in a very moving letter to an American journalist when he said, 'We are all embarked in social welfare and we let all the people dream for us'. And when both a people and its leaders dream the same negative dreams and fall in a trance, then it becomes very dangerous. I'm thinking of Hitler and the Germans. Jung himself witnessed that collective delirium from the very beginning, even before 1914. Did he feel the danger and the madness of it?

Yes, he felt that danger acutely because, as a Swiss German, he was part of the German culture. He told me how troubled he was before the 1914–18 war. He was getting very strange visions. He had visions of a tide of blood covering the whole continent of Europe and rising up until it stood level with the top of the Alps in Switzerland, and in this sea of blood he saw mangled corpses, bodies without heads, arms, bits of legs floating about and he thought, 'I must be going mad!' But then he realized that he was having these visions whenever he was travelling to a place called Schaffhausen in Switzerland – that's where his wife came from – and Schaffhausen is on the Swiss–German border. And he thought, 'This is very strange but it's always when I go towards Germany that this awful vision intrudes.' He was so worried by this that in 1914, towards August, he was invited to lecture at Edinburgh University. He very nearly said he would not go because he thought he was going mad and might just spread the madness around. But he went, and on his way back from this conference, in Holland, he opened his newspaper and read the declaration of the First World War. Then immediately he understood. He was almost relieved, for at last he knew what his visions had been about.

And the fact that it came through Germany influenced him enormously. I'll try to offer an explanation. Jung believed that the unique achievement of Western Europe, particularly Christian Europe, was the creation of an individual who would be sufficiently individual and integrated to take the burdens of his community and the world upon himself, to resist this collectivization of the spirit – a throwback of the spirit to primitive man and the 'tribal' Europe of the past. All those hordes out of the East which poured over it – the Huns, Goths, Turks – were all collective, compulsive and demonic phenomena. He suddenly saw this now as an inner danger and saw the renewed significance of the coming of Christ, the emphasis his example put on a human being and his task to make what was universal specific – to make what was collective, individual. This was the creation of individual man, and he suddenly saw the individual imperilled in Germany. Hegel said that before Christ there were just peoples, after Him, individuals. But Jung was profoundly more explicit, and saw it all as a split in the German soul. He began to suspect that Germany, the Germany which had led the last invasion of Goths and Huns out of the East and tumbled Roman civilization, and was also the last to become Christianized, had never really struck a balance in depth between its Christianized self and its primitive, collective self. It was as if Wotan and all the *Furor Teutonicus* of the Romans were erupting again in this First World War. This is why Faust was such a profoundly important symbol to Jung. He said that this was fundamentally a German myth, and that Faust expressed the split in the German soul – that this highly scientific, philosophic and consciously determined Germany had a dark aspect, which was not integrated and in a proper, proportionate order above. It was growing great with anger because it was neglected and unrecognized below in the underworld of the German soul. He quotes Burckhardt, the great Swiss historian, who was at the University of Basle when Jung was there. Burckhardt had a great influence on him, and also on my own father. When Burckhardt heard the news that Kaiser Wilhelm I had had himself crowned at Versailles, he said, 'There is the doom of Germany, it is just beginning.' In other words, he was foretelling that this was the beginning of the German inflation, the madness and hubris of supermen. From that moment of revelation in 1914 onwards, Jung saw this element orches-

36

trating. Day by day the German individual was being dissolved into this collective, archaic mass. He always put the emphasis on the archaic, for this was a retrogressive and not a modern phenomenon, although technically contemporary.

This is our own danger: if you do not let the human spirit progress, it must regress. If you will not let it go forward, it goes backward; and so when it transformed itself into the great totalitarian collective madness of Hitler, Jung saw this as the great danger for modern man. We had created societies which encouraged a shallow, collective person as a substitute for the agonizingly difficult, integrated Christian individual. And this individual was in mortal danger and increasingly losing touch with the religious self which had raised and upheld him, to make the universal specific and the spirit whole.

What kind of relationship did you have with Jung?
We became friends. I used to drop in on him and made a habit of seeing him as often as I could. And when my wife Ingaret was studying with him I saw him all the time. Then after we came back to London – in those days I used to go to Africa a great deal – I always used to go to Africa by way of Zürich, and would spend some days with him. On my way back I would call on him again.

Could you describe him? Wasn't it true that he had a great love of life, was a man of the here and now, as well as of the before and after?
Oh yes, he had a tremendous love of life, which he radiated. Physically he was the best possible credential for his psychology. During the 1914–18 war, which was a very troubled and difficult time for him, he said to the people who were interested in psychology, 'We ought to have a non-solemn side too, a social side.' So they started a club which still exists in Zürich, the Psychological Club. They used to meet at this club once a week and have jolly good food, and drink a little bit too much. They would dance and sing and wear fancy dress – I've seen some marvellous photographs of Jung dressed up as Bacchus.

His face was a bit like Pan's with those laugh lines around his eyes?
Yes, that's true; he was always close to nature. He felt physical separation from nature very intensely when he went away to university. He said his bitterest experience was that he went to university with a

country mind and he suddenly discovered there was such a thing as a town mind, and that the whole of life was divided between town and country minds. There is a great deal in that. It haunts me, and is what I feel very much about western society. Western Europe was once governed by a country mind – even city states had a keen country awareness – but the country mind has greatly diminished. People who know nothing about the land suddenly sit and rule like gods over the fate of other men. They think they can just pass a law and create a new state of being. Any farmer would tell them you cannot do that, there are no short cuts; that everything is a process of growth, and growth has got its own time and laws and seasons, and is not man's time. It takes ten months between the conception and birth of a calf and there is nothing you can do to speed it up. We know that. The abuse of time which goes on in towns is terrible, particularly in industrialized cities. People live in them as if time were theirs to command, although they pay a terrible price for it. Jung was aware in all these things that he was confronted with a vital dilemma: that his duties to the town and its community were in conflict with his love of nature without and within. He saw man as a partner of nature.

What do you think Jung would say to you today, at this stage of your life and evolution in your books?

I know the first person who would reproach me if I did not get on with my individual story would be Jung. He would say, 'You go and finish what your work demands, before you talk about me.' Yet, wherever I go and wherever I have a chance, it has become part of my life to bear witness to the reality of Jung by speaking about him. I do that continually. I have only just this morning had a call from America again asking if I would come back to talk about him. I add what I can when I can to his story, seeing myself as a kind of messenger-boy keeping contact on my beat around the world between people who continue his work – a sort of deliverer of telegrams between people who think themselves alone and separate but already are a 'pilot scheme', a model of something greater to come.

I did not discuss profound things with him by letter except occasionally, for instance when his wife died. Then I wrote to him. He answered and I wrote back. There are significant elements in those exchanges to which I refer in my book. But they do not really contain anything which would shed new light on Jung's thought and work. I think they would not justify my breaking off what I'm doing now.

Who was Jung really for you – friend, master, father?

He was a friend who gave me much, to whom I owe more than I can say, and who was also great fun. I must stress this: he made me laugh more than anybody else I know. But above all he was a kind of lighthouse to me. In that way he made me feel that I was not too far off course, that I was more or less on the right passage and in convoy. It gave me a feeling of confidence in what I was trying to do myself. He threw light on great areas of darkness of our time, indeed all time. Perhaps you know that lovely poem by Baudelaire, '*Les Phares*', where he goes through the great painters of all time and he talks about art? I think Jung was a lighthouse, *un phare*, for ships navigating on the great seas of life.

Did you ever meet anyone else as interesting as Jung, someone of his stature?

No; I've never met anybody of his immense stature, where the man or the woman measured up to the achievement so well. It always amazed me – his immense appetite for life, his zest for living. When one stayed with him – the abundant and delicious food served, the fine wine, cigars for those who smoked, the sense of sane well-being – there was a great love of life there. I have met many who are in their own way great people, who mean a great deal to me, but they are almost all anonymous and not persons the world thought 'great'. Some of them are black, and coloured people. I think of those I knew in the war who were truly great, in the sense that they rose to the challenge of their own lives. They were integrated within their own destiny and they did not try to evade it. But Jung was also great in that he lived his own unique destiny. He accepted it as his proper task in life, and so his life was full of an inner eventfulness. But he also had a scale about him which you could say some of the anonymous people lacked. He had the extra quality to match his unique performance. I don't know how one, to use a terrible modern word, 'quantifies' greatness, but he had a scale, a measure, which matched his quality. That was a tremendous achievement.

And he had a rare ability to question himself.

Oh, all the time! I remember, about two years before he died, when Ingaret and I were at Ascona one winter to be with him, he and I went for a walk. I remember him saying to me, 'You know, it's terrible when I look back on my life how little I've done.' He added, 'I've done so little when I see what remains to be done! In order to do my job properly I should have been a mathematician as well, I should have been an artist, a physicist' – and so on. He said he should have been all these things and really felt he had failed. We happened also to be talking about one of his books and I said, 'If you'd only written this one book, your life would have been worth more than most other lives I know of in the last 500 years. How can you be so ungrateful?' Yet I knew it was a sign that only he was great enough to realize how small a distance he had covered.

Did he talk to you about Freud and why they broke off their relationship?

I think what he felt about Freud was that he could not have gone any other way but to accompany Freud in the beginning. He never complained about Freud, and he never spoke about Freud to me with anything except gratitude, saying what a great man Freud was. It was only when I asked him once about it directly that he told me how for a long time he had had doubts about Freud. These doubts had come to a head during their last visit to America. I think it was round about 1911 when they were doing a tour of America together. As usual they were interpreting each other's dreams. Freud told Jung about a dream he had had and Jung said to Freud, 'I cannot help you with this dream until you tell me what your associations are, your personal associations, with a certain aspect of the dream.' He picked out something from the dream and Jung said Freud blushed, and replied, 'I'm afraid I can't tell you.' When Jung asked, 'Why not?' Freud replied, 'It would be bad for my authority.' Jung said, when he heard that, something in him snapped, because he felt that if a man set his personal authority above the truth, then he could not keep him company any longer. That really precipitated the final break. It had been building up for a long time.

However, the break between Jung and Freud never surprised me. The surprising thing was that they should have been together so long, because they were totally unalike and they worked differently. Jung was quite frank about this. He said, 'I had not been honest enough with myself. I was in a way deceiving both Freud and myself by our collaboration.' I think that shows how deeply Jung looked to himself and felt in this a self-betrayal, and that, like St Peter, he had failed the light.

40

And yet like Peter he was 'a rock' on which much was built and more, endlessly more, shall be built. If ever he saw a fault he corrected it. The errors he was afraid of were errors of the spirit, and those he corrected by confession in his soul and repentance of heart and mind. He never failed in that. He had many problems in his personal relationships because people, men in particular, found it almost impossible to have real, objective, personal relationships with him, and this hurt very much. He could not bear men working with him and then ceasing to be themselves and becoming an imitation of what he was; this drove him to enormous fits of rage.

There are many essential differences in mind and behaviour between Jung and Freud. Did this apply also to their attitudes towards drugs? Today, not only 'welfare societies' but also 'drugged societies' are mushrooming all over the world.

I do not know about drugs as a source of difference between them. All I know is that Jung was sceptical of their psychological value. When Aldous Huxley started experimenting with mescalin and wrote a book, *The Doors of Perception*, about it, Jung exchanged letters on that subject with Victor White, a distinguished Roman Catholic priest and, for some years, a friend and supporter, who asked him for his views. Jung wrote him a long letter in which he said that he did not really know much about experiences with mescalin and then went on to say:

'I don't know what its psychotherapeutic value with neurotic or psychotic patients is. I only know there is no point in wishing to know more of the collective unconscious than one gets through dreams and intuition. The more you know of it, the greater and heavier becomes your moral burden, because the unconscious contents transform themselves into your individual tasks and duties as soon as they begin to become conscious. Do you want to increase loneliness and misunderstanding? Do you want to find more and more complications and increasing responsibilities? You get enough of it. If I once could say that I had done everything I knew I had to do, then perhaps I should realize a legitimate need to take mescalin. But if I should take it now, I would not be sure at all that I had not taken it out of idle curiosity. I should hate the thought that I had touched on the sphere where the paint is made that colours the world, where the light is created that makes shine the splendour of the dawn, the lines and shapes of all form, the sound that fills the orbit, the thought that illuminates the darkness of the void. There are some poor impoverished creatures, perhaps, for whom mescalin would be a heavensent gift without a counterpoison, but I am profoundly mistrustful of the 'pure gifts of the Gods'. You pay very dearly for them . . .

'This is not the point at all, to know of or about the unconscious, nor does the story end here; on the contrary it is how and where you begin the real quest. If you are too unconscious it is a great relief to know a bit of the collective unconscious. But it soon becomes dangerous to know more, because one does not learn at the same time how to balance it through a conscious equivalent. That is the mistake Aldous Huxley makes: he does not know that he is in the role of the 'Zauberlehrling', who learned from his master how to call the ghosts but did not know how to get rid of them again . . .

'It is really the mistake of our age. We think it is enough to discover new things, but we don't realize that knowing more demands a corresponding development of morality.'

I find that passage, which begins with the question, 'Do you want to increase loneliness?', and comes to an end with expressions like 'the thought that illuminates the darkness of the void', not only charged with the truest religious feeling but full of the sense of poetry one only experiences when one is talking from the heart of the truth that is not just literal, linear and partial but utterly whole and total.

Did he make a distinction between the primitive peoples who used drugs for religious purposes and the curiosity of intellectuals in the West?

I do not think he really went very deeply into all that – nor do I think he looked for large audiences. Towards the end of his life he wrote me a European anyway. He did not believe in short cuts or anything unearned. Again and again he emphasized that you must find your own way and earn your enlightenment. He was against a growing Western superstition that healing, even of the spirit, was just chemistry, that the answer was a chemical one – although he knew the tradition of alchemy as nobody else did. In fact he rediscovered it and its meaning. He was aware of how the alchemists' approach was of great religious and symbolic importance, but was still limited by its own one-sidedness which used chemistry for a purpose for which chemistry was not the answer. Both alchemy and astrology greatly interested him; he saw them as forms of projected psychology and felt the alchemists were symbolically acting out the spiritual search in their quest for the philosopher's stone. He believed that the spirit was all-important – and that the physical world could be the spirit seen from without. Jung had so much to do and was so intuitive, he very quickly knew if a fork in the road was a genuine choice of main road or a sort of side-track. So he did not have to go far down for his intuitive sense to say, 'Ah, this is not for me. I must follow my own road.' But he was terribly insistent on this – that work, earning, sacrifice in a contemporary way – all were necessary. That is why he was not surprised when people did not queue up to take on his psychology. He did not offer instant redemption. His approach calls for the hardest of all human tasks, the task of individuation. It presupposes the hardest road man can travel and there is no other way. The true road is a hard road.

Do you think, however, that Jung's message has been correctly transmitted and received?

I do not think it has. I think it was correctly transmitted by Jung and by some of his followers, but I think what has prevented Jung's message from having its full impact yet – and that is one of the reasons I wrote my book – is that some of the people who convey Jung's message are professionals and try to think of that message as purely psychiatric. I think the Jungians are a wonderful breed, and, after all, Jung was a psychiatrist himself, but psychiatry was not his end but a way on which the object, the direction, was all-important.

If you look at Jung's autobiography, *Memories, Dreams, Reflections*, you see that there are several chapters before the encounter with his work. Psychiatry was a means to his work but not the ultimate work itself. To write about Jung purely in a psychiatric context, important as it is, is not enough. Jung moved on to be much more, but they confine him to psychiatry, depriving him of his universality. On another level, think, for instance, what would happen if one confined Christ purely to the parables of healing the sick and left out the Crucifixion and the Ascension? The meaning of his coming would have almost been totally lost. In a different dimension this is what so many books are doing with Jung. They leave him in the wards with the sick. I have read books by eminent psychologists which end with a chapter on Jung's contribution to psychiatry, as if that were the end of the story: but it is really only the beginning.

Did he want to communicate with the greatest number of people, with a larger audience?

No, he didn't. He was quite content to work in a small way and always felt that if there was anything worth while in what he was doing, it would take care of itself. He did not believe in having followers. He did not believe in having great institutions. He was modest in the way he worked. Numbers were never, never important to him. He really never looked for large audiences. Towards the end of his life he wrote me a very moving letter. He said, 'I am an increasingly lonely, old man writing to other lonely men.' And I took him up on that and he said it was not meant to be a complaint. He said he found great comfort in a remark Christ makes in one of the very early apocryphal gospels. I have forgotten which one it is exactly but it is where Christ says to his disciples, 'Wherever there is anyone who is truly alone I am with him.' And what is very significant for me in Christ's last years is that he spent all his time with just twelve apostles, implying that if he could really get his meaning through to twelve it would be as much as he had to do. He spoke to the multitudes only once – thereafter concentrating on his twelve, and the odds and ends of humanity he encountered on the way.

Jung mistrusted numbers. He saw great danger in numbers, because numbers are a danger to the individual. He saw in our modern world that we did not realize the peril in which sheer numbers were putting us, the peril of what he called giantism, the sheer size of operations, the size of our cities – our confusion in thinking of growth and expansion as synonymous. All these things were a form of hubris, of quantity as opposed to quality and he saw them as a great threat to the human spirit. So his whole instinct was to work on a small scale where you could be precise and clear.

I shall never forget – I once went to America and told my friends, 'Look, I'm very tired and shall be grateful if you could keep our meeting small.' It was on a Good Friday. I had just arrived in New York and was exhausted. Then I opened the *New York Times* and saw a whole-page advertisement, 'Laurens van der Post on The Destiny of the Human Spirit'. This was not what I had meant or had been promised at all. But I felt I had to go and I was dismayed; there were hundreds of people there. When I had finished talking I was uneasy – I had been ill-prepared. I realized I had been saying things unconsciously, more to accommodate the audience than really what I wanted and needed to convey. I had been seduced from speaking with precision. Later, when I told Jung about this experience, he said, 'You have been warned. If ever you have to talk to numbers like that you must write it down beforehand. A manuscript is the only protection you have against the devil of numbers.' So he had obviously thought about this and realized the peril. He wanted none of it himself.

But numbers can also be magical, conveying infinity, love, music, within them.

Oh yes; each number, as a number, and not a collective amount, was in a sense sacred; to Jung there was an archetypal element in each. That is why he could never do mathematics. For instance, he told me that if he had an equation to the effect that if A is equal to B, and B is equal to C, then A is also equal to C, he found this a highly immoral statement because how could A be equal to B, let alone C, since they are all different. A is A, B is B and C is C. He had this enormous respect for the identity of things.

What did he think were the great evils of our time beside giantism and numbers?

Well, the great problem of our time for him was man's failure to know himself, to recognize evil and deal with it within himself. That is why he was always at war with a Roman Catholicism which held that evil is only an absence of good. This, Jung thought, was blasphemy because evil to him was real. There were these two great opposites in life, good and evil. How relative they might be to a man's state of awareness, and what they represented, were absolutes on man's pilgrim way. To diminish the stature of evil as a reality in life, therefore, was to make man more vulnerable to evil. As he said in his correspondence with Victor White, 'You can't call Hitler's massacre of the Jews merely an absence of good. Nor can you call Stalin's massacre of the peasants in Russia merely an absence of good. These are evil things and we must call them by their right names. This is a sure fact.' And he said, 'Man is only free insofar as he chooses good rather than evil.'

But didn't Jung believe evil was necessary to good? Like Mephisto to Goethe's Faust?

Yes, I think he fully accepted that evil was part of the reality of the universe and had a very important role in that, in a sense, if man did not have good and evil to choose between, life would lose its meaning. But I think one must be at one's most aware when one speaks of the reality of good and evil and not be over-confident, because the problem of their presence in life is only capable of articulation in part. All we can say with a certain instinctive authority is that consciousness, good and evil, all three, burst into life at once; they are interconnected in the most subtle, mysterious and enigmatic ways. The gift of consciousness compels us to recognize good and evil, however provisionally, and with all the awareness we are capable of we have to choose between them. There lies the greatest freedom conferred on us by consciousness: the freedom to choose between good and evil; and as we choose, so shall we increase or decline.

It seems man is always tempted to bite into the forbidden fruit of the tree of knowledge of good and evil; and more so now that he has immense powers at his disposal.

Yes, and this is what worried Jung. He felt that this increase of power demanded of man a greater ethical responsibility in its exercise. He often said that the prevention of another world war, of another nuclear holocaust, depended on the rate at which individuals could be made into true individuals, incapable of being seduced by the mass collective urges of the human spirit, as the Germans were and as the Russians are today. He said we must not forget that the Russians are the primitive peoples of Europe. He said we must not attack them – they must be left to defeat themselves; but we must be ready at all times to defend ourselves.

Again, this would indicate that the only possible evolution is a spiritual one.

Jung was very much aware of the profound meaning of Christ's remark, 'Resist ye not evil', but he tried to see reality whole and recognize that there are moments when man has no chance to choose between good and evil. He did not hesitate to say that often he had to

46

choose the least of evils. The key word was 'choose', and he made it clear that the would choose rearmament as long as there were totalitarian threats to be contained.

Jung himself may have had the power to resist numbers, and evil. But what about the average man?

Jung didn't believe in the 'average' man. He called him a 'statistical abstraction'. No, he believed that man could be overcome by collective urges in himself and the only safeguard was an individual who would not sacrifice his individual sense of right and wrong to the crowd. This was really what it was all about, that the individual had to be made modern. The individual for him was not an individualist. All 'ists' and 'isms' were wrong to him. Individualism was wrong; the individual was a man who was individual in the service of life and the community. It does not mean that he was not a 'community man' but that he was in the community. Jung viewed the community as rather like a congregation in church: whereas at a football match you could say you had a crowd, you could not say that you had a crowd in a cathedral, because every man there is an individual and is merely reunited, through the Eucharist, to something beyond himself. That sort of communion is what Jung believed in: you cannot fix the rules – you obey them. This to him was the task which we were neglecting, which we had forgotten. For him the first warning sign, almost, in the European spirit, was the French Revolution. The Revolution in France filled him with horror because he had a great love of France and the spirit of France, and he felt that this thing which came to a head in Paris was a betrayal of all that was good in France.

Yes, there is a tendency in France to cut off heads, to kill – and be killed – for the defence of ideas.

Yes, and it was this French Revolution that made revolution respectable in a sense – it's only now that people are beginning to realize that revolution really is anti-life. In the first book I ever wrote* I quoted Goethe, and Goethe witnessed the French Revolution: 'I hate those who make revolutions as much as those who cause them. I believe that far more good is destroyed by revolutions than is accomplished by them.'

* *In a Province.* The quotation in German is: '*Ich hasse jeden gewaltsamen Umsturz, weil dabei ebensoviel Gutes vernichtet als gewonnen wird. Ich hasse die, welche ihn ausführen wie die welche dazu Ursache geben.*'

And the French Revolution, what it represents, is far from over yet, either in the French spirit or in the modern scene. The goddess of reason it raised and crowned in Paris is still enthroned, and in the spirit of the contemporary world and in the social scene it still commands and incites millions, all over the world, with Russia its most fanatical convert.

Did Jung attach any importance to the teaching of history?

Yes, he did. He had a great sense of history. He believed profoundly in teaching history, but again, as with everything that Jung conceived, he felt it had to be done in a contemporary way. For him history was transformed from the school level to the story of the soul of man. That was the only history that ultimately mattered to him, yet today this important dimension of history seems to matter less and less. He was trying to bring the human spirit back into contact with history before it was too late. He was dismayed by the loss of soul and meaning already caused by this loss of history. All around him in Europe he saw this loss of soul and meaning orchestrating, and he wanted to stop it because he saw it as the way to catastrophe.

But is it possible to change man, particularly through education? What were Jung's views on education?

He was a man born with a cause, so much so that he never had a chance to be young and irresponsible. He was fighting for and with his own ideas and discoveries so that he hardly had time. He had to delegate many of his tasks to his wife Emma. He was in a sense crucified to his own genius. He was so busy I do not think he had time to be a conventional father. Although I do not think his wife would have changed roles with anybody in the world, she herself was so moved by what her husband was doing that she joined him in his work when their children were educated and off their hands. She did a good deal of research into the legend of the Holy Grail. It is particularly touching because all his life Jung had wanted to work on this, but he felt he should not trespass on his wife's ground and deprive her of perhaps her best chance to contribute out of her greater feminine self to his work.

=====

What is your own view on education? You were one of a family of thirteen children and you yourself have children and grandchildren. How to open windows, how to broaden the horizon, how to multiply chances for the young?

I think the great thing is to awaken the child, the mind of the child, the imagination of the child, to give it a light, to respect, not spoil, its own identity, and it will soon find its way, because life itself is a process of educating the universe. Well, this is not the modern trend; it's all too rational now, and of course this is not education at all, it's the opposite of education, it is a blinding, this hubris of the mind, of the rational. It is a kind of not loving, of not caring. When the human being loses interest in the child, he is in great peril. And we are in great peril because more and more children are being thrown into schools, into the hands of professionals. People give them money and material things instead of giving them what they want – our love and imagination. That is, awakening their imaginations to the experience of love. Once you've done that you can leave it, it will take care of itself. The education of the parents is really the education of the child: children tend to live what is unlived in the parents, so it is vital that parents should be aware of their inferior, their dark side, and should press on getting to know themselves. To the extent to which they emancipate their shadow, they set their children free to be themselves. So in this sense it is the education or re-education of the parents that should be our main concern.

But what kind of future do we prepare for our children – if we assume that they do have a future? With the advent of the nuclear age nothing and nobody can be the same as before. For our own good everything perhaps should be considered as atomized, even words. Don't you think all professionals in the use and exchange of words, such as politicians and journalists, should now treat words as if they were nuclear products, that is to say in a careful, meaningful and responsible way? In that sense the 'thousand suns' of Hiroshima and Nagasaki should have opened our eyes.

I certainly think that the lesson we learned from Hiroshima and Nagasaki could be used for the good of mankind, just as I think atomic energy can be used for the good of mankind. There is an enormous symbolic importance in the fact that the source of this destructive energy was nuclear – that it came from the atom – because it shows that the

49

greatest energy in the physical world is in the smallest unit . . . Just as I have been saying to you that the source of power, transforming power, in human society is in the smallest unit of human society, which is the individual. The individual is the atom of society and therefore these two symbols are in a sense complementary. What is most threatening and destructive in human society today is the human being who is split in his own nucleus: it is the fission in the modern soul which makes nuclear fission so dangerous – he is a split atom. He has got to heal himself, make himself whole.

So many things have been said and so many books have been written about the atomic bombing of Hiroshima and Nagasaki that, somehow, we tend to forget the context of it in the Pacific War. A sure fact is that that holocaust saved your life and the lives of hundreds of thousands of prisoners-of-war and civilians in countries occupied by the Japanese.

Yes, I know we were saved by it, because we have evidence of the fact that we were all due to have been killed by the Japanese. Actually the bomb was dropped in August, and the massacre was timed for when the real invasion of South-East Asia would begin.* Mountbatten's forces were gathering to invade South-East Asia on the 2nd September. So we were only saved by a few weeks. But I am convinced that millions of other lives were saved too. Because if the war had gone on, hundreds of thousands of American lives would have been lost, millions of Japanese lives would have been lost – you can imagine the number of *seppukus*, the ritual suicides, that would have gone on, and the numbers that would have been killed in a last battle . . . It's unspeakable.

Do you agree with the argument that says if the Japanese had produced the atom bomb first they would have used it without hesitation?

Yes; you know them better than I do. I think that people were caught in such an extreme cycle of their own spirit that they could have done anything and believed it justified. It was an extraordinary war they fought; it was a sheer fantasy, you see, but in a way the same thing applied to Germany. I am certain that it was a *Götterdämmerung*, that Hitler conducted the war in such a way that he had to be defeated. If not, why did he ever invade Russia? Why did he invade Russia? He could not

* See *The Night of the New Moon*.

stop. It was just like Napoleon: why couldn't Napoleon stop? Why did he have to go on and on. It was this blind collective urge which once it is released is a form of madness, collective madness, that only this deep mythological mechanism of proportion and self-correction can arrest and dispel, even in Hitler's as in Napoleon's case, by unconsciously forcing them to conduct war in a way that will defeat war and so make them instruments of their own destruction.

What is your opinion now about the bomb? Do you think the Americans were right to use it?

To me the interesting thing is that the bomb has only been used twice. You could have said that in the Korean War, which was a very dastardly war, another sort of Pearl Harbor was organized: I mean, when MacArthur's back was turned and the Americans were nearly pushed into the sea in Korea, there could have been a tremendous temptation and indeed argument to use the bomb, but it was not used. I am quite certain that what we call the western world will never drop an atom bomb first. But I feel it is important that the western world should have sufficient power to do so in self-defence, so that any country which may be tempted to use the bomb against us will know that it will get more in return. And we must not persist in thinking of nuclear problems as only a United States–Russian dimension. Soon all sorts of maverick states with money to burn are going to have atom bombs. The number who have them already or are about to get them is alarming. We must get away from looking at life partially and hysterically. We must, as the Greeks enjoined, look at it steadily and whole, and life will never forgive us if we neglect any defence reality demands of us, for the sake of a fine gesture that merely warms the egotistical lust for feeling ethical and superior: but the emphasis is always on defence, not aggression.

Remember, too, that in the psychology of war there is an element of proportion, diabolical proportion. You can see it, for instance, in the use of poison gas. In the 1914–18 war the Germans used poison gas with great initial success and everybody assumed in the 1939–45 war that it would be used again. We and the Americans had gases that went far beyond the original poison gas that was used. We were ready to use it in a big way against the Germans. But somehow, because everyone was conscious of it, it was never used.

But in the 1914–18 war gases were dangerous to use even for the users. Wind could blow it back to the trench.

In a small way that happened, yes, but in the '39 war there were other ways: for instance, dropping the gas from the air where you could not be imperilled by it – but it was never used. It is an interesting observation. But I do feel that in regard to war, in the West anyway, the whole psychology of our time towards war has changed. The approach of the human being to war can never be the same again. In 1914, I can remember that my eldest brothers in Africa were terrified they would not get to Europe in time for the war – which we came to think of as the last of the 'romantic wars'. But the last world war, as far as France and Britain were concerned, was a police action. Very sadly we donned our uniforms and took our guns and we went off to war. There was no jubilation, no cheering and laughter and excitement. To me what happened in the Falkland Islands is very interesting: you could look at the people in the Argentine singing and cheering and screaming in the streets. There were no such demonstrations in Britain. Our forces looked like a lot of policemen going out to put down a riot – one saw just one great grey ship of war after the other, slipping their cables by some quay on a grey English afternoon without bands or flagwaving, with only fathers, mothers, children with sad haunting faces waving goodbye. But by contrast there broke out in their wake a barracking of hate and distrust and anti-Britishness among the British themselves, even a pro-Argentinianism – more disturbing than any outright jingoistic or chauvinistic display could have been, because this was the same thing only darker and more dangerous because it was in reverse.

But this war was close to the Argentinians and quite far away for the British.

No, but it was our people who were going away to war in our unique historic way. I mean the British throughout their history have fought wars far away. The Falkland Islands were nearer to us than South-East Asia where we fought in the last war in the Pacific, very much nearer. But people were going off quietly, without any fuss, without drama, without rhetoric.

———

How did you survive when you were a prisoner-of-war? What were the essential factors which contributed to your survival?

Well, it is a fact, it is a law of life that you should fight for life truthfully and honourably as long as you can, and that you as the individual cannot decide to abandon life – that is a thing which is left to God and therefore we had to do everything we could to go on living. The only weapon we had – because we were completely helpless – was to live truthfully and not to allow the madness which surrounded us to distort our vision of the truth. I could have been proved wrong at any moment, but I felt that as long as we lived truthfully we had a chance for survival. And the proof is that we did survive.

Your prison camp in Java was a microcosm of the world with Dutch, British, Australians, New Zealanders, Indonesians, Chinese and, of course, the Japanese and Koreans enrolled by force in the Japanese army. Was there any interaction, and did any changes take place in the hearts and minds of all these men?

Well, I described what happened in my books,* and what was interesting to me was the way in which the ordinary soldiers of all races and colours got on with one another, even when they could not speak the language. You'd see an English soldier and a Chinese walking about roaring with laughter at something they had seen, and having this feeling of togetherness that all prisoners tend to have. It was also interesting to me that the greatest problems we had were with people who were part of what you might describe as the intellectual classes. The people who had not lost contact with their instincts – they were our source of strength. They were the ones that sustained. The difficult people were among the officers – and I hasten to add how exceptional they were – because they felt some special treatment was due to their office, that they had privileges as officers necessary for the upholding of their rank and exercise of their command. And among the officers the trickiest were those who had been lawyers in private life. They were excellent men but seemed to find it difficult ever to command or obey. Everything was a case to be argued. The wholeness of the thing tended to escape them. All was argument, counter-argument and special pleading. But for the

* *The Night of the New Moon* and *The Seed and the Sower.*

most part everybody responded to leadership by example rather than command, and on the whole we were blessed in the quality of our officers and men. We came through, and though one would not like to repeat the experience, an enormous liberating influence for us all was the absence of possessions and the stark simplicity with which we had to lead our lives, so that only essentials mattered.

And everybody was forced to cling to one another, forced to be involved.

Oh yes, we did that, because our own command instinctively followed the great declaration of St John, 'In the beginning was the Word, and the Word was with God, and the Word was God.'

For instance, I joined the prison camp later than anyone else because I was captured later, and when I did so I was horrified at the state of disorder and dissension there. So when Wing-Commander Nichols, a great prison commander, and I took over, I started by writing a letter and getting a man to help me make copies of it, and we posted it in all the different places where people could read it. Its message, in essence, was, 'We must look upon imprisonment not as a tragedy but as a great opportunity. This break of continuity which life in prison appears to be, is more apparent than real. We all carry our true and unassailable continuity within us and we have only to follow it and we shall come through.' I went on to outline what I thought the opportunity was; and that is how we lived it, as if this were a great opportunity for re-education. So I created an educational system in the camp and people had never been so busy. I meet people now who, I am sad to say, after the many years since they were in prison with Nichols and myself, get a look of intense nostalgia and they say, 'You know, those were the days . . .' It is rather tragic because it reflects the failure of so-called peace and its inadequacies which are the causes of war.

This experience of 'togetherness' can happen in time of war or in time of great urgency or emergency, but how can it happen in everyday life? How can we be wiser when money, power, status count for so much?

The only way you could do it would be by being an instrument of the truth, and then human beings would respond.

For instance, in the camp, one of the first things Nichols and I did was to confiscate all the money in the camp – and some of the officers parted with their money under protest. In fact, one of the most senior

54

threatened to have us court-martialled after the war for what he called this insubordination. We used the money for the welfare of the camp as a whole. There was no private money henceforth. And in many ways like that we showed that an officer's condition was not created to give him special privileges. If anything, an officer in these circumstances should have less than his men. That is what being an officer meant: to lead by serving more than anyone else. That was why the British forces were for me so movingly called 'services' and why, contrary to their television image of today, they were not reflections of class and capitalistic systems but great brotherhoods; indeed monastic orders of sorts.

But to return to money, I can tell you an interesting story about money which reflects our prison approach to it. You see I had six weeks after the Japanese capitulation in which I had to represent the British Government in Java and, in all immediate issues, govern it through the Japanese, in a Java which was in a state of rebellion. And then the first contacts with Mountbatten came through an exceptional Admiral, Wilfred Patterson, a sensitive, humane and far-seeing serviceman. He was joined by General Christison, a soldier-statesman of a high order, who was going to take command when our troops arrived. I told him all I had learned, what I thought should be done, and how dangerous I thought the ignorance we seemed to fight in was, back at High Command. Characteristically, he made up his mind immediately, and said to me: 'You must go back and see Lord Mountbatten at once.' So, dressed in my old prison clothes, I was flown in a reconnaissance aircraft to Singapore. I arrived there late in the evening as everything was closing down at the airport. I told the RAF officer in control that I had most immediate authority from my Admiral and General to go in the first available transport to Ceylon the next day.

After a startled pause and a glance at the General's note written on a torn-out page of his pocket dispatch book, the officer said: 'That's all right, I can get you onto the transport but I am rather embarrassed, I don't know what to do with you for tonight because Singapore is full of ex-POWs, full of people, I don't know where to put you . . .' I said: 'Do you mind if I just sleep on the floor of your office?' He said: 'No, but . . . what about food?' I said: 'That doesn't matter. I can wait until I get to Colombo.' 'But', he said, 'that won't be for another twenty hours!' I said:

'I've gone without food for days in prison.' So he gave me some water to drink and left me. The next morning I flew to Colombo in Ceylon. I arrived there at four o'clock in the afternoon and found I had to wait for some hours for a plane to fly me on to Kandy where Lord Mountbatten's headquarters were. So I went into what we called a NAAFI, a restaurant organized by the services for people passing through. I went and sat at a table and a NAAFI girl in uniform came along and asked me what I would like to have. I was looking very odd in my improvised prison uniform with shaven head and emaciated features and she looked at me very strangely as I said, 'I'd love some eggs and bacon.'

So she went and got me eggs and bacon and toast and coffee. But then she came along and said, 'That will be five shillings.' And I looked at her in amazement and exclaimed, 'My God! Do people still use money?' 'Well, I'm afraid we do,' she replied.

I had not thought of equipping myself with money for this journey, for in our prison world private money had been so utterly abolished that it had been eliminated from our personal reckoning. So what could I do? Almost in a panic by the enormity not only of my thoughtlessness but this evidence of an abyss opening up between the values of our prison world and the 'free' world, I threw myself on the mercy of an officer sitting at a table near mine. I explained what had happened and said, 'Could you please pay for my tea? Give me your name and address and when I get back to London I will take you for dinner at Claridges.' He gave me one glance and said, 'Certainly,' and gave me my five shillings. I paid the waitress and went off on my journey to Lord Mountbatten.

But that shows you how we came out of prison and the way our lives had come to presuppose a world where these things were no longer necessary.

And did you also try — you yourself and the other six thousand prisoners with you — to understand your captors and tormentors, the Japanese?

I have often thought about this question. I realize that when I first went to Japan in 1926 I was really little more than a boy. I was tremendously changed at a very profound level, in my psyche, as it were, in my soul. That experience has been one of the great and most creative influences on my life, a meeting at a deep level of metamorphosis. And it has not come to an end yet. I notice changes are still going on. Today, I can see a lot of it consciously but I am not seeing anything that was not there unconsciously. So although this process of understanding started inevitably as an instinctive reaction, its conscious consequences were profound and have gone on all my life. Looking back on my encounter with the Japanese in Java I am amazed by how much was already unconsciously present in my imagination, which would have a decisive and protective fall-out in all my dealings and doings with the Japanese. I know, for instance, it saved my life that day in 1942 when I was caught by Japanese soldiers on the mountain, Djaja-Sempoer in Java, with almost all that I had known of the Japanese language forgotten – because unfortunately I could not read Japanese to keep it alive in my mind – and yet the right reaction came out of me in this moment of crisis, and I said to them, 'Would you please condescend to be so kind as to wait an honourable moment?'

In the best Japanese!

Yes! And from this little knowledge came more food for understanding. Particularly so when I came into contact with the Japanese again in prison and confronted their dark, shadow side. We all have a shadow within but here I was meeting a specifically Japanese shadow, the aspect of their character aroused by the violence of their transition from the pre-Meiji Empire of Japan, moving overnight, as it were, from a medieval culture and structure into the modern age; and making the mistake we continue to make, in spite of all the evidence and warnings, of thinking that you can make men and their societies contemporary by merely heaping our terrifying technology and its horrendous power on them. They did not realize what damage they were doing to their instinctive selves. And here in the war it was bursting out, presenting itself in the most brutal way. Yet it was never something which was totally inhuman to me. It seemed instinctively that I could understand it. Even in its most frightening forms, I could understand it in a way that I could not understand the Nazi phenomenon. It seemed important somehow that our salvation in prison depended on enlarging this process of understanding.

This is what I tried to do. I tried to tell people what I knew about Japan and Japanese history. I gave lectures in prison on these things, and then I relearnt, very rapidly, Japanese. I started teaching Japanese classes, and that was the biggest class that I had. Now this is a very strange phenomenon. To me it was profoundly symbolic that there were so many of the ordinary British soldiers who wanted to learn the language of the enemy. That was a tremendous bridge to understanding. I had these large classes and I found I only had to ask the Japanese and they gave us books in Dutch about the Japanese – and in Java there were a lot of people who knew Japan well. Holland had a very ancient connection with Japan; after the Portuguese were thrown out of Japan the Dutch were the only people allowed to trade with them, and there were a lot of books about it.

So that was strange. Everything that the Japanese inflicted on us was always balanced by something they gave us, through these books, out of their minds and their spirit. And I am certain that that is one of the reasons we came out of the experience with no bitterness. Very few people came out hating the Japanese. It was a remarkable achievement, particularly when I hear what happened at other places where the bitterness was much greater. It was a great triumph really on both sides.

Of understanding.

Of understanding – I can only put it down to this fact. You see, if you meet something with truth, no matter how disagreeable the truth is, it is always a meaningful and creative experience. It seemed to be so not just for my own British soldiers, but also the Dutch, Menadonese, Ambonese – they all came through with this unique understanding which I think, looking back on it, is in a sense also a tribute to something in the Japanese – a sense that we were all victims in some cosmic process.

Yes, but on the other hand, didn't you feel that there was a pitiful lack of knowledge about the Japanese on the western side?

Oh yes.

And that you were trying to catch up with this lack of knowledge?

That too – yes, of course, there was that. But in the conditions in which we were, it was the human aspect – the human contact, you know. After all, none of us was in our native country – we were all on foreign soil. We were condemned to play this role of people at war. And make no mistake about it, this is the most ancient theatre there is, where man dramatizes himself into a state of war.

And the paradox is, you felt freer than your captors.

58

Once we began to understand and to learn from the experience, yes.

Have you ever met any of your captors, after the war?

No, never again, because the military who ran the camps were immediately called up and sent back to their combat units. Although for about a year I saw quite a lot of the Japanese army people, they were not the people who had been involved with the prisoners. And I had a very remarkable experience with the Japanese army after the surrender. But I never had the chance to go back immediately to Japan because straight-away I went back into active service for about two years. Then the moment I returned home I got involved in African matters. But I felt I could not abandon my relationship with Japan. I owed it to life to go and see Japan again and I did, I went back to see my Japanese friends.

And on that stage, of the camp and the war between the Japanese and you, you felt the experience had been positive on your side. But what about the other side? Did you have the impression that one of the Japanese, or two or three of them had somehow changed their behaviour, their psychology or psyche after being in contact with you, in relationship with you?

Yes! First of all, I think that if the Japanese had not been changed by their contact with us, our fate would have been much worse. I think that in putting understanding of the Japanese so much in the forefront of our prison lives we were in fact saving our lives all the time. Though that wasn't the object of the exercise, I think that had an enormous bearing on the way we were treated. That is the indirect evidence compared with other camps. There was, for instance, a young Japanese interpreter, who appeared towards the end of our captivity, and when I was being confronted on very critical occasions by the Japanese military and he was acting as interpreter, I always felt that he was on our side, and that in interpreting, as far as I could judge, he was improving on what I had to say. He was almost an accomplice after the fact. He was putting my case in the most convincing way possible.

Once the capitulation came about, I worked a great deal with him. One day he felt free to tell me what he had not been able to tell me before – he had had an English mother. I saw then that it had been his mother who was always pleading for us on these occasions. How mysterious! Tears came to my eyes when he told me this and I said, 'Please thank your mother,' and he said gravely, 'I will do so next time I go to her shrine.' Another interesting thing was that he had heard from the Japanese how much they had respected us really. Apparently ours was the most unusual camp they had come across on the island. He said they had picked up a lot of things from us. He did not want me to think it was just the Japanese who had had an effect on us – we had had a very strong effect on them. That was very nice to hear.

I seem to remember other examples of how understanding the Japanese character helped, particularly after the surrender.

Yes. One in particular stays with me. I had to order the Japanese general to use his forces to protect the Dutch against the Indonesians. I remember his look of horror and the anguish of his reply, 'But it would be dishonourable for me now to fight against people I myself urged to rebel.'

'You can have no honour rooted in dishonour,' I told him simply. 'You will have to discover, as I did under you, that there is a way in life of losing all in such a manner that it becomes a way of winning.'

Deeply moved, he bowed, hissed between his teeth and said almost in tears, 'That is a very Japanese thought.'

And from then on I had their full co-operation.

You suffered at the hands of the Japanese, but still you make a distinction between the Germans and the Japanese. Why?

Yes, I always distinguish between the Germans and the Japanese in the war, although there are resemblances. I think the problem was totally different. You know, Japan was thrown open so quickly to the West that it really had a modern, western technology and power before it had the psychology to go with it. They were people who had not cut the umbilical cord between themselves and their medieval past; they were caught in their own history. Whereas the Germans had all the illumination possible but they deliberately rejected the light that we all shared, for this mission of darkness, this discredited, primitive, collective upsurge. And this was the terrifying thing about the Germans to me, and this in a sense makes the Nazi phenomenon different from the Russian one, although the Russian is also a totalitarian phenomenon. There is a certain natural element in the Russian collective vision. That is why it has gone on for so long, because the Russians are a primitive people,

60

pliant to command and in a way trusting of authority. The Russians do not have the German enlightenment, or the German philosophic and scientific structure. They are very largely a tribal people. They had collective values in their villages. I describe in my book on Russia* how the elders of the village controlled the life of the individual, whom he should marry, whom he should not marry. It was a collective existence so one cannot quite compare it with German life. But I think what one can compare with the Nazis are the leaders in Russia who make use of this natural primitiveness for their own ends.

Isn't it a bit strange that you admire, respect and even love the Japanese who were your enemies and inflicted pain and torture on you?

It is a paradox, we are all paradoxes, and when I first came to Japan I saw it all the time. I had the feeling that all that I loved was not the whole story. It was a great source of strength to me in prison to draw on my first experience of Japan and I think that made the difference between life and death, not only for me but for thousands of other prisoners, because I kept saying to myself, 'If I remember this other Japan very, very clearly, the Japanese who come in contact with me here will also have to remember it.'

And you know – the modern concept of 'love' is in any case restricted, sloppy and debased. It is really an heroic dominant in life. Those who experience it are almost always in battle with the 'not love' in themselves first, and then in their life and time. And the core of this love is a form of total and truthful knowing which is unshakeable and unswerving, perceiving the faults of its object as precisely as its virtues but yet coming out of that difficult and contradictory perception intact.

What is your explanation for the cruelty of the Japanese during the Pacific War? Were they conscious of evil and their evil acts, or were they victims?

I think they were really caught in a trap of their own history. Really it is almost as if they were asking the world to stop them. They behaved in such a way that they had to lose, which is almost proof to me that unconsciously they wanted to lose the war. This is the only way in which they could get rid of the dark side of themselves. And I have Japanese friends; they do not talk much about the war but when they do talk about

* *Journey into Russia.*

it, they talk about it as their revolution. They see it as a kind of evolutionary revolution.

You once confessed to me that if you could be born again and had a choice, you would rather like to be born Japanese. I found that quite astonishing! Why Japanese?

You must remember this was said in the context of our discussion on Japan as an alternative civilization. But I do not know what the reasons are, it is just a fact of experience. I think the most wonderful things in life are beyond reason, that is why I think 'why' is often such an irrelevant question, it is very limited. The real things of life have nothing to do with 'why', they are just 'so', they are just 'thus'. Life is a 'thus', and until you realize this 'thusness' of life you are stuck.

I remember Nagisa Oshima told me, when he first read your book The Seed and the Sower, *he read it through in a single night and he could not stop crying. There is one proof that the Japanese also feel very close to you.*

I feel close to them, naturally very close to them. I always feel happy when I see them or when I think of them, I feel very happy and content that there are people like the Japanese in life, because if there were not people like that we would have had to invent them.

But how did you come to make that journey you mentioned to discover Japan as a young man in 1926?

It happened sometime in the winter of 1926 when, after an exhausting hockey tournament, I fled from the team I had successfully captained and went off alone to a café in Pretoria where you could still get coffee and waffles in the national manner. My mind could not have been further from Japan because I was then deeply concerned about what I was going to do to help William Plomer and Roy Campbell.

Suddenly I was wrenched out of my deep train of thought by the shrill voice of the proprietress shouting, 'Get out! I can't have any niggers in here!' I looked and saw that two oriental-looking gentlemen in khaki macintoshes were staring amazed at an enraged, rather fat Afrikaans lady. Something immediately made me jump up and go out to confront her, and ask, 'Why are you shouting?' I think she would have gone on shouting had I not addressed her in her own language. Instead, she explained in a rush of words that she could not have coloured people in her coffee-room because if she did she would lose all her custom. I replied, 'If you do not serve these gentlemen immediately you will lose my custom and the custom of all the teams in this tournament.'

Before her look of amazement even was complete, I bowed to the two men and asked slowly in English if they would do me the honour of joining me at my table and sampling some national delicacies. So began my meeting with Mr Shirakawa of the *Osaka Asahi* and Mr Hisatomi of the *Mainichi*, two of the most distinguished Japanese journalists in their day. Through them I met Captain Mori and received his invitation to accompany him on his ship to Japan.

And, what is more, although I did not know it, when out of my instinctive self I defied that formidable Afrikaans proprietress and the custom of my country, I was saving my life in the jungles of Java in 1942. Well, you could say that is something that happened by accident. But on the other hand I think it is something that came to me because of the kind of person I was. I think the kind of person one is is a kind of magnet which draws certain inevitable things to one out of all the possibilities that chance and circumstances present. And when one looks back later in life it is almost like looking at one of those magnetic charts of the Earth where all you see on the surface conforms to a hidden magnet underneath; and one's own magnet is one's character, one's disposition and what one's made of. So I think that my nature predisposed me to these happenings, which we might call accidental, and in particular this meeting with the two Japanese journalists in the interior of Africa.

From your long experience of the Japanese at war and at peace how would you characterize their psychology? For an outsider the Japanese are still difficult to understand. They can easily cut heads or cut themselves open, but they can also cry when they hear a cricket singing . . .

For this I must refer again to that voyage to Japan in 1926. I had a very strange experience then because I went to Japan by way of Sumatra and Malaya, and already I was in touch with volcanic earth, the earth of earthquakes. And because we had Malays in Africa, I knew about this Malayan phenomenon of *'amok'*, and I was wondering what the relationship was between the nature of the Earth which looked so green and peaceful above and yet had these hidden fires beneath its surface. I was wondering about this all the time I was in Japan. Although I saw the beautiful and the lovely side of Japan practically all the time, with one or

63

two exceptions that I mentioned in my book, I was beginning to wonder if it wasn't just the Japanese earth but the Japanese people who were full of lava and earthquakes. From what I knew of their past, I was already aware of a certain paradox of the Japanese spirit.

———

You speak of life and destiny as if they were a chart or a map. You have just now made a parallel between the Earth and the human spirit, as if it were a landscape. How much part of the world and the cosmic forces are we?

All I can say in that regard is that I do feel that whatever is represented in the universe around us tangibly and visibly, whether it is the Milky Way, black holes, suns or movements of stars, all are somehow duplicated within, reproduced within. Somehow I feel there is a very profound intercommunion. We may not be able to put it into words. It is beyond words but there is something in me which tells me we too, every human being, is a universe with these phenomena inside. It is also an enormous responsibility because in the beginning things always start as feelings, intuitive feelings, as an intuitive groping after a very fugitive sort of idea; so this need to make metaphors is already a way of beginning to grope with the framing and expression of the great mystery of a new area of human awareness. I think we are all poets and artists and astronomers when we are searching for our true self and trying to express it.

Do you think there's nothing new under the sun and everything has been said in the past?

No, I do not think everything has been said and rightly said. I do not think we could say that, because in my opinion the story has hardly started. If you look into the great statements of life, the things which you think have been truly said, and then look at them again in fifteen years' time, suddenly you say, 'But it means something else! Something was said there which I haven't seen before!' So this to me is the element of surprise that always comes later and is always present in great truth. It is never fully grasped and it is something one is always climbing up, or going down into, or working at – you never come to the end of it. And I think here one is entering an area of the unknown where one follows. I feel very much with Guillaume Apollinaire where he says, '*Pitié pour*

64

nous qui combattons toujours aux frontières de l'illimité et de l'avenir' ...
('Have pity on us who always fight on the frontiers of the infinite and the future').

If these 'frontiers of the infinite and the future' are difficult to look at and to describe, how can we at least experience them? This mystery of mysteries, what is it?

God and love. 'God is love.' And for me nothing more beautiful and nothing truer has been written since what St Paul wrote in his first epistle to the Corinthians, particularly the thirteenth chapter. I can only tell you that, ever since I was a little boy when I first read this thirteenth chapter of Corinthians – and that to me is almost supernatural because I am the thirteenth child in the family, I was born on the 13th December (and I am sure if there had been a thirteenth month I would have been born in that) – it has been to me the most important thing written in the Bible.

And it had also a special significance for Jung too.

That's right, yes.

Could you quote him? I think it's in Memories, Dreams, Reflections, *isn't it?*

It's quite a long quote but I can read it to you certainly. I think it's very beautiful because the whole meaning of life is there:

'... the fact forces itself on my attention that beside the field of reflection there is another equally broad if not broader area in which rational understanding and rational modes of representation find scarcely anything they are able to grasp. This is the realm of Eros. In classical times, when such things were properly understood, Eros was considered a god whose divinity transcended our human limits, and who therefore could neither be comprehended nor represented in any way. I might, as many before me have attempted to do, venture an approach to this daimon, whose range of activity extends from the endless spaces of the heavens to the dark abysses of hell; but I falter before the task of finding the language which might adequately express the incalculable paradoxes of love. Eros is a *kosmogonos*, a creator and father-mother of all higher consciousness. I sometimes feel that Paul's words – "Though I speak with the tongues of men and of angels, and have not love" – might well be

65

the first condition of all cognition and the quintessence of divinity itself. Whatever the learned interpretation may be of the sentence "God is love", the words affirm the *complexio oppositorum* of the Godhead. In my medical experience as well as in my own life I have again and again been faced with the mystery of love, and have never been able to explain what it is. Like Job, I had to "lay my hand on my mouth. I have spoken once, and I will not answer" (Job 40:4f.). Here is the greatest and smallest, the remotest and nearest, the highest and lowest, and we cannot discuss one side of it without also discussing the other. No language is adequate to this paradox. Whatever one can say, no words express the whole. To speak of partial aspects is always too much or too little, for only the whole is meaningful. Love "bears all things" and "endures all things" (1 Cor. 13:7). These words say all there is to be said; nothing can be added to them. For we are in the deepest sense the victims and the instruments of cosmogonic "love". I put the word in quotation marks to indicate that I do not use it in its connotations of desiring, preferring, favouring, wishing, and similar feelings, but as something superior to the individual, a unified and undivided whole. Being a part, man cannot grasp the whole. He is at its mercy. He may assent to it, or rebel against it; but he is always caught up by it and enclosed within it. He is dependent upon it and is sustained by it. Love is his light and his darkness, whose end he cannot see. "Love ceases not" – whether he speaks with the "tongues of angels", or with scientific exactitude traces the life of the cell down to its uttermost sources. Man can try to name love, showering upon it all the names at his command, and still he will involve himself in endless self-deceptions. If he possesses a grain of wisdom, he will lay down his arms and name the unknown by the more unknown, *ignotum per ignotius* – that is, by the name of God. That is a confession of his subjection, his imperfection, and his dependence; but at the same time a testimony to his freedom to choose between truth and error.'

And I find in this the key to all Jung's seeking, to all his work. From beginning to end it was a labour of love. Love is a mystery and ultimately, for us men especially, it is a feminine mystery for our guide, our way to it, is always through the great objective feminine. I have always said that as a natural scientist Jung made the journey which Dante undertook as a

66

poet in *The Divine Comedy*. At the end of both journeys, as they both were in the presence of God, they experience what all the traffic and travail of life and creation has been about – this love, which for Dante joins intellect and feeling and reveals itself as that which 'moves the sun and the moon and all the other stars' and for Jung it is the divine gift of God to man, the awesome freedom to choose between truth and error. Dante's guide was a beautiful feminine face – Jung's the rejected, the despised, the suppressed, the metaphorically 'dirty and ugly and averted face of woman'. By looking for the meaning in the fantasies of a certain permanently alienated Miss. Miller, or of Babette, committed to an asylum whom Freud dismissed as an 'ugly old woman', as well as in the lives of hundreds of others, he was led into and safely through the depths of his own hell, to become, like Dante, a freeman of creation and, as Dante had done, reintegrated for the future the scattered and neglected, trampled and bruised fragments of the life of our disintegrated time.

This was Jung's ultimate achievement that, like Dante, he achieved a condition within himself of a total objective love. The totality is proved in that it included the ugly as well as the beautiful. Dante followed a beautiful feminine face, and that is perhaps the easy way for a man; but Jung followed the face of a woman of whom Freud said he could not understand how Jung could waste his time with such a disagreeable person. That is one measure of the innate distance between the two men. Jung thought that to understand was 'beauty' of a transcendent kind because from the beginning his nature had so predisposed him that he had to live his life in love, in search of a cosmogonic love that included all, and I for one believe he found it not only for himself but for us all and showed us the way and means to do likewise for ourselves and our time.

Now also in the same chapter Jung refers to St Paul, who wrote, 'When I was a child I spake as a child, I understood as a child, I thought as a child: but when I became a man I put away childish things.' And that seemed so true because as a boy I knew that one day, very soon, I too would have to put away childish things. And this concept of love, of which a lot of people have a sentimental idea, is to me not sentimental but the most heroic of all concepts, because it is a call to battle.

I am sure you still hear Jung's voice ringing in your ears. What do you think his tone would be if he were reading this instead of writing it? Would it be a sad tone?

No, it was quite different. When Jung talked about these things you felt the weight of the mystery in him. His voice would get very deep, and he always tended to talk as a person who is on the frontiers of our world and our knowledge where these things weighed very deeply and where anything could happen at any moment.

On the whole, was he an enlightened pessimist or a sober optimist?

No, neither. He was different, you see. I think he summed it up, as he would, very modestly. He said that he thought on the whole that life was on the side of meaning as opposed to meaninglessness. He believed in life and he certainly was not despairing. I do not think he would have done what he did in his life if he had been motivated by despair. On the contrary, one of the things about hope is that hope fears all things but at the same time hope ceases not. In Jung, you see, the hope was strong because love is hope. Love is the hope that ceases not, and ultimately love is certainty.

At this stage of human evolution what do you think will be the next big event, the next encounter between God and man?

Well, I don't know – one's got some inkling about it – I believe very profoundly myself that I can see it at this stage – the feeling comes to me in the following way. I hear people everywhere saying that the trouble with our time is that we have no great leaders any more. If we look back we always had them. But to me it seems there is a very profound reason why there are no great leaders any more. It is because they are no longer needed. The message is clear. You no longer want to be led from the outside. Every man must be his own leader. He now knows enough not to follow other people. He must follow the light that's within himself, and through this light he will create a new community. You see, wherever I go in the world, this to me is a general trend. I am aware of the fact there are already people in existence today – take us – who really belong to a community which does not exist yet. That is, we are the bridge between the community we've left and the community which doesn't exist yet.

In this future community, how shall we be ruled and governed? By a group of wise men?

68

I do not think it can be that. It has got to come through the creation of more and more individuals who will take upon themselves the task of leading themselves, and to the extent to which we can lead ourselves properly and decently other men will follow. It cannot come collectively; it cannot come through groups; not yet, if ever.

You say that as if you were not quite sure. That 'if ever' seems to strike an almost pessimistic note, compared with what you have been saying.

No, it is not that. I am never in doubt when I think about the wider plan of life. If I have any doubts at all they are, as it were, tactical; but never in the strategic outcome of life. No, it was merely that I have been thinking about the extraordinary feelings of fear and helplessness that I encounter increasingly on the collective level as I go around the world. I think it was characteristic of the generation into which I was born that we were just as afflicted by doubt over the values and condition of our societies. We too felt that the world was in many ways terribly, terribly wrong; but at the same time we had a sort of instinctive feeling that we could go out and change it; and I have never wavered in that feeling. If anything, it has gathered pace and force in new dimensions. But now I meet many groups of people who live in a kind of dumb despair and state of helplessness, and it seems so unnecessary: if only people would stop cutting themselves off from their natural instincts and intuition, and increasing the divide between themselves and their own predisposed natures.

But this really rounds the whole circle and brings us back to our discussion about God; I feel the theme needs orchestration, even at the cost of repeating some of the basic notes. I am certain that if only man could increase his awareness and renew his relationship with this whole pattern in himself, which theologians call 'God', all that feeling of helplessness would go.

May I illustrate it from something else that happened to me in the last war? I was standing at nightfall looking out of my prison. It was what I believed to be my last night alive, and I had fully accepted that I would be executed by the Japanese in the morning. An enormous thunderstorm had broken outside and the heavy rain – which always, in my drought-conditioned African senses, brings feelings of relief and music – was falling. The lightning and the thunder was almost continuous. I thought

I had never seen lightning more beautiful – it was almost as if I were in the workshop of creation where lightning is made – and it was so charged and intense that it seemed to overflow its own zig-zag thrust at the jungle and come more like a great stream of fire out of the sky and make a delta of flame in the black. But there were also great purple sheets of lightning in between, that swept like archangelic wings over my prison. But it was the thunder which meant most of all. I had never heard the voice so loud, so clear and so magisterial. And suddenly, quite unbidden, a great feeling of relief came over me. 'That's it!' I thought. 'The Japanese are ultimately not in overall command. There is witness of a power greater than man which, in the end, will decide all.'

I express it very badly because the experience was totally beyond the capacity of words and is one of the most overwhelming emotions I have ever experienced; and in that moment all anxiety left me and I was, in the deepest sense of the words, no more troubled. Through nature outside I had been reconnected with a kind of powerhouse inside myself of which I had been unaware.

Mind you, I do not want to imply that these feelings of helplessness and fear are not understandable. The world is full of the most terrible, awful and awesome happenings and portents. For the first time in human history every portion of the world is, simultaneously with all the others, in a state of profound crisis and increasingly in the grip of national and international outbreaks of violence on a scale that it may never have known in the past. Confronted with this, people not only feel helpless but they are also troubled because they do not understand what and why it is all happening to them in an age of so-called progress and enlightenment. It is as if the modern spirit is moving increasingly into an atmosphere of deepending gloom, and people do not see any certainty, let alone a glimmer of light, by which to guide themselves. The dominants in their respective philosophies, the dominants in religion, in art, and ethics, all seem to have vanished or to be vanishing. It is not only that churches and temples are almost empty, it is also that all the great tributaries, all the great streams of creation which contributed to religion, and from which humanity had derived its greatest meaning, have run dry.

It sometimes would seem that the brightness of our age is an illusion,

70

and that we are living not in the vast cities and palaces of the mind which St Augustine knew so well, but in some lonely outposts at sundown on the fringes of what had once been a certain and forward-moving world. Out there in the darkness there is a horrendous tread and a reverberating thumping on the gate. There is something trying to enter but we are afraid to open the gate because of all the horror we have witnessed in our time. It does not seem to occur to us that all this emptiness, all this evidence of breakdown, all this decline in values, this diminishing awareness and sharpened sense of insecurity despite the obvious proliferation of material security in our lives – that all this might be the messenger or the forerunner of something new, and what is knocking at the door should be invited in.

I have a suspicion that these tributaries I spoke of as running dry because the waters, the energies, that had been at their disposal are no longer directed at maintaining what has already been established, all are massing ready to bring the future in, to bring something new into our midst. And this all seems to me evidence of a state of mind and heart which has always presided over great moments of transition: transitions which, if not accomplished freely with all that we have of awareness and wholeness in ourselves, would lead to a total destruction and blackout of all that has gone before. This constitutes the greatest of all challenges that face not only the individual, but his society and its institutions, since they have, in a sense, to die in certain aspects of themselves in order to live again. They have to renew themselves, not by abolishing what has been in the past – this is the classical heresy of the revolutionary who, in order to add a new storey to the house that he has inherited, begins by pulling out the foundations on which the house is built – so much as reappraising the past in the light of what is coming, and so giving it a contemporary and immediate meaning.

This is the highest task of man, to preserve the continuity of creation, to preserve what is true of life in the past as far back as the twilit area where his consciousness disappears with the first light of the beginning. The present has to be made a bridge to the future, when fear will go out of the window and the gates and door are open so that the future can come in, however problematical, as an honoured guest.

Somehow we should learn to know that our problems are our most precious possessions. They are the raw materials of our salvation: no problem – no redemption. And it is only by bringing to our problems the whole of ourselves – which means all that we have rejected in these specialized aspects of ourselves we call civilization – that life can be renewed in a greater dimension of itself. But these in-between moments are frightening; and they are the moments that the first people of Africa, who feared them most, attributed to 'a loss of soul'.

Now the question is, what do you yourself mean by this 'loss of soul'? I ask not in the spirit common in modern argument, which would be to ask you to define your terms, but I would like you to say more about it.

The 'first people of life', as I prefer to call the primitive, had a lively sense of what we call soul, and feared the loss of it as the greatest calamity that could befall them. I would like to enlarge on it through telling a story of theirs, because that speaks directly to the sense of creation that man has deep within himself where nothing, ultimately, is impossible, because for hundreds of years now all understanding of the spirit has been narrowed and restricted to what can be rationally expressed about 'the spirit'. The spirit is no longer seen as a gift that we hold in trust from life but as something that is narrowed to a conscious, wilful, rational egoism. The spirit is not only reason – although it includes reason; it is not only feeling – and of course it includes feeling as well: but it is for me, above all, intuition, which is a profound compass, bearing on our origin and our destination. And this is ultimately what religion is about: 'origin and destination'. The result has been that the spirit has lost, for the moment, what made it one of the greatest of all human passions. So it has abandoned the human being in his narrowed, rational state, indulging the greatest pastime and speciality of our time, which is finding first-rate reasons for doing partial and wrong things.

This truly is one of the most marked characteristics of modern man; hence this babel of voices and tumult within and without each one of us. Every man has tended to become, as it were, a walking piece of organized chaos, incapable of communicating any more in a total way with his fellow human beings. So I have to turn to the story, from a time when life was young, and which talks through images and symbols even to the man behind the bars of his clinical intellectualism.

The story is very simple; it is the story of a man who lived on his own, a primitive man who lived on the edge of 'The Forest of the Night', and he lived by keeping cattle. It was a wonderful herd because the cattle were a roan of black and white which, among the people who told me the story, had a profound symbolic meaning. You remember the great Chinese symbol of wholeness which is a black whale with a white eye, curled up, and a white whale likewise beside it with a black eye, enclosed in a perfect circle. As a symbol of wholeness black and white are both necessary in the imagery of the first people of the world to constitute both life and a means of living.

Now this man lived very happily with his cattle until one morning he went to milk them and found that they had no milk to give; in other words, the story is telling us he had arrived at a moment in his own life when the life he was leading had no more sustenance to give him in the old way. He thought, 'This is very strange, because I have given them everything I could possibly have of the knowledge of grazing to make them produce milk and I shall take particular care today that they are properly fed.' So he took them to one of the better grazing grounds and fed them well and he thought, 'Tomorrow morning I shall get a wonderful lot of milk.' But next morning they still had no milk to give. He did this repeatedly until at last he thought, 'No, there is something more to it than mere grazing; something else must be happening.' So he kept watch on the cattle in their kraal, and in the middle of the night he saw a cord come down from the stars and down this cord came a number of very beautiful young women, of the people of the stars; and they ran with containers to his cattle and started milking them. In other words the nourishment, the food, was already being withdrawn from him in the context in which he lived towards the stars where the light of the future comes from.

Well, he ran out, and the star people scattered immediately and ran up the cord as fast as they could, but he managed to catch hold of one of the girls and pull her back: he succeeded, in other words, in catching a portion of the future to live with him and become his wife. She had, of course, her container with her still, and she said to him, 'I am happy living with you and I will work for you but only on one condition: that you will never look in this container without my permission.' And he promised her that.

73

This went on happily for some months. He went out to look after the cattle by day; she went out to work in the fields and they met at night and he apparently was perfectly content with that portion of meaning that had come down from the stars. Then one day when she was out and it was very hot he came back and was very thirsty and had a drink of water; he then saw this container and was suddenly very irritated by it and thought: 'This is ridiculous. Why should I not look in it?' He went and took the lid off, looked inside, put it back and laughed. That evening when they met again the woman gave him one look and exclaimed, 'You have looked in my container!' 'Yes, I have,' he answered, and added, 'You silly creature! Why did you make such a fuss about the container when the container all the time was empty?'

'Empty?' she uttered, distressed.

'Yes, empty!'

And at once she became very sad, turned her back on him, walked straight into the sunset and was never seen again on earth.

It did not matter him breaking his word so much. What really mattered was that he could not see anything in the container, the other things which she had brought from the stars for both of them.

This is an image of the terrifying moment in our own lives when we can no longer see what we have naturally in the container, which is soul. It is not that we have not got a container full of starlight, as it were, but that we have lost the capacity to look into it and see what nature has put there of new meaning when that which has fed us can feed us no longer. That for the first man of life was a loss of soul and implied a living death thereafter.

The story is very moving. I see and feel very much the tremendous sense of loss that it leaves behind in the listener. But is that really a complete image of what is meant in the modern sense by a loss of soul? It is in the story essentially a feminine loss, and is it not therefore a partial representation of what is meant by a loss of soul?

No, it is not, because throughout in the story the masculine and the feminine elements of life are closely interwoven and dependent, even totally complementary to each other. It is possible that if a woman told a story about the same tragic deprivation in her own spirit, she would use a different imagery and the man would play a different role. But in the first

74

place the story – although often told and elaborated upon by the woman, particularly the mother – issued from the man. In the beginning the woman acted out and lived her portion of the soul and it tended to the man; while the man was far more consciously concerned in the implications for his life and the future through following the images and symbols evoked in his imagination. Also we must not forget how, in western civilization, our great compass stories have come from men – men, moreover, writing in the context of what until now has been largely dominated by the spirit and will of men. And for man all the evidence tends to show that the soul is feminine. I could therefore easily have drawn on myths and legends from our own, Western past which portray this loss also through the loss and abandonment of the woman in man. You just have to think, for instance, of Ariadne abandoned on a rock in a sea of her own tears; an image of the feminine so imperative in the imagination of one of the greatest of Renaissance men, Leonardo da Vinci, that he was inspired by it to paint one of the most moving portraits of the mother of Christ as a virgin on the rocks. And long before that there was the legend of Orpheus and the shattering tragedy of the loss of the Eurydice that was the image of his own feminine soul. And do not forget Dante who, in his meeting with the Mother of Christ, greeted the manifestation of the feminine element in Christ which mothered his spirit of infinite love, with that unforgettable salutation, 'Virgin Mother, daughter of your Son.'

When you think back there are countless other examples to the same effect and you realize how the loss of the woman in this, the primitive story, is dealing with something which proves to have been true for man not only in the beginning, not only in the world of Greece when the gods themselves walked in the streets with common men and women and inhabited the forests and the streams and conveyed their presence and message for men through humble shepherds and mountain folk, but also today in a world where the gods have vanished into the heavens beyond the Milky Way and the whole meaning which was conveyed by a total acceptance of the reality of a creator called God is increasingly denied.

From early on I found myself wondering why I was more interested in Greek than in Roman civilization, and the answer, in a sentence, was that at its greatest period the Greek spirit acknowledged the feminine as much as the masculine, while the Roman civilization was entirely dominated by the man of mind, out of touch with its feminine self. The Renaissance for me was precisely so significant an event in world history because in it the Greek totality of masculine and feminine, particularly its feminine inspiration, was brought back into a world dominated by its Roman inheritances. But since the Renaissance all the caring, feeling, loving values, which the sense of the feminine in man promotes in life, have diminished until only an arid, rational, masculine intellectualism and a power-obsessed urge have taken over, and the moment of the container in the story, when its lid is lifted by the man and he declares it to be empty, is upon us.

What I think is so significant in the imagery of the story is the fact that this man in his clearing in the Forest of the Night lives by the milk from his herd of numinous cows who, in their uniform of skin which is both black and white, represent a living partnership between feminine and masculine – yin and yang as the Chinese would put it. The cow, after all, is an image of the primal feminine in life and this man, in living by this primal feminine, and caring for it, is obviously doing something of universal significance; this is established in the story by the fact that what feeds him also is needed as nourishment for the stars, hence the raid on his herd by the women of the people of the stars. There comes a moment, however, when this primal nourishment is not enough and it needs transformation into a less collective and more individual evolution of the feminine in man. This, I think, is the meaning of his capture of the most beautiful of the women who have come down from the stars to draw on his own primal feminine element.

This is a sort of Jacob's ladder situation in the imagination, a proof of the reciprocity between the life of man on earth and the forces of creation in Heaven. It is interesting that when I first came to read Dante and Wordsworth for myself, the story immediately came vividly to my mind as it has done since on so many other occasions. The Dante association was just this: that his *Divine Comedy* begins the fateful descent into Hell, which has to precede the ascent to Heaven, with the lines, 'Midway through my life I found myself on a path through a dark wood.' Dante too had his forest of duka-duk. Wordsworth seemed to give me an answer why it was a woman from the stars who was allotted a special role in the story. I quote the lines from his 'Intimations of Immortality':

> 'The Soul that rises with us, our life's Star
> Hath had elsewhere its setting,
> And cometh from afar:
> Not in entire forgetfulness,
> And not in utter nakedness,
> But trailing clouds of glory do we come
> From God, who is our home:'

You can see also the profound logic of the true symbolism of meaning which makes it inevitable that it was a star in Heaven which led the shepherds to Bethlehem.

At the risk of sounding flippant I would say that I believe you, but thousands wouldn't. How do you answer people who would say, 'Yes, this of course may well be so spiritually, but we are practical people, and what has all that got to do with our practical lives? We have heard all this before and it seems to us to make very little practical difference to how people behave.'

Modern people who so pride themselves on being practical and realistic are really not being practical at all. They express a partial state of being as if it were a whole, and express an extremely narrow condition of consciousness. Man is not realistic and practical unless he first acknowledges the immense importance of realizing that pragmatism begins in the human spirit, and unless man is spiritually pragmatic as well, however successful he may appear in the short term, he is impractical to the point of destruction in the long run. It all begins with the pragmatism of the spirit and with as great an awareness as possible in this dimension of himself wherein all that we mean by religion is experienced. If you read Jung's case histories you will find that almost every one of the disoriented and alienated spirits who turned to him for help were sick because they had failed to be aware of this dimension, and the pragmatic role of its reality in their own lives. Jung said, over and over again, that he had never effected a cure in a human being without restoring in them a capacity for this sort of spiritual experience we have been discussing.

I think this, in a backhand sort of way, is proved throughout history by all the peoples who have overthrown whole cultures and civilizations.

They have done so first by denying in themselves the god or gods who represent the highest value of the civilization or society they seek to overthrow. They proceed then to attack and destroy, before they do anything else, the contract of trust and faith which the men of that society have with this value in themselves. It is not for nothing that in the French Revolution, God had to be the first casualty, and a Goddess of Reason be enthroned in Paris in his place. It is not for nothing that you cannot be a member of the Communist Party of Soviet Russia without being an avowed atheist. And that one of the stock Russian questions asked of astronauts in Moscow when they have returned from outer space is, 'Did you see any sign of God and heaven up there?' – and the mocking reply, always to a roar of laughter, is of course that they did not.

So what we have been discussing is of the greatest and most immediate importance and urgency. But we have to realize that we cannot recover for modern man the capacity for this sort of experience and awareness by the kind of exhortation he has had to endure for centuries and still endures in the churches of today. It can only come to him with the reawakened sense of the myth which is already stirring in his dreaming self. That is the reason why one of Jung's most important books is called *Modern Man in Search of a Soul*, and this is all that a life of meaning is about.

All this brings me to the part of the pattern of creation and continuity of creation which I call to myself something like the 'evolution of God', not in a Darwinian sense but in the sense of what evolution means in the ordinary English language. It is an overwhelming feeling that God himself evolves through a continuing process of creation and re-creation in which we are chosen instruments and partners, and that in measure through an increase of our awareness of this partnership, through accepting, as it were, divine obligations in our life on earth, we help and speed the evolution of God and His act of creation. It is perhaps what distinguishes our western Hebraic, Roman, Greek and Christian culture from that of the great cultures of the East, such as that of India, where the creator, creation, the infinite, is a kind of unchangeable absolute and man has to adjust and conform to an absolute pattern – for good or evil. But whether we go to church or not, whether we are believers or not, we are part of a culture which has had at its centre a completely and totally different concept.

There has been an effort among fundamentalists to deny this – and in all religions this has had a transitory validity – wherein creation is an absolute and mankind has to conform; as if creation is an act which is totally behind us and men just have to find their way towards whoever created us and all that has gone before. But Homeric stories at the beginning of our civilization, like the *Iliad* and the *Odyssey*, and of course the New Testament, already hint at a different kind of searching of the human spirit. But this fundamentalism, which still persists, inflicted a totally different view of life on us which imposed a kind of static absolute on the culture to which we belong. We may have to start off, therefore, with the concept of a creator who said, 'Let there be Light', and there was light, and this creator, for a period anyway, in various ways gave the man he had created, as it were, his marching orders, and all man had to do was to march. And if he did not march according to the way he was told to, he was definitely in trouble. But there came a very great moment when this God ceased to be one who merely gave orders and he revealed the change – one of those mysterious and inexplicable leaps forward that defy orderly evaluation and scientists call mutation – and it came in the form of a dream.

For the first people of the world, like the owner of the numinous cattle, the dream itself is a manifestation of God; if you act from the area of the dream you are in the area where one experiences what theologians call 'God'; where one experiences a sense of origin and direction, and you have inserted in life a kind of radar, an inbuilt ability to discover direction towards new and greater meaning.

I refer, of course, to the dream of Jacob's ladder; perhaps the greatest dream that has ever been dreamed in the history of man because it is a dream which conveys both its own message and at the same time tells us what dreaming is. And the dream, it says clearly, is a ladder between man and God, a ladder where angels descend and ascend. '*Angelos*' is the old Greek word for messenger. Jacob has apparently broken all the moral canons of people, clan and family; has sinned, betrayed his brother, stolen his heritage, and betrayed his own manhood by flight from the consequences of his deed, and is there helpless in the wilderness on the way to a strange land, on the way to an unknown future, as we here are lost in a strange land on our way to the future. At this moment there comes the dream to comfort and reassure him, and profoundly alter the relationship between man and the creator. The creator said, 'Through this dream I tell you henceforth there will be communication between you and me. As I communicate to you through this dream, you, through your prayers and obedience to your dreams, can communicate with me. What you say and what you do henceforth can also make a difference to me, your God and your creator. Together we shall transform creation and life on earth.' It is an immense leap forward in human meaning, because God has taken man into partnership and commands that as man conforms to the act of creation he will be blessed.

The implications of this are enormous and of infinite possibilities, for in this totality of creation God submits himself, like every thing and creature in creation, to the laws of his own creation. Through this leap forward, life is instantly more dynamic. For man is no longer a thing merely to be ordered about. He is not just left to his own stumbling and to a kind of blind-man's-buff way of life. He has now the opportunity of placing all his natural energies at the disposal of creation, and a new sense of conscious, discriminating direction which he did not have before to help him on his way.

Yet like all meaningful changes, the revelation in the dream has to be lived before it can be fully understood and served. There is an apprenticeship of centuries to be served. There are still long, painful years in which this partnership has to be developed, for it is still lacking in certain things. God is still unpredictable, and is held responsible for strange disasters and undeserved catastrophes, not to mention afflictions on people – even people who are dedicated, or try to be dedicated; and so by human standards at times God is frightful, cruel and unjust, and therefore more of a dilemma to man in partnership.

This dilemma is expressed in that unforgettable and as yet totally inadequately understood Book of Job, where God's greatest servant on earth is inflicted with the most appalling catastrophes. If the story has any meaning at all it is that, if one stands fast in the midst of the fumblings and gropings in which we are involved, there is an answer because there is a portion which is the justice of God; a paradoxical sense of justice which, through this act of divine injustice, comes alive not only in life on earth, but comes alive in the overall process of creation. Through it the act of creation has a kind of new lawfulness restored to it; there is a kind of divine intercession born and a new kind of advocacy in heaven where God takes the part of man, as it were, against the God he was.

Another great stage in the evolution has been reached, and from that moment comes the feeling that God is increasingly dedicating a portion of himself to represent man in the divine course – until the greatest revelation which we have not understood properly yet: the incarnation of the Son of God, the element which is his future self. Christ became man to put himself at the disposal of man, and with him came the great, transforming power of the universe – the love of God, which has not yet figured so prominently on the scene.

So already we can see it is more than just a question of communication between the creator and man. If we read the message of the coming of Christ truly as it is, what is happening is that the creator is relegating ever more significant elements of his own creativity and divine power to man. He is making it possible for man alone, man living on his own in the heart of himself, to be a portion of what is ultimate and divine in the agony and glory of performing what has hitherto been solely a divine function. And the emphasis is as much on the agony as the glory, as so uncomfortably portrayed and symbolized in the crucifixion: no agony – no glory: no sacrifice and suffering – no transformation or renewal. Now we know that suffering is the lot of God and hence also the lawful lot of his partner. It is bearable always because it is divinely shared, and, in the measure in which man freely shares it, it is transformed into the love which transcends all and is the light of darkness that leads man and God to the final wisdom.

So when this great figure, who has brought such good tidings of great sorrow, has been resurrected and has ascended and been withdrawn, there is something else that we are given clearly, to take man and creation another great step forward. The New Testament rightly calls it 'the Holy Spirit', but it has many names. For Blake and Coleridge it was the imagination, but whatever the name, man now has a clear and certain guide: he only has to follow it. It leads to a pattern of spirit within himself which puts infinite energies of transformation and creation at his disposal. Starting as a kind of sergeant-major-God, it has led man to a God partner who has made man responsible for some of his powers, clearly implying that man, and what he does, is of the utmost importance to creator and creation, and his own evolution is bound and interdependent with the whole movement of creation. Would we but allow ourselves to know what is already known in creation about us, renewal and greater new meaning is ours and life full of power which no longer corrupts but reintegrates our infinite diversities for another mutation we cannot yet discern, but whose promise and existence sings in the congregation of our blood. How sad, how irreligious that, just here, the churches established for the promotion of creation step in and, almost as if they forget the Holy Spirit, they say, 'This is the final revelation; this is the final act; this is all that we need to know about God and creation; there is nothing more to know. All we have to do is to imitate and copy Christ and that is all there is to living' – leaving out the tremendous way we have come and the fact that it was Christ himself who said, 'And ye shall know the truth, and the truth shall make you free', attaching so much importance to truth that one believes that, if he were here now, he would say: 'I was the revelation, I was true revelation, but even so only revelation on the way. There is more revelation to come.' It is this absolutism of dogma and rule of establishment that have caused the spirit and the Holy Ghost to leave us; evolution, to the point where God sent his own son down to become a man, to show that he also – and we too after his example – could be men in the divine image, has been arrested. A cold and arrogant despotism of reason has frozen over the process in us.

This is the moment at which we stand; and contemporary man does not realize what the coming of Christ meant, and will fail it in a blind imitation of what Christ himself was. I think for me one of the most profound things Jung ever said was that human beings believe that they have to live their lives as if they were mere imitations and copies of the life of Christ, whereas if they truly sought the meaning of the coming of Christ, they would realize that they had to live their own seeking lives, their portion of the Holy Spirit of imagination which is in their keeping, their own true selves – just as Christ had lived himself without deviation, in a way that had never been seen before, to the end for which he had been born. And this is the reappraisal which confronts us if we are to evolve with God. We often ask ourselves: why is there no religious leader appearing to deliver us from stagnation and retrogression with some shattering new revelation? Why is there no great statement of cosmic intent which we can all try to follow? What has happened to all those great minds and leaders who used to guide people in the past? The answer is clear: the stage of great leaders has irrevocably gone and the task, the responsibility, is tossed on to each one of us. We are in our own theatre alone. We have to make our sense of what is collective individual, and live as individuals following the truth as our own natures predispose us. And how should we do that? Where should we turn to take the first step?

We should turn as always to this ancient ladder Jacob found in his dream, pitched between the great wasteland of himself and his creator Our responsibility now is to know ourselves and to determine what is good and what is evil. This is the debt that we owe to the Holy Spirit which is irrevocably conferred on us in our lives; and we are condemned in the cause of renewal and enlargement of creation to follow it as truthfully and utterly as Christ did. We now are bound to decide for ourselves consciously what is good and what is bad: to make what is meaningful take precedence over what is meaningless. It is the sense of this power, this sense of responsibility that we share with our creator; this sense of belonging to the universe that we have lost and that we must rediscover and embrace in a lasting act of remembrance of our origin to set ourselves and our societies once more on course.

It may be that there are other worlds with forms of being, with a greater awareness of this responsibility than we have, but this is what is on our doorstep and knocking so powerfully to be allowed in. For the moment this is our unique role. We have already got power enough to destroy the whole of human life; but we have not yet got the moral obligation, the sense of good and bad, to match it and follow it as our instrument of metamorphosis. We have not yet accepted that every act of knowledge, every increase of knowledge, increases our responsibility towards creation. We have been induced into believing that we are completely helpless in the grip of powerful new forces and that we are caught up in a process that is meaningless, and just sweeping us along like the swine of a new Gadarene. But we have the power to be creative if we turn back to what I can only call 'the dreaming process' in ourselves, and we put our imaginations and our lives into this area where the dream occurs; then we can 'do', and we can change life.

But the message is clear: the power which does not corrupt comes to man not in multitudes, it comes to him as an individual man, as it came to the man alone with his cattle, his natural self in the Forest of the Night and which, by his failure to recognize it, lost him his soul. It comes first to the individual alone: the individual who has to guard his individuality in an aloneness that is not loneliness but, as the Zulus say, a house of dreams. There he can discover the greatest of freedoms, to live out his own gift of life without diminishing or imperilling, but enriching his association with the society of man. And the dreaming to which I refer is not some lush, comfortable, pink marshmallow kind of concept. It is a voice of steel, calling us to live and fight for truth not in hate but love, for love. But it calls in a language to be decoded, since it is – as someone I know in America, who left his church to do just this, put it – 'the forgotten language of God'. We have no excuse any more, and it is the greatest scandal of our day that neither religion nor science acknowledges it, that we have the code to read the ancient instructions inscribed in our dreams – and we do not use it.

All this reminds me very much of one of the last letters I ever had from Jung, when he wrote, 'I cannot define for you what God is. I can only say that my work has proved empirically that the pattern of God exists in every man, and that this pattern has at its disposal the greatest of all energies for transformation and transfiguration of his natural being.'* And this is the challenge and the immediate call of truth. The sin of our time is not that we do not know. We do know where we have to look for the power and the energy and the sense of their direction, but we are so intellectually oriented that this seems a non-rational, even superstitious thing to do because we persist in the preposterous illusion that we must know rationally, in advance, where we are going.

We have been so conditioned that modern man wants to have a

* Quoted in *Jung and the Story of Our Time*, p. 216.

hundred years' plan before he moves. Think of the arrogance of that: of imagining that we can plan the next hundred years, let alone the next two days – we who cannot even complete an airport before the blueprint is out of date, and our present is littered with the remains of what we once so brilliantly invented and planned that is now obsolete.

I have often felt that it is as if there has been only one modern man and we crucified him two thousand years ago. We still have to make his example truly modern in ourselves and be individual and specific in terms of the totality of our own natures, as he was. This is the way we have to go. But we now have to do our own leading. We have not to wait on masters; we do not have to wait for foolproof spiritual exercises; we can go to people and seek what they seek, but we cannot do it wholly their way and be stereotypes of one another. Like the leaves on the trees, we are compelled to be each our own way, again and again. We have, for this, to turn inwards – to look into ourselves; look in this container which is our soul; look and listen in to it and all its hunches – incredible, silly, stupid as they may appear to be. It might tell us to make fools of ourselves in the eyes of our established selves but, however improbable, just listen, just give it a chance in yourself, particularly at this moment when everything is increasingly impersonal. Until you have listened in to that thing which is dreaming through you, in other words answered the knock on the door in the dark, and discovered your estranged self, you will not be able to lift this moment in time, in which we are all imprisoned, back again onto a level where the great act of creation is going on, whether we heed it or not. We can join in with increased awareness, thanks to the creator's evolution, or stay out. If we stay out we perish; if we join in, we live for ever.

You ask, 'If it is so simple, then what prevents us?' There are, history teaches us, many impediments, but for me the main obstruction at this moment remains this European hubris of mere knowing, this wanting to look egotistically before we leap – failing to remember that those who look partially and over-long never leap at all, and betray the evolution of the spirit that is gathering force in the wide prophetic soul of the dreaming of things to come – which is preventing us from recognizing that our revelation will no longer come in one overwhelming and unchanging revelation from one great man. Humbly and contritely it is to be sought in the mirror of the universe within each individual soul, and the message read there lived out with the whole of an honest self where in time we shall rediscover the propinquity which is at the heart of all things and the most dedicated and caring reciprocity of giving and receiving between creator and his all.

Do you think that new technology, like super computers, intelligent robots, new ways and means of communication, can make man more human, more reasonable?

New technology can only be used as an instrument if there are individuals who can use it responsibly. What the computer is utterly incapable of doing is to give us a value judgement. It is utterly divorced from meaning. It can work statistically and it can quantify, but it cannot deal with meaning – and certainly not create it. And do not forget, it is a law of creation that that which is created can never be greater than the thing that created it. That is why we must submit ourselves to God, because we cannot be greater than our creator, and we are safeguarded in this too from domination by our own inventions. And I think the other side of the contract of life, the contract we have with creation, is the fact that the creator, as I mentioned a moment ago, is subordinate to the laws of what he has created.

This is very significantly illustrated in Greek mythology. The great law of life in Greek mythology is Fate, and it is the one thing that Zeus, the greatest god, cannot interfere with. This to me is a profoundly religious thing, that the god himself, by creating, commits himself to be bound by the laws of his own act and deed of creation.

As you travel to Africa quite often, how do you perceive it? We all know that Africa is plagued by problems – drought, desertification, hunger and political instability. How do you see the African landscape changing?

I think that Africa has a very, very hard, desperate road ahead because it needs an urgent, enormous and sustained act of education. I think we should admit that in a way Africa was given a form of political government for which it was not ready and for which it is not yet prepared. The democracy we gave it on the whole failed, since it did not possess the prerequisite of a spirit in which one cares as passionately for the rights of the person disagreed with as one's own. It is a question of relations with the ultimate values in life. We are, in a sense, betraying democracy in the modern world by putting all the emphasis on numbers and not enough on values.

May I give you one example? Some years ago I went to see an African leader whom a number of us had worked hard to bring to power in a politically emancipated country. I went to see him because he had just confiscated the farms of a score or more European farmers who made a significant contribution to the self-sufficiency of his country, and who had all opposed their own colonial government's effort to deny the country independence. I had come to think of him as an ally and a friend, but when I met him it was clear that he had no time for me and my purpose and regarded me, now that he had what he wanted, as irrelevant. In the end I broke off and left, saying: 'Until you create Africans who will fight as hard for the rights of their fellow European countrymen as we fought for theirs, you will be something grossly inferior to what you have replaced. And until you are ready to do so, I do not wish to see you again.'

I believe one of the greatest sources of error and disaster in our lives today is the assumption that all great social problems must have political solutions. All the solutions of our problems must also, sometime, have a political expression but in the first instance they are apolitical, and no instant ideas, ideology or new law can bring them about. They arise

87

first as intimations in an area of spirit where our master values have their origin. They must be nursed, grown, lived and fertilized in the imagination of men everywhere before they can become decently political.

Politics by itself cannot create and initiate solutions; at best it can create the climate which makes the growth of solutions possible; and Africa, with rare exceptions, as its post-war history shows, has still a long way to go before it has the right climate for such growth.

You said before that the time for great leaders has passed, and individuals must now take responsibility for new growth and change. That may be all very well in the so-called advanced countries, the 'haves'. But what about the 'have-nots'? Don't the Africans in particular need good, new leaders?

Of course there are exceptions; that is implicit in our basic concept of democracy as the most evolved of political philosophies. All people who have been born in the twentieth century are not necessarily, psychologically, twentieth-century people. They may still have a medieval or pre-medieval psychology, it depends on the culture. It is not to denigrate the rest but it is merely to state a fact to say that, on the whole, the people who dominate the world, who have the power to destroy or renew the world, are people of the West.

How would you rate Mrs Thatcher as a prime minister, and as a world leader?

Well, you are asking me about a personality who is evolving at such a rate and whose circumstances of office change daily, so that anything I say is liable to be inadequate and out of date almost as soon as it is uttered. But tentatively, and provisionally, I feel she is a woman who always gives of her best and expects the best from everybody else. I think she is a very rare phenomenon in the modern world: she is a woman who is doing what she is doing vocationally in a man's world, without losing her femininity. She has really been called to this role: it almost seems that her whole personal story has been a preparation for this and – as happens when people do the thing for which their nature is destined – she has all the energies surging in her that enable her to do more than most people could because she is not going against her own grain in any way.

88

So why is she criticized so much, even in her own Conservative Party?

I think this is the penalty of being so outstanding a person. Since the war, Great Britain has not been properly governed. The British, both under the Conservatives and under Labour, have been led along by promises of a well-being and a prosperity which they had not earned, and all the fundamental differences, for instance about what kind of a Britain there should be, which are normal in a healthy democracy between the opposition and the government, all these differences were fudged. When a government was in office it fudged its own so-called programme and the opposition fudged the opposition. So we have had a fudge situation; everything was blurred. Then Mrs Thatcher came in as a young Member of Parliament, almost fresh from Oxford. She had been reared in a very political sort of upper working-class family; her father was very interested in local affairs. She was born with a great sense of duty, of discipline and of self-respect. She believed profoundly in these things and she saw them totally absent from the scene. She looked at it very simply. I mean, she looked at the economy of the country, for example, like a woman newly married at her future household. The economy of a country is nothing but national house-keeping, and to her horror she saw housekeeping at its worst. She saw all the issues first in terms of the microcosm of her own life: she saw the whole thing from its smallest to its greatest dimensions and she was determined to put it right. She had a strong sense of English history, and the values she believed in were essentially fundamentally English ones, and should be so observed. She believed in these things profoundly, and she is not a hypocrite, she is very straight. She is one of the most direct and honest Prime Ministers this country has ever seen.

There are a lot of people who wish perhaps that she was a little more devious rather than always exercising her tendency to do things directly. But she really set about reforming the things that needed reforming in this country. Well, the moment you start reforming, every situation has people who have a vested interest in resisting change. That is where a lot of the criticism is coming from – from lazy, pampered, intellectual people who have got vague, easy-going, idealistic dreams. They have been living on Britain's capital, because this was an enormously wealthy country, and they lived on its capital of brains, of money, of economy, until it ran out. This is the situation which Mrs Thatcher inherited, and she has started to put it right.

She inherited a situation, for instance, in which the trade unions in this country had become far more powerful than any medieval baron had ever been. They were doing things which were against the fundamentals of English law. They were interfering with the freedom of the individual, with the human aspects of the situation, and against the spirit of the rule which is vital to the British soul. They had become brutalized organizations. We have an example of it with the recent miners' strike where an important vested interest of workers was defying the good of the nation. Everything in this country needs reforming, and she is trying to renew everything. Once you start that process you make a lot of enemies.

But for the first time since the war I, personally, feel that Britain is being governed again, and of course in a country where you have a generation of people who have never been governed at all, they think this is brutal, this is tyrannical. To me it is the release, the return to freedom – freedom which only discipline can give one. I think of Dante's transcendent sense of this truth, 'In his will our peace'. But the people who have a more chaotic view of society, people who have never experienced government before, they do not know what has hit them. But it really is a brave effort to try and restore government on the classical, European model and correct an alarming decline.

There has been a great deal of criticism of Mrs Thatcher in that she does not perhaps conform to the idea of what a great world leader should be. There is a feeling she should be more like another 'Iron Lady', Catherine the Great of Russia, and should protect the arts and culture more.

Well, this may be how she is seen from abroad but more modestly in her own country: she is living in an age when you cannot really, as a leader, perform everything on a world scale. You can only really lead by example within your own country, and I think her example is great – her family life, everything she does. She is an integrated personality and this is of enormous importance. Trivial people and false, unreal things break against her; so that I am not surprised at all that some people, particularly some intellectuals and socialists, criticize her, and would by-pass the here and now, all the discipline of growth, for some frantic, instant utopianism. To my mind, the so-called liberal socialist elements in modern society are profoundly decadent today because they are not honest with themselves. They ought to know by now that they release forces in the world and society which they can never control, and this is immoral. They release expectations which they can never fulfil, and this is immoral. They give people an ideological and not a real idea of what life should be about, and this is immoral. They project onto other societies and countries solutions for problems they do not have to live themselves, and this is obscene. They feel good by being highly moral about other people's lives, and this is immoral. They do not realize that all they have of ethical energies are needed on their doorstep and that ultimately they have nothing to spare. To think otherwise is vain and immoral too. They have parted company with reality in the name of idealism. I think any 'ism' is a poison. They should look at the consequences since the war of their preaching, their pharisaical stancing, and the way, when the logical casualties of their philosophies lie bleeding and dying in millions on their way, they pass by on the other side.

I think it is right to have a vision of where you want life to go, but never have any doubt about the real, hard, slow way in which you can accomplish this vision. Think of all these phoney new disciplines which have been created in European universities, all these new faculties about subjects that do not really exist. I mean, 'political science' does not exist; 'social science', what is that? There is no such thing. There is science, and it has many branches, but none are 'social'. Solemnly teaching these non-existent subjects only increases the atmosphere of unreality in which modern people live. People qualify in a non-existent subject and then in the name of this unreal thing tell other people how to live and what to expect! They have caused enough assassination, killing, revolution and destruction in states which are not stable enough or sophisticated enough to tolerate the nonsense and the poison they emit, and you would have thought the so-called radicals would have learned something from this, but no: they carry on as if they alone possessed the secret to the ultimate good. I find them more incomprehensible and dangerous than the outright revolutionary.

Then there is this enormous trend which accompanies industrialized societies, which is to produce a kind of collective man who becomes indifferent to the individual values: real societies depend for their renewal and creation on individuals. Mrs Thatcher has taken up this battle. She has tried to reduce things, to make things smaller. She has understood the perils of numbers and giantism. She has tried to give people back their sense of responsibility. She was criticized. 'Why doesn't she do anything in the miners' dispute? Why doesn't the government interfere?' She refused and said it was not for government to interfere. It was the job of the Coal Board, not the politician. They employed these people, they had created the situation, they had to fight it out. So gradually she is trying to get people to face up to the consequences of their own actions. In the past the government has stepped in between people and the consequences of their behaviour. There is a limit, she realizes, to what government can do. Governments cannot really reform people; all they can do is to create an atmosphere in which certain things are more likely to happen than not, and this she is doing very successfully. The number of new, small businesses that are starting up in Great Britain is just astonishing.

And she took over at a time when the whole world was in a state of recession. People blame her for the unemployment in this country, but there is not a country in the world which has not got millions of unemployed at the moment. It is not peculiar to this system. In fact, what we have had in Great Britain for a long time is unemployment disguised as over-employment.

And the other factor which may distinguish her from other prime ministers is that she really has contact with the people. Her strength is not in her party, it is in the people, in the ordinary people of this country. She really trusts the people and loves them, and they trust her. The people who are so vociferous against her are an élite group, a very mixed élite of privileged people in the modern world, vested interests of mind and power, of which one of the greatest is trade unionism.

Being a woman doesn't create difficulties for her?

Yes, it does. Although she is not aware of it herself so much, I think it creates difficulties for her. Many men still find it very difficult to accept a woman as a leader, and they find it very difficult particularly to be ruled by a woman with a better mind than theirs, and to find a woman who is much more capable in an area of life which they regard as singularly a man's area. Amongst the more traditional people a certain amount of unconscious envy and jealousy has been directed against her. Much of the opposition and criticism of her from within her own party stems from this. The opponents, of course, would deny this: they wear hypocritical compassionate hearts full of fatty degeneration on their sleeves and accuse her of a lack of caring; but it is plainly the archaic, if you like chauvinistic, jealousy of men reared in a man-dominated culture.

There is, in fact, a very disturbing, pathological element – something totally non-rational – in the criticism of the Prime Minister. It amazes me how no one recognizes how shrill, hysterical and out of control a phenomenon it is. Nothing goes wrong, or is wrong, in the eyes of her critics which is not her fault. She is blamed for all the failures in the British world of today, and the list is too long for me to give it in detail – and I think you will recognize it only too well, seeing us more objectively than we can see ourselves. But the extraordinary thing is how even the people who are supposed to be on her side have a sneaking, sleazy, unconscious sympathy with her critics and therefore are helping it along in a way which could lead to the destruction of the first classical manifestation of government we have had since the war.

Of course, like all governments, her government has its faults, but one has only to think of the alternatives to see that none of them is valid at the moment. I think socialism, which has a nineteenth-century inspiration and was valid really only in a nineteenth-century context when the working classes had no vote, has long since been out of date and been like a rotting corpse whose smell in our midst has tainted the political atmosphere far too long.

The third-party alternative has an absurd justification. Heaven knows, Britain needs a powerful, wise and intelligent opposition, but not something based on premises so ludicrous as theirs: because what is the main argument which sums up all the arguments for the third alternative? It is that Britain should have a third party to rescue the country from party divisions. Think of the nonsense of it: it is coolly suggested, with great deliberation and plausible rationalization, that instead of Britain being divided between two parties, it should now be divided between three – or rather four because the alternative is really a coalition of two. I do not know how this gets by in the minds of so-called thinking people, and can only ascribe it to this decadence of the liberal spirit, this slack, permissive, armchair utopianism which makes people feel good in their soft-cushioned rooms. It should be obvious to all that even the best of third parties will still be a party of human beings, with all the human fallibilities and capacity for errors built deep into them, and merely in another way repeat and add to the errors of others.

Besides, it is totally against the great democratic traditions of Britain – the greatest democratic tradition the world has ever seen – a tradition that was great precisely because it was rooted deeply in the psychology and nature of people. This sounds complicated but is really simple. All human beings are born either introvert or extrovert; they are either Greeks or Trojans; Apollonian or Dionysian; Classic or Romantic. This is the divide in the human spirit which produces the opposites and the tensions that provide human beings with their energies of change and renewal; one group of people whose natures dispose them to serve the forces of change in life, and another group whose nature compels them to shape and contain in the interests of civilization and culture the forces of change that have been released. To abandon this deeply-rooted part of our tradition can only lead to more of the confusion and the loss of creative energies that we have suffered in modern Britain. We do need another regrouping in the political life of Great Britain that will return to us a valid and loyal form of opposition, and for me the worrying thing is that neither the old Labour Party nor the third alternative shows any signs yet of doing this.

It is this sense of failing themselves, and political life, unconsciously which is projected upon the Prime Minister, because, ultimately, one of the hardest things in men is that they cannot bear being responsible for their own errors, and they try to find a villain in the world outside on whom they can unload them. Another symptom of this pathological condition is the decline of quality in Parliament. I was born into a political family, and though I do not think I have a political mind I cannot help being automatically interested in the political life around me, to the extent that I often wish, for the sake of the story-teller that I would really like to be, that I did not have this compulsion. What has depressed me for many years about political life in Great Britain is how, in the fifty years or so in which I have been able to observe it, its quality has steadily declined. But even after the war, under Attlee and Churchill, it had a health and sanity which would be totally lost today if it were not for the present leadership. This health and sanity was apparent from the fact that Parliament was not just a place of abuse and hysteria, but an assembly which was also a place of wit and fun, stimulating rather than diminishing serious debate. There was not a day, almost, in which a good, funny story did not come out of Parliament.

Where has all that wit and fun and good humour and inter-party respect gone? All is bad temper, hysterical denouncement and attribution of bad faith and villainy. I do not know how people can tolerate the way in which some of those in the Opposition talk to a woman, even when she is Prime Minister. There is a deep, natural obligation in men who are really men to be chivalrous to any woman in a way they need not be chivalrous to one another. Yet I cannot recollect a single leading article in any of the newspapers in this country which has corrected the members of the Opposition for the way in which they address the woman who is Prime Minister – a way in which they would not dare to address a man.

Great issues demand – and there was a time when they received it in Parliament – to be discussed quietly and to be argued in depth with words that are listened to with attention. That no longer happens, although quintessentially the democratic spirit demands, as an article of faith, that one accepts that men and women can differ over issues without being guilty of bad faith, lying and deceit; it demands grace and courtesy from one another; it demands a certain standard of good political manners. Manners are an age-old condition of the civilized mind, in order to have a system of behaviour which prevents human contact from sliding into chaos and old night. The primitive peoples of Africa that I have known have wonderful manners and the most courteous and orderly forms of debate. One of the most significant things for me in Dante's great journey down into Hell and up into Heaven was that in Hell there was an absence of good manners; when he emerged and arrived in Purgatory he was amazed how grace and courtesy between the spirits he encountered were already present, and increased with a breathtaking and inspiring acceleration as he neared Paradise.

The fact that these things have vanished from Parliament and our political scene is, I believe, a sign of political sickness, and part of the explanation of the pathological opposition to a woman who, through the mere fact of her womanhood, stands for the caring and feeling values of life. Indeed, those of us who have known the Prime Minister intimately, and have worked with her, know that she is full and over-flowing with them, although she is more incapable than most of wearing her heart, in masculine fashion, on a sleeve that no instinctive woman sports.

Happily, she herself so far has had the strength of character and purpose not to allow her vision to be distorted by any of this. She says there is a job to be done, and she does it. The Falkland Islands crisis was a striking case in point: nothing illustrates her character and range better than this crisis. The whole thing came to her as a very great shock. There was nothing that she knew that prepared her to believe that the Argentinians would do this to us, and she only heard about it on a Wednesday night, at nine o'clock. She was called out of Parliament and she was told that an invading Argentinian fleet was heading for the Falklands. She rang up President Reagan and told him, and he said, 'Margaret, you are surely kidding!' Newspapers, people all around her clamoured, 'Why didn't the Foreign Office listen to the American intelligence?' But this is the truth: they did not know. She immediately got busy. She got Reagan to warn the Argentinians what the conse-quences of their action would be. Reagan did all he could, but he could not stop them. And between nine o'clock on that Wednesday evening, and Saturday morning, she organized the British counter-attack in the Falklands. On Saturday morning the fleet sailed with the troops who threw the Argentinians out. It was an astounding feat of organization. It shows how well this country was being governed that within a moment's notice the troops were on their way there, and it was a brilliant enterprise of war. It was not on a very large scale as an operation, but it was launched 11,000 miles away across the Atlantic with the Antarctic winter coming on, in the darkness and the storms of the Antarctic, with logistical problems, with a shortage of aircraft carriers, against an airforce that was eight times the size of the planes she could muster: it was great in quality and in danger. She not only undertook this enterprise but, far from revelling in the enterprise, she spent her days trembling lest at any moment she should hear of a British battleship being sunk and hundreds of lives being lost. She carried it all, she carried it incredibly well and bravely and she carried the country with her against terrible accusations of jingoism and God knows what automatic radical and liberal slush. I think that was a typical example of her courage and stamina.

This Falklands war seems to have taught several lessons. It has shown up weaknesses in the Western defence system in the areas of intelligence and communications. On the other hand, the role of the press was decisive, not in stopping the war but in accelerating the decision and negotiation process. But the press and Mrs Thatcher, that is not what you would call a love affair. It didn't even start with a honeymoon. Ever since she took power she has had a large segment of the press in England against her.

Yes, even where officially a newspaper might support her in its editorials, the staff are often against her, and it comes out in the reporting and the photographs and the way they cover the news. There are always people getting at her, but she goes on doing what she thinks is right and she has, so far I think, carried the country with her. Unfortunately too, from what one knows of human nature, people get tired of leaders after a while, however good they are. They want a change. Even in a Japanese prison-of-war camp towards the end I felt that we were going to have serious problems with this non-rational urge if our imprisonment lasted much longer.

That even happened to Winston Churchill, who was so good at the art of survival.

Yes, and Winston Churchill really was never in the unglamorous position of having to put a run-down house in order. Mrs Thatcher has to do the political equivalent of seeing to the drains, and the rot and the holes in the roof. She has to budget so that she can save money to bring the plumbing up to date, make the house modern and send the children to new and better schools. All her main jobs have been unglamorous and long-term, and she has never promised the impossible. People try to get her to promise things; 'When will you get unemployment down?', 'When will you do this and that?' and she says, 'I cannot say. It does not depend on me only, it depends on you, it depends on the nation, it depends on what we decide to do with our fate.' I think a kind of strength is coming through to people from that.

You have known a great many people of outstanding stature. What would you say was the common denominator of these personalities when they were in power? I am thinking of Mrs Thatcher, Winston Churchill, Lord Mountbatten.

Well, the ones you have mentioned all had one characteristic in common, and that is courage. Then the divergences start, but I think that Mrs Thatcher shares a great many things with Churchill. First of all, her love of her country and her love of the English-speaking world, her sense of the history of the English-speaking world. She admires Churchill, and if only she had a feminine, prime-ministerial model to follow, as she follows many great male ones, she would happily do so. The lack of one, I believe, accounts for her interest in the life of Elizabeth I: she is open to historical guidance and influence. And she is as dedicated to public service as Churchill was. Churchill could never imagine life outside Parliament really.

Yes, he was by nature a political animal.

That and more: the most apolitical-political animal ever seen in Britain, in the sense that he was almost mystically committed to Parliament and the spirit of democracy in its English evolution. At heart he was not a party man: he was always a national figure, a national politician and statesman who made a great mistake when he accepted leadership of the Conservative Party. I think Mrs Thatcher has got a sense of immediate, everyday detail which Churchill may have lacked. She would have made a very, very good commanding staff officer because her grasp of detail, of the sheer boring detail of what modern life is about, is astonishing. I place her virtues in the order of those Milton wrote about as won in the heat and dust of the running of an immortal race and not akin to 'a cloistered and fugitive virtue' he refused to praise.

Churchill was assisted by a brilliant team, but Mrs Thatcher gives the impression of being a rather solitary figure . . .

Well, Churchill still had a great tide of history flowing with him. She is dealing with a generation which has lost its sense of history and is charged with bringing it alive if it is not to be lost for good: her task is more difficult. There is on the European scene a very, very alarming thing and that is what I call historical amnesia; alarming because history in the real, living sense is our only guide to the future.

There are still some world leaders who have this sense of history, but very few are left who experienced the Second World War. Roosevelt, Truman, Eisenhower, Stalin, Churchill, de Gaulle, Franco, Tito, the Emperor Haile Selassie, are all dead. The only survivor is the Emperor of Japan, Hirohito.

Yes, they are not around. For instance, since Stalin, no country has been more leaderless than Russia. Russia is run by the most depressing collection of committees.

But don't you think, in the special case of the Soviet Union, these committees act as safety valves? What would it be like if the power was concentrated in the hands of one individual? Would it not be too dangerous?

Well, it may be a fortunate coincidence, but it means that there is never going to be any vision in Russia because you cannot get vision from a committee. I was told the joke in France that a camel is an animal that was designed by a committee!

For us there is a tremendous amount to be said for this quiet, steady form of government. When I think of what Britain was like under the previous government, and where it had got to – it is quite frightening how far we had gone down the slope. But there is a sign now of something emerging, a new kind of awareness of a need to recover self-reliance and self-respect. I think, for instance, one of the things this government of Mrs Thatcher's will bring about, not by design so much as through what it is, will be the end of the Labour Party, the Socialist Party in Great Britain, as a political force. We shall see another kind of opposition emerging. I do not know quite what it will be – we do need an opposition, a loyal opposition. But no new ideas have come out of the Labour Party since the Manifesto of 1848. There is nothing that is of the modern age – not their structure, their concept of trade unionism, their concept of life or their concept of society. Their concept of society is a partial society ruled by social workers. I mean, this is so out of date, so out of touch with reality, so anti a life of increase of spirit and its means.

Is Mrs Thatcher calling for this 'loyal opposition'?

She is. She has been longing for a loyal opposition, but there is not one at the moment. In this desperate miners' strike that was dragging on week after week, the House of Commons attracted surprisingly few

Labour members to its debates. They were all out doing something else.

I think one day she will be seen as a very great Prime Minister and a Prime Minister of reform, because the interesting thing in Britain is that the Conservative Party, which is a party of conservation, has really changed roles with the radical parties. The Conservative Party has become the party of reforms and change, and the others are trying to conserve, trying to anchor us to outmoded and discredited patterns of society.

———

Do you, because of your Huguenot descent, take a special interest in French affairs? Were you, for instance, interested in de Gaulle as a leader of the national resistance or as a statesman?

Who could help but be interested in de Gaulle? He was, after all, more than a resistance leader and statesman, he was a voice of history, a warden of the spirit of his people, and after a fashion saved and helped to remake it. And also I was interested in de Gaulle because some of my French friends personally believed in him. Pierre Maillaud, who was his first Minister of Culture and Information, was one of my greatest friends, and I was terribly sorry when he was drowned in the South of France; and Siriex, who was one of his people who became Governor-General of French Somaliland, was also one of my friends. But I was interested in the phenomenon of de Gaulle. He was in a sense more of a phenomenon of a certain religion, a high priest of a faith of history – that is the nearest I can get to it. You must know how eighteenth-century rationalism, which led with a logic of the divided soul to the Revolution, deprived France as a nation of a religion, and how in a profound sense this was replaced by a religion of French history and civilization. One believed in France rather than or instead of God.

But after Hitler and Vichy, even faith in France in this sense was the greatest casualty, and there was nothing left, only a great vacuum in the French spirit. De Gaulle, however, had neither lost his god nor his love of and belief in France, and he set about with a superhuman passion which was as fiery as it was cold as ice. For instance, if you had asked the generals in Algeria, whom he betrayed for his faith, they would have testified to the ice that served the fire in him. I think he lifted history and his love of France into the absolute. They were not relative, they were absolutes. Even against the French. I shall never forget – I do not know if you saw a rather remarkable French television film called, '*Français, si vous saviez*'?

About the collaboration of some French with the Germans during the war?

Yes, and also about the resistance. Now there was one young resistance person who went to see de Gaulle. He had been out and suffered in the Maquis. He was only about twenty. And he came out of the Maquis to meet de Gaulle. He was vibrating with excitement at meeting the great general, this symbol of a free France whom he had heard about. And de Gaulle greeted him, said he was glad to meet him and thanked him rather stiffly. Then the young man asked, 'What can we do now, General? We must get it right this time. What can we do?' And de Gaulle replied, 'Your work is done. I have come now. You can leave it to me.' When this same young man was interviewed many years later, and asked about de Gaulle, he answered with great sadness: 'I can't help thinking that de Gaulle felt very deeply that the French were not good enough for France.'

That was the paradox of this very great man of history, a man who, like Churchill, had been profoundly prepared for his work. He educated himself and, like Churchill, had years of schooling in the wilderness. He was a great reader . . . I remember Adenauer saying once to a friend of ours that he had been staying with de Gaulle. And something that Adenauer liked to do when staying with people was to look at their library. He had had a chance to have a good look at de Gaulle's library, and commented, 'He is the best-read man I have ever met in my life. I have seen a lot of libraries, but that is the best one ever.'

But I was more interested in de Gaulle because of his implications for Britain. I thought his anti-Britishness dangerous for us as well as for France and Europe. It was utterly disproportionate and turned him into a sort of reincarnation of Joan of Arc, without Joan of Arc's justifications. And why? After all, we had been through such a lot together.

You mean because of the Common Market?

Well, it was more than that, but certainly it demonstrated itself during our effort to join the Common Market. There was a friend of mine at the

Foreign Office who, with Heath, conducted the negotiations for Britain and he said that finally there was nothing rational left to stop us from going in; we had met all the objections. We had satisfied everybody. The only way to keep us out was for de Gaulle to veto us. And he vetoed us. He would not have us in.

Then, I knew Malraux slightly, through Stephen Spender, and we had been in correspondence. So when we were staying with our ambassador in Paris – he and his wife were special friends of ours – I thought that I must see Malraux about all this. We have talked about this odd compulsion of mine to try and help anonymously about things, even in the most unlikely circumstances, when I feel I can. And I asked Malraux straight, 'Look, what is going on? Will you let me meet de Gaulle and talk to him because I want to ask him what is wrong with us, what is this hatred? So that he can tell me and at least we can understand it and try to do something about it.'

Malraux said, 'It is not hatred. He had better tell you the story himself. I will try and arrange for you to meet.'

I left feeling happy that afternoon, certain we were going to meet. Malraux could not have been more understanding and, for him, warm and expansive. But that very night the disturbances started on the Left Bank.

May '68 and the students' uprising?

Yes. And, as you know, it ended in de Gaulle stepping down.

It's too bad. You missed the chance. But did Malraux offer any explanation of why de Gaulle was acting as he was?

We met again, and Malraux said, 'You know, it would be a very good thing if we could arrange for you and General de Gaulle to have a discussion on television about all this. I have suggested something on those lines to him and he likes the idea.' And I remember saying, 'I know the BBC will gladly do its part, but television or not, will you please pass this message on to him. I think great evil will come out of this stance of apparent hatred. It looks dangerously like the evil of the centuries coming alive again. France and Britain should never have been separated. Reconciliation between France and Germany is of the utmost importance but not at the price of separating from Britain and keeping us out of Europe.' But although I did not know it then, de Gaulle was already broken. What little there was of political verve and nerve in his apolitical and superhuman soul had left him. So nothing came of it, and poor Malraux himself was bound too for the dark.

I only really saw the light later when de Gaulle, on an official visit to Canada, got no further than Quebec, where he cried out, '*Vive le Québec libre*': he cancelled the rest of his visit to Canada. Then suddenly I realized it was not hatred of Britain so much: it was a fear born of his immense, personal and obsessional love of France, its language and culture. Quebec was a symbol of a profound conscious and unconscious fear of the power and the spread of English, and of a rapidly increasing Anglo-Saxon world in which France was as vulnerable and powerless alone as Quebec was in Canada. Of course, it was an historical deafness and dumbness and not a contemporary spirit that went with this archaic love. It was congenital, and somewhat pathological, as the young Maquis leader realized. It was an area where nobody could reach him, really, certainly no one on the English side. And I thought, if only I could talk to him and say, 'What the hell is wrong? Please, General, tell us what it is.'

That would have been very interesting. But somehow I feel more objective as a Frenchman on the periphery. And I do not think de Gaulle was especially anti-British. He was against all the Anglo-Saxon cultural bulldozing, and he was naturally opposed to the mistakes the Americans had been making all over the world since the Yalta conference – to which he had not been invited. His resentment certainly never ceased to grow after that.

I find 'bulldozing' a strange word. No one will ever want to 'un-French' France: we need France, for France gives to life something that no one else can. That is why I mentioned Quebec, you see. Quebec can always be Quebec as long as it wants to be Quebec. So can France, and so it shall always be, even when not as a world political force. Our invincible fortress of ourselves must always be in the spirit and not just in our political and geographical shapes or political power.

Don't you find that, generally speaking, French intellectuals are more oriented and more attracted towards German thinkers than English ones?

Yes, Malraux and I touched on this. I did say to him, 'You know how much I admire your work but I have always been sad that you do not know England better. In your autobiography, *Antimémoires*, almost the only British person who gets any notice of approval is T. E. Lawrence.

You do not even mention Shakespeare. You are full of Goethe and Nietzsche.' And was it, I wondered, because his favourite uncle was a friend of Nietzsche and accompanied Nietzsche to his lunatic asylum? But Malraux was exceptional; he was from Alsace and had strong Germanic influences bearing on him. And I could not help adding, 'You do not know us at all. You should read your Alphonse Daudet, and his son Léon of *Le Voyage de Shakespeare* and *Le Stupide XIXème Siècle*. They are good French guides to the English and represent a France that understood and knew the English, and realized how we need each other.' He looked quite stunned at me, and said, 'Yes, I've always regretted it. That's my Alsace upbringing. But you know how many English friends I've got.' And I said, 'Yes, I know', but I did not add that they tended to be left-wing or fellow-travellers who really hated their own country.

I should like to add to what I said earlier about de Gaulle and the Americans: he was certainly not anti-American. And he believed in the Atlantic alliance. He demonstrated it when he was among the first of America's allies to side with John F. Kennedy during the Bay of Pigs incident and the row with Fidel Castro. The French seem always to have been fascinated by the Americans. Are you not somewhat, as well? Your family and ancestors were not only Huguenot rebels and idealists, they were also nomads; is that perhaps why you feel close to the Americans, those devourers of space, from their rush to the West to the big jump to the Moon?

I think there are certain parallels between our history and American history and that may well have something to do with it. I do like Americans very much indeed – in fact there are very few people I do not like – and it may well come from the fact that they are still in touch with their pioneering spirit.

In America, as in socialist or communist countries, the biggest problem is how to protect and develop individual rights. Do you agree with Orwell's vision of the future as he described it in Nineteen Eighty-Four?

I think Orwell's prediction could be provisionally true but it is not an absolute; it is not an end, it will not last, there is something beyond it. I do not believe that life would allow it to last, and I think that there are all sorts of new things coming alive that will deny it. Among young people everywhere there are new kinds of values emerging, new emphases put on different sorts of things compared to my own generation. I think the Orwellian prophecy may be fulfilled in part as a phase, but no more than a partial and highly provisional phase.

Forces of oppression and coercion can be aided and abetted by new technology, new weapons – but it would be hard for them to control everybody and everything at the same time. Besides, they can be contaminated and finally vanquished by very crude but very aggressive kinds of ideas and weapons. We all know that a handful of guerrilla fighters can resist and even defeat the most sophisticated army.

That is true, and I also think the modern human being is beginning to care about the preservation of his own identity and the values it implies as he has never cared before. He is beginning to realize he is in peril. He does not even know what it is, and so his sense of the search, the ancient urge of the quest of Spirit, is becoming increasingly important to him. This is a very significant thing. For young people, one of the favourite expressions in the Anglo-Saxon world, if faced with something they do not like, is: 'It isn't me', or 'It's not my scene', and so on. They are beginning to think about the 'me' in themselves, whether they are conscious of the direction or not, as we talked about it in our discussion on the evolution of God. It is a moment, I believe more than ever, of which the Greeks in a great crisis of being and spirit said, 'Called or not called, God shall be there.'

Also I am very interested in the new attitude of my friends towards their children, and how the children have changed. Many friends have children who in the past would have been pushed into business or into becoming barristers or doctors; they are now learning to be carpenters and craftsmen and even cooks because they find that in that way they are fulfilling themselves and are much happier. The question of individual fulfilment is now being posed for people in an everyday and matter-of-course way, and they no longer follow automatically in a family pattern or a social pattern. Suddenly all is wide open and everybody is going for an area which will enable him to do what he calls his or her 'own thing'. These are good signs.

And then there is a tremendous reaction against bigness. People have realized that sheer size can be a form of hubris, imperilling the human spirit, and they are rebelling against it. They are realizing the immense distance between quality and amount, between giantism and creative power, and hence that there is no size or distance in meaning.

Yes, it does seem that small is beautiful now to a growing number of people. Is it not true that Switzerland is beautiful and strong because it is small? I was surprised to read in your book on Jung that the Swiss were offered an opportunity to enlarge their territory and borders, but refused it.

Yes, that is a fact. At the beginning of this century there was a tremendous row going on between the Italians and the Austro-Hungarian Empire, over the Tyrol, which is German-speaking. The Italians passionately claimed part of Tyrol as being part of Italy, and the Austrains said it was part of Austria. It was then proposed that the territory in dispute should all be given to the Swiss. But the Swiss said, in effect, 'No. We said at the time when the Swiss Federation was formed about two hundred years ago that our frontiers would for ever be those decided then. We never want any more land and would never accept less.'

How nice to know there are not only wise men but wise nations as well!

Well, I think the Swiss could not have their particular qualities if they were not a small nation. I think you could put the whole population of Switzerland into one-third of London or half of Paris, it is such a sparsely populated country. And this gives their lives a personal identity; there is still a personal involvement of every human being in Switzerland and you have there what you do not have in larger countries: they are all neighbours and friends.

So towns and cities should shrink in size to be comfortable to live in, or at least to be manageable?

Yes, towns have got to grow smaller, not bigger; then, paradoxically, in terms of real meaning they will gain by becoming less. I think all the reasons which once upon a time made a city desirable, now make a city undesirable. Cities no longer fulfil the purpose for which they were invented. One of the reasons for a city was to make communication between different elements of the community easier and more effective; so, putting them all in one place where exchange could more readily be attained, seemed to be the right thing to do. Now the last place where communication is easy is in a great city. You have only to look around you! You only have to watch a motor-car designed to do 120 miles an hour go through London at one mile an hour. You can see how people have to fight to get to their offices. The waste of time, the waste of energy that goes on! Exchange is not made easier by a city – it is made more difficult. People have to communicate as if they were living in different continents, that is, by telephone. They never see one another face to face. It is an illusion to think if you live in a city you see your friends. We find we only see our London friends when we go down to the country and invite them to come and stay. And from the point of view of defence, which was another prime reason for cities, nothing could be more dangerous than a city now. In the old days, of course, a city offered security, but now it is the most vulnerable part of the nation, and at the first hint of war it has to be evacuated.

Some cities, or parts of them, have gone totally out of control. Even policemen do not dare enter these areas.

This is a terrible thing. One is frightened . . . even here in London, which is comparatively peaceful, we have riots now. I watch London. Just this afternoon as I was coming to see you, caught in a traffic jam, I realized that I was caught up in something which was out of control – even the traffic is out of control. There are aspects of daily life which are out of control and we simply accept it: there are masses and forces entangled hopelessly around one, for which no one will accept accountability. This is social madness. When people in Great Britain talk about rehabilitating the inner cities, my answer is: pull them to the ground and make parks and fields out of them. Let's settle the people somewhere else where it is smaller and healthier and they can once more lead a recognizable life of their own and live unafraid of the responsibility of their actions and discharging of their affairs.

And when we talk of 'inner cities' let us give thought to the real inner city, called the city of God, the city of light and meaning, because it is neglect of the city within that starts decay of the city without; crime, disorder and violence all have to do with loss of meaning socially and individually. The greater the absence of meaning in the life of the individual, the more violent and disordered his life becomes.

Again, proliferation of the human species is an immense danger to us in the future. Size and great numbers are the enemies of modern man and of the earth. If, for instance, in South Africa the population goes on multiplying as it is doing now, in the year 2020 there is not even going to be enough drinking-water because, with its erratic rainfall, scarcity of rivers and uncertainty of subterranean water-levels, there simply will not be enough to go around.

What are the solutions? In the Middle Ages there were epidemics, hunger, wars, infanticides and so forth. But today?

Well, we want human beings who will take responsibility for these things. Already individuals all over the place are beginning to do it. We want also a very pure form of government. Of course we are seeing these problems now on a bigger scale but they are not new. The Athenians in Greece had all these problems. When you read Thucydides' account of Pericles' rule, you find he had all of these problems. Some of his great speeches to the Athenians are even more relevant to our time than his. It is because the Athenians got to the point where they would not face up to them and deal with them that they declined and fell. The Macedonians took over and they fell, and the Spartans took over and ultimately they all fell – as all civilizations fall – because there was a vital problem of their time, a challenge to reappraise and renew themselves and reach out to another meaning beyond themselves, as in reaching out to the one they had established was the unknown in the beginning which brought them about, to which they failed to respond. The one saving thing today perhaps is that there is not a society in the world, not a country, which is not being challenged in this way and condemned to put itself back into a way of new meaning or perish, because the ultimate lesson of history for me is that men and their societies can endure and surmount any enormities except a state of meaninglessness.

Is what you are saying also valid for Soviet Russia?

My sad and overwhelming feeling in Russia when I was there was that it was just about the most depressing country I have ever been to in my life. The sheer hopelessness of life and mankind in Russia, the joyless-ness – the Russians seldom laughed unless they were drunk – there was no fun. You felt that people knew the life they were leading was dishonest. They did not really believe in the State, although they pretended to – and the pretence was ghastly. To see one man live a lie – to be guilty of a lie oneself – is terrible enough, but to see millions of people being governed by liars, by people for whom lying and deception are a form of faith, is just about the most frightul condition of man imaginable, particularly when he is in possession of vast power.

One of the Russians' main pleasures is not only to drink but also to have children. In some developing countries to have children can sometimes be a kind of consolation and revenge against fate and suffering. It is quite difficult to control that.

We must all re-educate ourselves for that. I think there is time. I think the only place from which I can see an answer coming is the West. Western man must renew himself in his full Christian image, which demands a heart that will go out with love to the rest of the world. I know it is fashionable to say the West is no longer Christian because our churches are emptying fast and our educational institutions are dominated by arid intellectualists who think religion is superstitious and a delinquent state of mind, but western culture is profoundly and incorrigibly Christian, and in its dreaming self preparing to make its established religious self new and contemporary. That is why I think that western man – with all his faults – still has the key to the salvation of the world within his culture, within his philosophy, within his spirit. If only he will go back to its source in his own story he can save not only himself but the world. Western man has the experience – through the experience of empire. He has an experience of eastern, northern and southern as well as western man. In his own context now, in his own heart, he has got so much of the whole world enmeshed, incorporated into the western spirit; his chauvinistic stage is behind him for good, and he has got all the bridges he needs to the rest of the world, if only he will cross them.

Founding the United Nations was a great dream and an attempt to solve these problems. But do you think we have the time left?

Time is always running out. It is in the nature of time to do so, but it is also in the nature of time always to provide more time. I believe it is never too late to do the right things. I believe in deathbed repentances perhaps more than other forms of repentance.

The United Nations now presents not just a political but quite a grave ethical problem. The world has experience of two models of world organization now: the old League of Nations and UNO. Both have failed and disappointed, and yet even in their failed state they have proved we cannot do without them. We must, as a matter of great urgency, reappraise our experience of these organizations and see how and why they have failed us. It will not be easy because a lot of the failures have been due to the members and not the organization, and reform will depend on our willingness to reform ourselves. But there is no doubt the constitution and shape of UNO is wrong. For instance, it should not be its own highest legislative and judicial body both at the same time; it should be subject to its own laws and the interpretations of the laws by its own independent judiciary.

Then members whose own systems violate the concepts of human rights of freedom, of democratic government, of peace, should be suspended and not allowed to sit in judgement on others. You cannot let it go on being a body sitting in judgement on the world, when the judges include nations like Uganda, Abyssinia, Russia – which has invaded Afghanistan – and Cuba, which is sitting in force in Angola. And incidentally, they continue to condemn us on the Falklands Islands issue. Those countries which have abolished democracy in Africa and the rest of the world, the despotisms and totalitarianisms who sit automatically on the UNO juries, make a mockery of UNO judgement, and justice as we know it. Like the traffic in London it is out of control and wrong, but we do nothing about it.

And meanwhile what of those people who put their hopes and faith in it? I will give you one illustration. The late Haile Selassie, who was betrayed by the old League of Nations in the Thirties and abandoned to Mussolini, told me one evening when we shared a tent behind the Italian lines in the Gojjam that he would base his policy after his restoration on three main ideas. The first was the restoration of the old League of Nations in a new and more effective form. Although it had failed him, it had yet been real enough to demonstrate how much the world needed a body of that kind. The second was to have a policy of total forgiveness and reconciliation with the Italians. The third idea was to educate his young people as fast as possible.

On the day he appeared in the hills above Addis Ababa to accept from an allied group of officers the restoration of his rule, he kept them waiting while he went off to a little wayside chapel of St George. There, deeply moved and in tears, he fell prostrate before the altar, gave thanks and rededicated his people to these three principles: and when he rejoined the resplendent allied group he said, still with tears in his eyes, '*Excusez-moi. J'étais trop ému.*' We all know how only the Italian part of his programme worked, how both his young and UNO, for a second time, betrayed him, and that even now it will not insist on getting innocent members of the Emperor's family, mostly women, out of scandalous gaols where they are scandalously kept, and does nothing to mitigate the reckless Marxist despotism which killed the Emperor and rules in his place. And the final irony of it all was that the young, whom he educated and in whom he believed, were at the heart of this movement that led to his assassination and the new despotism.

It should not be possible for another Amin's Uganda to exercise full membership rights, nor a Russia while engaged in an unprovoked war in Afghanistan. These are some examples of grave faults in the system. There clearly ought to be standards of human rights, freedom, non-interference in the affairs of others and so on, which should be demanded of members. I sat on a private commission investigating UNO reform and the need is as great as it is urgent. Of course it will take time. It will not be an instant solution but one to be developed. But reform should figure each year on its agenda, formally raised and discussed. Also there are a number of distinguished and dedicated UNO servants with long experience of its working. It would be the best possible start to select a body of them – men like Brian Urquhart, who has been with the United Nations since its beginning and has just retired as the most senior and distinguished of its permanent servants – and get them to report on the areas most in need of reform and the necessary means. Unless it takes its own reform seriously and gets to work on it, it will fail the world again even more disastrously than its predecessors. When it broke its own Charter, it lost its chance to grow into a new moral power and became just another political institution.

But isn't it always like that with every human enterprise? Look at Europe. We are trying to build a united Europe, but the European Parliament and machinery is not exactly a model of virtue and efficiency.

Yes, we might have the same bureaucratic problems as the United Nations but our roots are deeper, we share the same values, so our motivations, our moral foundations, our moral credentials are better. I think it is tremendously important that Europe should not fail. Europeans should set themselves a certain spiritual vision of the world and then, if we are a truly united Europe, there is nothing that we cannot do in the world. We can do better than either America or Russia because I think we have, ultimately, a longer and more profound experience of history. Our vision is deeply rooted in history; it has models of a united Europe in the past for which there is still a nostalgia in the modern spirit, a remembrance of a common language only a few centuries ago. So we just have to look back at what we have inherited from the past and start there again, instead of starting with these specialized fragments of our past which people today are telling us are the whole of our past. We must just look at our history again and see what sort of people we were, why we have come to this, and we shall be able to go on. So I think this is why the European experiment is of immense importance. I think in Europe we have the key to the salvation of the future.

Do you believe in some form of control of politics, of power, of science and technology and in the action of groups, committees, institutions like Pugwash, the Club of Rome, and so on?

Let us try these things in a small way, let people always do their immediate best, but let us be modest about it and realize the slow growth, the patience we need. We lack the type of human beings who can form proper committees of control. We are in the formative stage, we have got to remake ourselves first, then we can have proper committees of control. At the moment it is no good putting the wrong people into the right place. The Chinese say you must not only have the right means and the right motive, but you must also have the right person and the right time for something to work: these two readinesses are all. We have not got the right people at the moment. We are none of us right; we do not know ourselves sufficiently, we have not faced up to the fact that we ourselves, not our institutions or stars, are the source of the error, and that until we have dealt with error in ourselves we cannot deal properly with what is wrong in the world.

So for myself I do not believe in forming societies or groups – that way the message dies straight away. I think this is a moment in life when everybody must act in his own little area. Excluding the war and my life in the army, I have only twice joined, and in fact helped to form, a group. One was The Capricorn Society of Africa after the war, which was David Stirling's inspiration and which we formed with the purpose of preventing the sort of things that are happening in Africa now from happening; and we failed, as I thought we would fail. I realized then that it was this problem of finding the right people that defeated us because there were not enough right people for the sort of society that we had in mind. All I hoped was that we could perhaps have pushed things in the right direction. In our failure there was a sign of the decadence of the European spirit of liberalism to which we referred earlier – because among our worst enemies were the liberal and intellectual establishments.

We were talking about democracy earlier; don't you think we are sometimes terribly wrong to try to export our values, our models of democracy?

Yes, of course. We try to export democracies to the world as if they were a sort of spiritual machine which will automatically work to a desired effect. We do not realize that democracy is perhaps one of the most advanced states of the spirit of man that you could possibly have, and, as I said before, without this spirit democracy does not work. Ballot boxes are, in a sense, the least part of a democracy, for they do not create it by themselves. We ought to realize how since the war, in country after country, we have allowed the ballot box to be used as an instrument for the destruction of democracy. In fact a far less sophisticated form of government with people using it well would probably work better than democracy used badly. I have seen so much, since the war, of the abolition of so-called imperialist tyranny, only to see it replaced by far greater forms of tyranny under different names. I have seen, perhaps more than most, how what is called the 'emancipation of colonial territories' led to massacre, loss of freedom and greater tyrannies than those that preceded them, with the human being in the end having much less of a chance of fulfilment than he had in a colonial context.

If you look at what has happened even in India, you would be full of foreboding, although it is miraculous how much of the democracy imported by the British survives. But this new India came about at the cost of a monstrous and precipitous act of partition in which perhaps four and a half million people were massacred. It was more than we lost in two world wars. This price, exacted in the so-called cause of independence, still seems to me to have been disproportionate. We have to ask ourselves the question, has it been worth it from the point of view of the ordinary people of India? We must ask ourselves, too, if what happened was inevitable?

I know that there is always the argument that what has happened in life happened because it was inevitable. This may be true of events behind us, because obviously what has happened has happened and we must live with the consequences for ever. But the question is by no means academic because it is of great importance to the future conduct of human beings to know whether tragedy has been inevitable, and what the choices were. Not to ask this question is to deny tragedy its real role in human affairs because tragedy is really only tragedy if at the time it had not been inevitable and resulted only because of a failure of awareness in men and their societies. And I, for one, do believe it was avoidable in India.

I say this because it was, in a very profound sense and not in a political sense which annoys the classes governing India today immensely, a very special relationship. To understand this I think one must realize that India is not an oriental country. This is not merely a biased and subjective interpretation of history of my own. Nirad Chaudhuri, that remarkable Indian writer who wrote the autobiography of an unknown Indian and is a friend of mine, in his appraisal of the history of India, *The Continent of Circe* (which among other tokens of recognition won the Hawthornden Prize), argues at length and conclusively that India belongs to the western complex of nations and is a branch of the great drive westwards of the mainstream of peoples who overran Celtic and Iberian Europe from the East. The trouble is that the world has come to think of the West and the East as two valid opposites of human races and cultures.

I think it is right to apply this distinction to the West. I think if one stood on the Great Wall of China and looked westwards, looked towards Europe (which significantly is derived from the Sanskrit word meaning 'land where the sun sets', and is indicative of the direction which the invaders of Europe took, not only geographically but by which they set the compass of their spirit), there is a complex of people who share a culture and a way of life sufficiently integrated in its creative diversities to form an entity called 'the West' – a West which, of course, extended itself until it included also the Americas, southern Africa, New Zealand and Australia.

But if you stood, say, on Mont Blanc and looked east, there is no sign of anything similar in the Orient. The East is entirely a geographical concept and has no validity or reality comparable to the West. The failure to realize this has been a great source of error in Europe's approach to the peoples who live in the East. I found it extraordinary and reprehensible that even Kipling, who knew his India so well and to my mind was a far greater artist and writer than the world was prepared to acknowledge, should have written anything so silly as, 'East is East and West is West and never the twain shall meet'. The fact is that in this vast area we call the East there is a formidable variety of totally different races and cultures as, for instance, the races and peoples who rallied around the crescent moon and followed Mohamet and the Koran; there are the peoples who inhabit to this day the world of Malaysia which includes the old Dutch East Indies and the vast scatter of islands called Indonesia; there is the world of Thai; there is, above all, one of the greatest and oldest civilizations the world has ever seen in China; and there is Japan; all of which in their sum make it impossible for us to speak as if there were one 'East' culturally, and such a being as 'Oriental man'. All this is a fiction, and a dangerous fiction, which has blighted the approach of the West in its attitude to the peoples of Asia. And finally, of course, there is India which has least of all in its spirit and racial composition to do with the Orient. It is only geographically a part of Asia. Its culture is old, rich, for long self-sufficient, self-contained, creative spiritually, artistically and even in the sciences, since it gave an enormous impetus to the evolution of mathematics, algebra and arithmetic and was responsible for the concept of the role of 'zero', without which all our calculations would have been doubly nought. The measure in which India remained its own India is proved for me by the fact that the great civilization of China, whose power and influence extended so far in the ancient world of Asia, hardly touched India at all. On the contrary, India had an immense and seminal influence on the civilization of China, and ultimately Japan, by exporting Buddhism far and wide into the remotest parts of the easternmost realms of Asia and even its furthermost south-eastern regions.

Moreover, the people who invested in India, as their language proves to this day, belonged to the European complex of peoples and have always been and remain a Sanskrit people. What has always struck me about the peoples of India has not been how different they are in spirit from so-called western man, but how close.

In my youth when I first started out in the world I made many friends in the Indian communities of southern Africa. I was introduced by them to the myths and legends, the *Upanishads* and the sacred books of India. These ultimately gave me a far better account of the spirit and the inner history of the people than the most minutely compiled and documented history of events could do, and immediately I felt that I had discovered close new neighbours. It was a discovery of immense importance to my future life because it was my first intimation that many of my closest neighbours often lived farthest away.

All these impressions swarmed in time like bees into a single hive of productive spirit wherein the conviction was nourished that the West and India were in origin and destination designed to move through time in convoy and partnership. I think it is because of this congenital similarity that the British for a couple of centuries were able to reunite and govern India, on the whole happily and fruitfully, with a mere handful of people. For me, therefore, there was no real and organic reason why the relationship between India and Britain should have been so brutally and disastrously amputated. Moreover, I believe that the forces of nationalism in India were far less of an internal, spontaneous Indian product than the projection of Britain's own internal social frictions and problems into its Empire and, above all, into an India which was far more developed, articulate and conscious than Britain's other extensions overseas.

I emphasize this because I think it is important to what we have been saying about the situation in the world today, since it applies not only to Britain but to the rest of the world. The nineteenth century, which was so fateful and creative in many ways, seems to me to have been guilty of disastrous errors in its doctrine of self-determination, and an elevation of nationalism almost to a position of sanctity amongst its values. It nourished increasingly a trend in its political philosophies towards divorcing itself from the great, apolitical and transcendent religious values which give politics ultimately its direction and meaning, and to cultivating assiduously in men the belief that politics was itself sufficient, and that all the problems that faced modern man were capable of political solutions – a heresy so widespread today that there is hardly a country in the world which is not in its disastrous grip.

But worse still, the changes demanded in society in Britain by the need to abolish poverty and emancipate the so-called working classes, and all the internal turmoil and friction it caused, were exported to the colonies and dominions overseas where they immediately ceased to be the mere class-problem and inherently the indigenous and special problems they were at their place of origin, and became sources of conflict between imperial authority and the race subjected to their rule. For the British and European socialist, the working classes and colonial subjects were one, and had the same enemy in authority. This in turn, in Britain, caused the forces of reform – who naturally saw the established order as their enemy and were predisposed to be anti-authority – to identify with the colonial subjects and oppose their own overseas rule of law. It is not for nothing that partition and the abrupt departure of the British from India was fostered and encouraged over many years and ultimately set in motion by the first real socialist government ever imposed on Britain.

I think if both Britain and India could have been contained for longer in the total concept of their respective histories and if there had been an appraisal of the profound values they shared, something different from the complete break politically between the two countries would have emerged and a growth of genuine democracy, in the ancient Platonic concept, would have been possible in India, rather than the gradual erosion of democratic values.

Living as I have for many years in Japan, I find what you say about the European myth of such a creature as 'Oriental man' important and extremely helpful. It is a misconception I battle against all the time. But I would be glad if you could elaborate on what you called the export of internal European frictions into the rest of the world. Surely it must have some natural, endemic root to be

*grafted on, or it would not have caught on in so widespread a fashion as it has
today?*

No, of course I do not want to imply that all races and cultures, even
the most primitive, have not a natural longing for an identity of their
own. But I do not think that this longing need have been a permanent
cause of friction. Indeed I believe that in a modern, interdependent
world, this longing could have found a valid expression more in
partnership with the European peoples who had made their home
among them, than in a separation and dismissal of them as mere
exploiters and spoilers of the territories they had come to colonize. Ever
since the war I have had a great deal to do with the so-called emancipation of colonial races both in South-East Asia and Africa, and I think the
time for judging the changes we initiated, and reappraising them
objectively by their consequences, is long overdue. I think that the
radical and liberal spirit which played a great and constructive role in
Britain, and which helped the British peoples to achieve and transform
their societies comparatively peacefully and without the revolution and
violence to which other countries resorted, has today declined into an
effete and decadent form. It still proposes and promotes forms of
changes which it should know, from past history, release forces it cannot
control, having disastrous consequences, and continues to behave as if
change for change's sake were enough in spite of the disorder and chaos
that is brought about.

Examples are so obvious and so abundant. I feel I must only re-
emphasize that many of the horrors which confront us everywhere in the
world today are European-inspired horrors and the results of grafting
inadequate European models and 'isms' on a vulnerable world. The
killing we have seen, for instance, in Africa is not natural to Africa. Of
course there is a sense in which African history is a horror story, and it
certainly does not lack war and destruction between the different
peoples of Africa. But these wars have never been sustained; they have
been eruptions of an as yet undifferentiated, collective and tribal spirit,
seeking to free itself from an archaic aspect of itself. They have never
lasted long. But this sustained killing for political ends which character-
izes the African scene today is not African but is killing on the European
model, and killing inspired by European ideologies, to such an extent

118

that even the Christian churches can talk today of a 'just war' in Africa, and organizations like the Christian World Council of Churches support financially change by violence and terrorism.

But to return to India: India, happily, had some immunities to the forms of chaos which we can see in so many other countries of the world, and after the horrors which followed partition made a gallant and sustained attempt to rediscover a more creative aspect of itself. Some of these immunities were reinforced by changes imposed peacefully on the country by the British. One of the most impressive witnesses to this was Nehru himself.

When Lord Mountbatten, under whom I served, knew that he was leaving South-East Asia and was going as the last Viceroy to India, we thought it would be a good thing if he established personal contact with Nehru to prepare himself in advance, and also perhaps got Nehru to send some message to us in Indonesia which would help us in our dealings with the forces of nationalism in the islands, and particularly with Sukarno. We thought that Nehru could not fail to respond since we occupied those islands with a very distinguished Indian Army group, the 15th Corps, of Arakan fame. I myself was intimately involved with this movement and ultimately, with the help of our local Indian Government representative – a most remarkable man called Mr Punjabi who, with his family, had become close friends of mine in what was then called Batavia – we extracted, in great confidence, which I think can now be safely breached, a message for Sukarno from Mr Nehru.

It was to this effect – I speak from memory because I do not have a written record and I do not know where it could have been recorded:

'Tell Sukarno that nobody could have wished for the British to leave us alone in India more ardently than I did. But even now, I hope that they are not leaving too soon. However, they have given me three things of lasting value: a non-political and incorruptible civil service; a non-political and incorruptible judiciary; and a non-political army. Without the minimum of these three things a modern democratic government would be totally impossible. Tell Sukarno he has not even got one of these things and he had therefore better pipe down!'

I fear these three elements may not be quite as they were at the time when Nehru gave us this message, but they have been sufficiently valid thus far to stand between a modern India and the forces of nationalism within this proliferating and almost frighteningly diverse mixture of peoples and castes.

Are you pessimistic about the future of India? Surely there must be some other, positive elements to mitigate against all these negative phenomena you have described?

It is not that I am at all pessimistic about the future of India in the long term. My fear is for the immediate, political future and the extent to which a totally new generation of Indian politicians is using a sense of grievance over what they imagine was an injury inflicted – on their grandfathers and not on themselves – to keep themselves in power. This form of historical hostility is a process I have called 'the vengeance of history' and is in danger of forcing India into sympathy with totalitarianism, which would endanger its own traditions and its own natural spirit.

The most hopeful thing is that India has adhered to a policy of using English as the official language of the country. As a result, the whole of English literature – which in a sense is the finest expression of what is best in the British spirit – is accessible to the people of India, and today there is an indigenous English literature appearing in India which I find most exciting and which may even outshine, one day, the literature which is being produced in the rest of the English-speaking world. I think that in the end, far more than political power, ideology, political sciences and philosophies, Shakespeare and all he inspired may save India, as he will save the English-speaking world itself.

Why was Jung not as interested in India as he was in Africa?

I think much of the background of the answer is to be found in what we have just discussed about India and how, like Europe, India is a Sanskrit civilization. Jung was immensely interested in and fascinated by India. After all, he went to India and it was really in India that he had another revelation, almost, of how much he belonged to Europe and how urgent the work was that he had to do in Europe. But I think India, though it added a great deal to the mythological evidence he was amassing for objective witness to the epoch-making hypothesis of the collective unconscious that was taking shape in his mind and imagination, did not in essence add to what he already knew, because the mythological message in India conveyed the same message as the mythologies of western Europe. And besides, the spirit of Indian culture was abundantly accessible to him in the literature and history of India. Knowing the importance of Indian civilization to him, I would not try to diminish it by comparison.

But Africa was a different matter. Remember we are talking now about the Africa between wars when it was still a great keep and fortress of natural life and not known consciously and articulately through literature as India was known. For the world it was very largely still, in the spiritual and psychological sense as well as the physical, a vast territory that still needed exploring and discovering. Intuitively also he knew that, like Europe, the civilization of India was already so sophisticated, so entangled and intricate in establishments and so hardened in its mental and social shapes that, within itself, the incentive for and even the hope of redemption and renewal was in danger of being lost. Whereas in Africa he felt there was still the raw material of the natural human spirit which excited his sense of the future enormously. He felt that there he still had a chance of re-establishing contact with the spirit of man much closer to his beginnings, and that if it too gave him evidence of a collective unconscious in African man corresponding to the evidence he had collected everywhere else in the world, his great hypothesis would be finally proved beyond reasonable doubt.

And that is precisely what happened. In the course of the journey he made through Africa in the years 1925–26, and the time he spent among the Elgonyi at the oasis of primitive man which Mount Elgon was in those days, he came to know clearly that his duty lay in Europe and that he must hasten back to take it up at once because in every way he felt that Europe was in lethal danger of losing its soul in the way we have discussed before. It is very interesting, if you read Jung's letters, to see how critical he was of Europeans who left Europe to convert people in Africa, when it was Europe itself that needed conversion. For instance, he was extremely critical of Albert Schweitzer going out to Africa to redeem Africans. He felt it was a profound form of evasion and that, ultimately, Europe could only convert others by example and that it should not be guilty of what he already regarded as one of the classical and greatest sins of men: projection of the burden of redeeming themselves onto others, and being good in the lives of unsophisticated people instead of being good in the humdrum challenges on the doorsteps of their own homes. He felt keenly that it would have been far better if a man of such great gifts as Schweitzer had stayed at home and helped make modern European man aware of how he needed redemption and how his societies needed renewal. He thought to the end that what Schweitzer had really done – in spite of a certain, inevitable 'goodness' – was unload his own burden onto the black people of Equatorial Africa.

And one must admit that there was something enigmatic about Schweitzer's absorption in Africa. One worldly-wise fan and supporter I knew claimed it was the only way he could get away from Mrs Schweitzer. Whether this was true or not, one felt there could have been an element of evasion in Schweitzer's obsession. His hospital at Lambarene certainly was run on eccentric lines – ostensibly with the plausible object of healing the sick as much as possible in their own natural context. How valid that was I could never decide. I could see great pragmatic reasons for it but the spiritual and extra-dimensional claims were another matter, and I have heard them debated and counter-debated without conclusive results.

I would give just one illustration of the enigma and the difficulties of understanding it. I once accompanied two friends of mine, Sue and Michael, now Sir Michael, Wood, by air on the way to Lambarene. I left them at Brazzaville and rejoined them there some days later. They had met Schweitzer and liked him enormously as a man but, as the founders of the Flying Doctor Service in East Africa – which today has grown into the African Medical Foundation and does unique and substantial work of immense worth in Africa – they were puzzled by his medical establishment, although they were viewing it as kinsmen rather than as strangers or critics.

On arrival they noticed that the quay at Lambarene was stacked with the most advanced hospital equipment, from X-rays to intensive care units, from surgical and technological equipment to camp-beds and uniforms, but still all unpacked and rusting in their cases. To be fair to Schweitzer he had not only *not* asked for complicated hospital equipment but had discouraged its sending, saying it would damage the context in which he believed he should work. Yet it was there: and was it dogma, ideology of mission or valid reason which allowed it to waste away?

Then, going round the hospital, the Woods saw patients with advanced elephantiasis, and at dinner asked Schweitzer and his doctors whether they had ever tried to deal with it surgically. They not only had not but did not know of the operation. So Michael Wood offered to do a demonstration operation in the morning. To his and Sue's dismay they found none of the knives in the operating theatre was usable. Normally Michael had an emergency operating kit with him always, but he had left that with me in the Congo. Fortunately he never travelled without dozens of packets of Gillette razor blades. With these, and with Sue as operating sister, he performed a model operation, with Schweitzer and his staff watching it with the closest attention.

No one doubts that Schweitzer must have done his best and one cannot ask for more, and yet this story does not suggest that he really knew what he was doing in Africa. For if Africa called to the whole man in him, I cannot believe Lambarene could have been quite as casual, and implacably ideological, as this experience suggests it was. However, it was his going out to Africa at all that mattered. If one can only give in part, it is better to do so, than not to give at all.

It is a known fact that many students of developing countries who are trained in Europe or America very often become revolutionaries, or do not want to go back to their native countries, which are therefore suffering from 'brain drain'. What should we do in this situation? Stretch out our hands or turn our backs?

Neither. Look closer at our hands and what they offer. Much of the violence and unrest in the world are our unique export: we should heal ourselves before we export anything more. But that apart, I do not know what the ideal solution is. I think the meetings of different cultures with different traditions in history are very fateful occurrences, because neither culture can go back and be what it was before and pretend it did not happen. The consequences are fateful for both and for all. This is what is happening in the world today: we have the most incredible intermingling of cultures and histories taking place. Therefore I think invasion, physical invasion, of one another's countries is even more reprehensible, because every culture at this moment has enough to do in looking into itself and trying to make itself into a contemporary culture before it interferes with anybody else. That is why the European experiment is so important and significant a sign, almost a token of health restored. We should integrate ourselves in Europe before we take the next step. We have got so much, we Europeans, but we must realize that we can ultimately renew others only by example.

———

In your book The Dark Eye in Africa, *you insisted upon the necessity of building a 'footbridge' between Europe, the Western world and Africa. But I think you yourself represent this kind of footbridge between Africa, Asia, Europe and the Americas.*

Yes, I felt, or rather hoped, very much that I could be not a bridge in a grand sense but a sort of little rope-bridge between estranged cultures. That is why I felt it was so important, as I say, not to be a halfway house, as my native country had begun in history, but to be a full house.

What are the reactions of Africans to your books, generally speaking?

The response has been very encouraging; although I think now there is a new kind of African for whom my books are not political enough – you know, the ones who have become bitter and sour. They want one to take sides, which I cannot do because I feel I am committed to a vision which makes the question of taking sides irrelevant. They are making the same old mistakes.

So it seems that we always have to go back to the fundamental questions: what is good, what is bad and evil, what is truth, what is man, what is the value of man, how much does he weigh . . . perhaps only the weight of a feather?

In this connection, I love the story of the quest of the white bird by the hunter who at last dies content with a feather of his dream bird, the great bird of truth, in his hand. Wasn't that one of the stories told by your Bushman nurse, Klara?

Yes, and I also mentioned how the Egyptians used to weigh the soul on its way from the body to the beyond against a feather: if it balanced, the soul could go on its immortal journey. I think that is a very beautiful concept of a great transforming truth.

Do you believe in reincarnation?

124

No, well, again one is pushed into an area about which I cannot pretend to know. But, strangely enough, I have met many people who believe in reincarnation and who tell me they have known me personally and recognize me as someone in their previous lives. One man, for instance, assured me that I had fought with him on the walls of Constantinople. I have met another man who said that I was one of the Knights of the Holy Grail and told me the name I had had at that time. I have wondered about the problems raised by these people's obviously sincere belief. I have, of course, known it also in the totally different context of India, but did not follow it to any conclusion. I have an immense respect for the boundary walls of human awareness. I know these walls are finite, but at the same time I know they are not opaque. There is a very strange light coming through them. But most of all there are strange events that come over these walls that I cannot explain and that I cannot ignore. I just accept them and they prove to me how great the area of unknowing is outside, and how important it is for our own increase not to reject it but just to allow the sense of mystery and wonder it evokes to preside over one's imagination. There is a dynamic reality beyond the here and the now.

And one of the consequences is that our notion of time is constantly being put into question.

Yes. I have just received a book from the author of *The Masks of Time*, about the feeling that time is not what we think it is. For me I find it the strangest sort of element in life and have never ceased to wonder about it and to accept that there is something overwhelming in it which finds even the most advanced concept of it as inadequate and believes that there is far more to it than dreamt of or even hinted at in our philosophies.

One night, after reading Dante, I wrote down, half-asleep, something that just fell into my mind. It was this: 'Time is the dream in between when time was not, and when time will cease to be.' There have been moments when I have not been sure whether the future is in front or behind, and have fallen back on a deep, instinctive feeling that there is a 'forever now'. So that time, in a sense, although important is not an absolute. All sorts of things happen in life that prove that there is a part of the human being, a part of the human soul, that is outside space and time, which is not influenced by what we call the laws of cause and effect, that behaves as if it were an instrument of something which transcends cause and effect.

Could you give some example related to your own life and experience?

Well, I think one gets this particularly in the realm of intuition. I do not know what it is, but I do know that, without looking for it, one is aware of something more . . . a feeling of something being prepared in the future when there is nothing around to explain that anything of the kind is happening. In fact, the whole of one's development at a given moment may point in the opposite direction, and yet one is aware that this direction is false, and that way over the horizon something else is preparing an introduction into one's life, a pattern of planning beyond the law of cause and effect. I think my whole life demonstrates it: my life has not been planned, I have always taken what was on my doorstep . . . and yet looking back on it, more and more it has a definite shape, a pattern as if planned in advance.

I will give you an example: I was born, as you know, deep in Africa and yet I always had a great longing to go to Tibet and climb Mount Everest. Somehow I had a conviction I would not die before I had been to Tibet. This was in the heart of Africa, and as a young boy. Now, where did this idea come from? Anyway, I never had a chance to go to Tibet and then the war came and I sometimes seemed to face certain death, as when I was condemned to death by the Japanese. Then the thought would always hit me, 'But I've not been to Tibet yet . . .' and this was a great, strange source of hope.

Now my wife, Ingaret, had a relation, an aunt, in London. I was reported missing, believed killed. For nearly four years everybody thought I was dead, but this aunt, who was what people used to call extremely psychic, kept on saying to Ingaret, 'Laurens is all right because he has got a Tibetan guide.' I had never discussed this with the aunt but she was proved right; I came out alive.

Now, in the year of the Queen's Coronation Ingaret and I were in Spain at the beginning of January – the Coronation was in June. One night I had a very vivid dream in which I was a member of the team chosen to climb Mount Everest. (Back in England they were, indeed, unknown to me, just planning the first successful climb of Everest at that moment.) In my dream I was told that because of my age I would not be allowed to go to the top, but I would be allowed to go halfway and be in charge of communications. Then suddenly that vision vanished and I was in a cave halfway up Mount Everest and there was a telephone in the cave – you know what dreams are like. The telephone rang and a voice said, 'This is *The Times* in London. We would like to know if they have got to the top yet?' I said, 'Just hold on a moment.' I walked outside, in my dream, I looked up and I saw two figures on the top of Mount Everest and a man coming towards me and shouting, 'They've made it!' And there the dream stopped. But it was so vivid that I said to Ingaret the next morning, 'They are going to climb Mount Everest successfully', and I wrote this dream down so that nobody could say I thought of it afterwards.

Now this was in January. Six months later, on the morning of the Coronation, Ingaret and I were going through the crowds at six in the morning to where we could watch the Coronation procession. We had had a special place given to us. When we came to the junction of Knightsbridge and Hyde Park Corner a policeman looked at our cards and took us through the crowds to lead us across to Piccadilly. Suddenly, as we were halfway through the crowd, the policeman looked at me and he said, 'I think you would like to know that they have made it' – and he had no need to say more. I knew at once what he meant. The news had just come through that they had got to the top of Tibet. What do you make of that? And all that on Coronation Day too!

From then on this feeling became stronger and more meaningful, that Tibet had a special significance in my life. It recurred in my dreams and at odd moments of the day when, consciously, it could not have been further from my mind. Significantly, it was very much with me when I went to Addis Ababa in Abyssinia for the twenty-fifth anniversary celebrations of the restoration after the defeat of the Italians. The Emperor Haile Selassie – Jan Hoy as those of us who were with him called him – had invited a small number of British officers who had fought behind the Italian lines in Ethiopia and served him personally when he came to join them there. Among them was an Indian Army Officer whom I had known and liked during the war in Ethiopia. He was – even in that extraordinarily diverse, rich and remarkable order of men called the Indian Army – an unusual phenomenon because he did not come from any of the military castes of India but was a Parsee, called Johnny Satarawala.

One day, when I was thinking about Tibet as I was sitting among a group of us waiting to go for an audience to the Emperor's palace, he suddenly said to me, 'You know, Laurens, I am now commanding an army group deployed at between seventeen and eighteen thousand feet on the frontiers of Sikkim and Tibet. You ought to come and see what we are trying to do.' Unfortunately, when I did have the chance to go, Johnny Satarawala had moved on to another post, but I mention him because he was the instrument of making me go to Tibet.

Once in Sikkim I made my way from Gangtok to the most advanced Indian Army post on the border and an officer took me to his last sentry post on the frontier where, as he said, 'You can see the Chinese on the walls beyond, eyeball to eyeball.' And indeed, from within this stone sentry box an Indian Army soldier, with the fearlessness which in my own experience seemed as natural to them as breathing, looked steadily across a strip of snow to a wall on which a rather plump Chinese officer, wearing, so incongruously as to make me want to laugh, a pair of white gloves, was ordering his own sentries to swing their machine guns on us.

The situation was not at all to my liking but the officer said to me and my one companion, 'Take no notice of him. This is our territory and we walk in it freely and wherever we like. Just you follow me.' So he led us across the snow as nonchalantly as if he were walking down a street in New Delhi. I was compelled to follow, no matter how great my trepidation. This became all the greater when the Chinese officer, in an obvious state of agitation and desire to prevent anything unpleasant happening, started waving us away with his white-gloved hands.

'Don't take him seriously, old boy.' The Indian officer spoke to me in the idiom of public school and British army, which was still used among themselves. I am afraid I did take notice but nonetheless followed. We walked almost up to the walls, where I could look across and down the far side of the Natula Pass – the Pass of the Whispering Winds – and there in the far distance I could see, in the grey-blue light of an autumn noonday, the sun filtering through the kind of haze you only get in the high Himalayas, turning the roofs of a series of monasteries into a sort of burnished gold. I could not go any further, but the earth on which I stood was the same as the earth on which the wall was built and the distant monasteries constructed. In a literal and political sense I was, of course, not in Tibet, but in a deeper sense I felt I had crossed the frontier and been set free now also to die. I had, at last, been to my Tibet.

My pilgrimage to Tibet had another and for me rather a moving and memorable end to it as well. I had always felt that between the nature of the earth which gives birth to a man, and man's concept of creation, there is a much closer link than we realize. I believe the earth has an influence on his spirit and being, and that the physical quality of his earth has a great bearing on his religious awareness. So from this place in Sikkim, where I stood on the edge of Tibet on the frontier of a new area of myself with all my perceptions heightened by what had just come over me, I suddenly saw that marvellous mountain which presided over the scene, Kanchenjunga, in a new way. It is the second highest mountain, I think, in the Himalayas, and it had never been scaled. It is sacred: they would not allow it to be climbed.* And I think it is rather wonderful to feel that there is a mountain where there is nothing to come between that mountain and God. Man is not allowed to profane it. And it was transformed for me instantly into an image of Buddha's teaching because I feel that Buddhism is a religion of the high mountains. It is a religion of altitude.

Christianity is a religion of serving creation in the here and now; it is very much of the earth, where man does his ploughing and sowing, his begetting and his suffering, seeking to find the great in the small, infinity in a grain of sand; so that it is very much in need of a special Cinderella earth called the desert, or wilderness – where man is alone and there is nothing except oneself with oneself in a kind of vast wasteland. I feel that reverence for the earth and all living things upon it – animals, insects, plants, grass and even the stones and humblest forms of matter – is implicit in our religion and at its best comes through very much in Christianity. But in that devoutly high mountain atmosphere it seemed to me very right that it should be one, devoutly Buddhist, land.

* Alas, the prohibition has been removed and the mountain has been climbed several times since; and the Chogyal, the King of Sikkim, has died after imprisonment by the Indians, so the last of royal line has been removed from the high Himalayas.

Significantly, not long after this, a party of ninety or more Tibetans came over the frontier from the Chinese side in the night, and I received a message that an officer-interpreter was coming to see these people, and asking if I would like to go along and interview them.

I went very gladly, and I can still see the little crowd before me. They had been more than three months on the march, walking at night, at altitudes of 18,000 feet, then lying up by day, hiding from the Chinese soldiery. The idiom of great suffering, endurance and all that travail and travel was like a fine script in the lines of their drawn faces. Several babies were born on the march. I can still see, in particular, the leader of this group; he was a very tall, ascetic-looking Tibetan, rather lean and with his hair in long black plaits: he rather reminded me of some of the engravings I have seen of Robert Louis Stevenson and his: 'To travel hopefully is a better thing than to arrive.'

When the interpreter had asked some questions, mostly military intelligence questions, he gave me a chance to ask them something as well. And I said, addressing myself to the leader, 'Well, there's really only one question I would like to ask: what made you undertake so terrible and incredible a journey into a strange country?' The man with the plaits seemed to be lit with flame within. His eyes sparkled and he said to me, 'Ah, but don't you know? We no longer have freedom of conscience in Tibet.' And I was moved as I was humbled, and cherished the experience as a parable of sorts.

Years later, talking to a large group of émigré writers in London where they were supposed to be welcomed and entertained by British writers, I remembered this again. Only two British writers had turned up: Rosamond Lehmann and myself. And in talking to these men and women who had suffered much I apologized and told them this story and concluded sadly that they had escaped into a world where writers won't even walk across the street for their conscience.

And I wished that we could know how much we in the West can learn from others. There is an arrogance about Europeans: they think they know it all. But consider the lesson implicit in this: it has become one of the key stories in my life, and I never find myself thinking about it without remembering how, even in their ordinary speech, to these humble people, who could not endure a life wherein the values of a

Chinese-made political ideology was in total command, religion was nothing if it was not a way, the way for them in life and time.

The place where I stepped into my Tibet was called Natula: the suffix 'la' in this name means 'way' – a way through high mountains. The highest honorific they could confer on mountains, kings or high priests or ordinary men was to add 'la' to their names, implying that they too had achieved something religious that was 'a way' for man. The wife of their ruler, the Chogyal, at the time was an American girl called Hope, and so she was inevitably referred to as Hope-la.

In this disposition of theirs a natural grasp of symbolism played an important role. For instance, I had a long discussion with the Chogyal about the origin of prejudice in human beings, particularly colour prejudice, and told him that I believed that the antagonism of white against black in South Africa was due to the Calvinistic heresy of taking symbolism literally and not seeing therefore that 'the black' they feared was a darkness in their own soul.

'You know,' he said, after a long pause – and it is important to add here that he had been educated in a monastery in Tibet – 'what you have told me explains to me for the first time why the Tibetans have always spoken of the Chinese as "the black people", symbolically, of course.'

Now that whole experience with Tibet is also an orchestrated example of what I call things coming over the walls of our natural perception which we cannot ignore. We would be stupid if we did, and that is where some scientists, particularly the applied kind, are so stupid. They say, 'Oh, well, this is only an isolated incident and it is of no importance.' I find that monstrous; it is introducing the rule of numbers into a field of reckoning where it is not valid. Exceptions prove the rule only in a superficial and abstract dimension of averages: in the deepest level of all, they question it. One incident is enough – it is real. What caused this incident?

The evidence for the sort of happenings I am telling you about is overwhelming: these things were taken for granted in the Renaissance and in the Middle Ages. It is only now that people pretend these things are superstition and are not important. How can they reject things that come so spontaneously out of the human spirit? Dante said the images which come to you naturally are your own; they are the material on which you alone can work and which it is your duty to follow to the end of your days, again recognizing the reality that out of life itself, not from our heads but out of life itself, something is presented to us that we have to follow with all our mind and all our intelligence. We should not want to do so superstitiously, of course: we have to do so in a contemporary way because this is what seems to me always decisive and final. We are condemned or privileged to make what is first and oldest, young and contemporary. This is always the prime duty of man. This is how he finds his meaning, because he is making a new area of awareness accessible to the human being. And suddenly, if we follow through in this manner, we get great new energies, for the moment we go into a new area of our spirit the energies are there to sustain us. The problem of our time is to stop bothering about the Manifesto of 1848 as if that were the beginning of all history, and to look at history along this unbroken thread of the imagery and the symbolism which has inspired mankind. We should follow that thread and recover the direction and dynamic to lead us out of a labyrinthine paralysis of spirit wherein we have made a despotism of reason.

Perhaps it is a mark of our time, but nowhere do we see great adventurers, great travellers. Is it that the world has shrunk and there is nothing more to discover? Or is it because we no longer know how to travel and open our eyes and our ears, like a Marco Polo or a Christopher Columbus could do?

Oh yes, it is quite clear: those people could not have done what they did if they had just been looking for cinnamon and silk. There was something else in it, a strange overwhelming drive at the heart of it all. Look at what they suffered. Portugal ruined itself economically in its traffic with the East. The whole decline of Portugal as a world power took place because it spent all its money and resources on maintaining an absurd and impossible trade in silks and spices between the East and Europe. But they also had a deep religious motivation; they had a Church and a necessity to convert, and I think the religious reason ultimately was the more important. This is where we see the danger of the churches because the Portuguese were promoting the cause of the Church, and not of religion. They were serving a particular Church which had become a sociological institution, although some of the missionaries were obviously doing it to serve God. Whatever one may feel about Francis Xavier, there is no doubt that he was truly inspired by a religious vision, and we must not forget that he belonged to a society which had tried to reform the church. He was part of the Counter-Reformation. It always moves me very much about the Japanese, how ready they were for this vision, particularly in the south, in Kyushu, and around Nagasaki. Hundreds of thousands of Japanese were converted, and one of the most terrible stories in Japan was the massacre of the Japanese Christians when the Jesuits were expelled. A lot of these Christians went underground and they became a very strange kind of Christian. I owe my life to a Japanese soldier who smuggled things into prison for me and looked after me – he was one of my guards. And the night before the morning when he thought I was really going to be killed, he said to me, 'I can tell you now but I couldn't tell you before: in my family we have always been Christians.' Even at that moment I was very moved because, although I did not know what his Christianity was like, something of it had stuck throughout the ages.

Captain Mori, the Japanese sea captain whom I wrote about in *Yet Being Someone Other*, was as a young boy very strongly tempted to become a Christian, although nobody had tried to convert him. It was simply that what he heard about it tempted him. I do not know quite what stopped him, because I think if he had had any guidance perhaps he might have gone on. But he was very much an individual; he felt there was something in his own religious inheritance of which he could make a synthesis which would be very important. To this day he is still a very religious man, and has a shrine in his house.

━━━━━

Besides Japan, there is another country in Asia which has played a great part in your life, and that is Indonesia. You were both actor and witness during the Indonesian struggle for independence. It is a sad story because it was a series of missed appointments with history on the part of the Dutch, as frequently seem to happen with colonial powers.

Yes; I think the story for me began on the morning after General Wavell and the Allied High Command had secretly flown out of Java because they knew it would soon be overwhelmed by the Japanese forces. This was round about March 1942, I do not remember the exact date. But I was left behind by General Wavell to carry on after the surrender of organized resistance, which he knew would soon come. I had come straight from North Africa some weeks before; now I was walking round their abandoned headquarters. The floors were littered with things that their officers had not been able to take with them: books, greatcoats, all sorts of things. Then I saw the sweepers who had been brought in to clean up, and there was something strange about them. Suddenly I realized that the turbans which they had worn for centuries as servants under the Dutch, made of brown and blue and white batik, had vanished, and they now wore the black hats of the nationalists. It had happened overnight! I went down to Bandung to the Hotel des Indes and all the servants there too had thrown away their turbans and were wearing the same black hats. What was more, if they had done it the day before they would have been punished for it by the Dutch and sent to change. But now the Dutch people pretended not to see it. Here was evidence of how deep the support and desire for independence had been before the Japanese arrived. The sign that their heads were as nationalist as their hearts had been all along, was unmistakable.

I thought how extraordinary and terrifying it was that people like the Dutch could live for 350 years in a country like Indonesia without realizing that the inhabitants wanted to be rid of them, were not happy to be colonized. So later, all during my time in prison camp in Java, one of the things I did was to talk to everybody among the Dutch and the Indonesians to gather all the intelligence I could, to try to understand what was happening, because I had a hunch it would all be needed after the war. I had no doubt that whatever the Japanese did to encourage nationalism, they were merely encouraging something which had existed for years. This was an irreversible tide in history. So when the Japanese surrender came and the war was over, the Dutch reappeared, wanting to use the British forces to help them suppress this struggle for independence in their empire. I thought, 'No. We cannot help the Dutch over this. We have just been through a world war and this is not the purpose for which we have been through it. We, the British, are dismantling our own empire. How can we fight a colonial war on behalf of the Dutch? We must stop it.' I pleaded and advised accordingly, and somehow we stopped it.

Your position must have been rather delicate, with your Dutch ancestry?

Well, not that so much, although it was a gratuitous complication at times; I was just one lone voice, but I knew the facts. I knew the people and had lived through the experience. By this time I had established contact with Sukarno, who all the way through collaborated with the Japanese. I knew the other Indonesian leaders too, who had never collaborated with the Japanese: Soetan Sjahrir, Amir S. Sjharifuddin, Darmasetiawan, Hadji Agoes Salim, and to a lesser extent Hatta. People think that only the Dutch suffered under the Japanese; they forget how the Indonesians suffered. They were just as anxious to get rid of the Japanese as we were, tired of their despotism, and angry because millions of Indonesians died in forced labour camps, in aborted military ventures, building airports that were never used, with scarcely any food and no medicines. So my whole effort was to inform, to let both the Dutch and the British know that they were not coming back to the Java they had left, that there had been a profound, irreversible change. So the British policy was directed to just one end, to try and get a peaceful solution between the Dutch and the Indonesians, which meant trying to save the Dutch from their retarded, imperial selves.

It was a heart-breaking period because the Dutch would not, or could not, see it. They believed that we were evil, and that if only they had their armies built up they could soon deal with what they thought were a few trouble-makers, and then they could have the islands back again, as before. Indeed, I believe myself that there was a moment when, if the Dutch had been prepared to confer dominion status on Indonesia, they would have accepted it – but the Dutch would not even do that. They missed their chance.

That was the sad story, briefly summed up. At that time none of my Dutch friends was even speaking to me. They regarded me as the person who had made this evil policy and they regarded me as a kind of traitor.

But now, forty years later, they should know better.

I do not think the new Holland cares about all that any more, and the older generations do not know or admit the truth – although there are some who every now and then pop up and try to blame and blackguard me personally, in the strangest of ways. The fact is that they tried, after we went, to impose their will on the Indonesians by force, and they failed. They failed because of the depth and the strength of the nationalist feelings in the islands, and also because it was a different world outside. They had no support for what they were trying to do. So they failed miserably and they lost it all when they could have made it succeed at that one moment.

But then to me there was the saddest thing of all. I remember the Dutch Governor-General, van Mook, saying to me one day, 'I cannot understand it. We've given them schools, medicines, roads, an honest administration, and yet they want to get rid of us. Why?' I said, 'Perhaps because it seems to be a law of life that there comes a moment in colonization, no matter how good it is, when it is no longer good from the point of view of the colonized. And then, Governor, could it also not be perhaps that you never had the right look in your eye when you spoke to them?' This is what haunted me; this is what I felt had been wrong: the neglect of human values, the utter failure to understand the longing that every human being, every group of people has, for a recognition of their own dignity and their identity.

What happened during the surrender of the Japanese Imperial Army in Indonesia?

We could not occupy Java immediately. Demobilization was going on, everybody wanted to get home, and the ships were full of troops going home. Java, Indonesia and Sumatra – indeed the whole of the Dutch Empire, which was the third biggest empire in the world – was made Mountbatten's responsibility overnight. He was not prepared for it, but he sent a cruiser, the *Cumberland*, under Admiral Patterson, to accept the Japanese formal surrender. He could not have chosen a finer or more imaginative officer. One day I hope to write about him properly and how invaluable his Celtic sensibility and sense of politics was to us.

Now he asked me to sit next to him when he was taking the surrender. I sat there on his quarter-deck in my old, tattered prison clothes and my shaven head. The Japanese general came and bowed to him, and I could see the somewhat startled look in his eye when he saw me sitting there. He came out of his bow and told the admiral that they had come to surrender, but had one request: the admiral must know how much their swords meant to them, how they were the most treasured and revered possession for every Japanese officer. Would the admiral therefore please allow them to keep their swords? And Admiral Patterson – who had very blue eyes, which then became stern and full of a light that was not inhuman but as firm as the occasion demanded – replied, 'It is the irrevocable command of the Supreme-O, Lord Mountbatten, that you will surrender the swords you have done so much to dishonour.'

And I saw a tremendous rush of emotion into the Japanese general's face, and the faces of all his officers. I felt desperately full of pity for them, they could hardly contain themselves. But they made an enormous effort and unbuckled their swords and laid them down.

What were the true feelings of Lord Mountbatten towards the Japanese? It's notorious that he did not want any Japanese to attend his funeral. He could not forgive them, officially at least. This is the general opinion. Do you share it?

No, I do not, and I did not know that. I was abroad when he was assassinated, and I did not know he had put that in his will. But it was quite a common phenomenon that the people who had not suffered under the Japanese were more bitter than those of us who had gone through the experience and lived through it. People who came out from England after the war, like the War Crimes Officers, were much more bloodthirsty than we were. I would find it odd if Lord Mountbatten thought of them as beyond forgiveness because he was a magnanimous man. Yes, I would find it most strange . . . Mind you, you should have seen the prisoners when they came out of prison. Lady Mountbatten went round among them, helping them, and the stories they told about the way they had been treated and the numbers who had died of neglect and cruelty would have shaken anybody except the people concerned, because we were used to it, we had an immunity to it. But people seeing it from the outside were very upset and shocked. That may have been the cause of it.

I always think of Churchill's words: 'In defeat, defiance; in victory, magnanimity; in peace, unity.' 'In victory, magnanimity' are striking words. It seems to me you want to make a new beginning at the moment of victory when you have won apparently all you have fought for, and you want to start afresh. One must not keep the past alive by giving it a place in the future through punishment. My own instinct would be to wipe the slate clean and say it was a moment of madness in life and let us get back to sanity and re-begin as soon as we can.

At least we do not carry the responsibility for starting that war: it was forced upon us. Our responsibility perhaps lay in neglect, in omission beforehand. I mean, if the war had started ten years earlier it would have been less of a war. That really is the lesson for the unilateral disarmers and for everybody: we have been through this pattern of lying down before people who want to conquer the world and it ends up with more killing than if you deal with it step by step as it arises.

One of the great weaknesses of democracy is that it does not deal with things in the beginning. We wait until they have built up into great pressures, which matter in terms of votes but have become very difficult to handle. Then they have a will and character of their own and are almost impossible to control and resolve peacefully. But in the beginning, when they are small, vulnerable and pliable, there is a time of innocence, when all, with imagination, would be oh, so easy.

This is an aspect of the present UNO complex I find so terrible: it has eliminated the small. Now issues are no longer contained, minimized and brought into their own natural focus, but spread all over the globe and, by way of UNO, turned into world issues. When UDI [Unilateral Declaration of Independence] was declared I was in Canada and immediately, through newspaper and television interviews and the most expensive cables I have ever sent, begged all my friends in the Wilson government not to take the issue to the United Nations – but in vain. It became a world issue and it was a sobering experience at Lancaster House how difficult the resolution of the problem was made by the fact that almost every country in the world wanted to have a say in it and it was not just left to Britain and what is now Zimbabwe to sort out between them.

One of the roles of the United Nations Organization is precisely that – to try to defuse conflicts and wars. But it cannot play this role if the nation states do not believe in it, support it and concede some of their power. They could at least keep the United Nations informed and consider it as a partner. If you had the floor at the UN General Assembly, what would you say?

Well, I have never had any personal experience of an international bureaucracy. I think, although they may help in applying vision in the world once it has been presented to them, they cannot create or initiate the vision.

There is a movement with which I am concerned, called the World Wilderness Foundation. It is a movement founded by a great friend of mine called Ian Player. He is one of the outstanding conservationists of our time and has received almost all the major conservation awards in the world. It is due to him that the conservation of the white rhinoceros has become one of the great success stories of modern conservation. When I was a boy there was not a handful of white rhinos left in Africa – a continent they had overrun in the beginning. Today, from this great reserve in Zululand where Ian Player worked, rhinos are not only being reintroduced to their ancient areas all over Africa, but exported to zoos all over the world. And what is more, out of all his conservation work in Zululand, Ian was struck by the fact that conservation is a deep need in the soul of man, that man needed it almost more than the animals did, and that once he brought modern people, so estranged from nature, back into contact with animals in their natural wilderness surroundings, people were changed by it for good. As a result of this experience he founded the Wilderness Leadership School, which blossomed out into the World Wilderness Foundation with branches in Australia, Britain and, above all, the United States of America.

As we get more and more experience we find the only way forward is not through groups but through individuals, so our whole aim is to re-create, or re-educate, individuals through nature and to see life from nature's point of view, so that wherever they go they take this vision with them.

So, for instance, if they were working inside the United Nations, they would themselves, within that organization, apply that vision, and that is the only way I can think that we can do it. That is to create a new type of individual, one that would appeal to the United Nations, to help us to promote our vision of nature not only conserved but rehabilitated. I would ask them from within, because you cannot do it from without. You are powerless in this sphere. You cannot promote our vision on a group basis but you can encourage the people who are deprived of nature, by example. You can get them, through nature, to join freely in this task of re-educating man through nature. Just as you invest money in the United Nations in the education of the Third World, we would ask it to look upon this as the most valuable and urgent form of education that modern man needs, and help reinforce us in preserving and creating new schools of wilderness. These schools of nature, where the voice of nature alone re-creates man, work miracles – as I know from experience.

I am quite sure you can attract vast numbers of individuals, but how can you persuade decision-makers, politicians or leaders to abandon their power and leave their offices for one, two or three weeks in order to go back to nature and find a new inspiration, a new vision? That would be the last thing they would do!

You would be surprised, nonetheless, at the numbers of politicians who do come to us and believe and understand. But our main thrust is towards the creation of a new kind of individual. No leader has power in himself or herself in a democracy: they only have the power we allow them. I mean, an artist has a power that comes through him or her to change man, but political power groups have not. And that is why we try to convert to this vision, as many of those who delegate power as we can, and leave them in their own spheres in life to use their own unit of power by example, by vote, by persuasion, to support this wilderness vision.

What would be the ideal geographical distribution of these wilderness sanctuaries? One per country at least?

No, we need as many as possible. Every bit of unspoilt nature which is left, every bit of park, every bit of earth still spare, should be declared a wilderness area as a blueprint of what life was originally intended to be, to remind us. When we do see that, it is like having a religious experience, we are changed by it. This act of instinctive re-remembrance sparks off a most dynamic sense of guilt and horror at what we are doing, and an immense longing not just to conserve but to rehabilitate the earth. But all is based on our belief that only individuals can promote forces of change in life; you cannot do it through groups. And by changing individuals, ultimately we will change the course of life.

Once man feels himself part of nature again instead of just exploiting nature – it is only man who has put himself outside nature – and once man allies himself to the evolutionary energies and forces of nature, there is nothing he cannot change, including himself – which is the hardest thing of all. And this is the lesson you learn in wilderness very quickly.

People often say that we are just another conservation movement, and there are so many already. We of course are all for conservation too, but we go beyond conservation; we see nature conserved and rehabilitated as more important even to man than to nature. Finally, nature will always take care of itself even without man. But man without nature is unthinkable and, known or unknown, his spirit needs it: needs it for its survival, sanity and increase, as his body does. We are the only people, I believe, who see nature almost as the last of our temples where man can hear, as it were, the original voice of creation and see life's natural witness and testament to it. And we have done our homework. Ian Player's great pilot scheme has nearly a generation of experience now and has proved that it works. Do you know the apocryphal answer Christ gave the apostles when they asked him, 'Wherewith shall we find the way to Heaven?'

No, what was it?

You know how he answers it in the New Testament, but in this apocryphal gospel He says, 'Follow the birds, the beasts and the fish and they will lead you in.'

You and Ian Player know an old Zulu, Maqubu, who is a depository of the cultural treasures of his people. He lives in perfect harmony with nature and talks to the trees, to the birds, to the clouds . . . A man like Maqubu certainly has an important message to deliver to us.

That is true. The people who go out with him into the wilderness come back completely changed. With Maqubu you immediately feel that you are in the presence of a new sort of man, a new sort of human being, because just to be with him without speaking his language makes you feel good; something just comes out of him which is pure goodness and harmony and purity. It flows out from him; and this he has got from nature. He is naturally a Zen figure who, wherever he goes, has only to be seen, even in the market place, to make those who still can see feel better for it.

I suppose you accept in these wilderness trails not only adults but also youths and children, especially when they have problems?

Yes, of course. For instance, a French merchant-banker came to us once. He had a son who would not speak to him – he was a complete problem-child. He asked me if I could help. So I said, 'Send your boy to see me.' He flew him over from Paris and I spoke to him about the wilderness and got his father to agree for him to go out in the wilderness with Maqubu and Ian Player in Africa. The boy did several wilderness trails and he stayed out there for six months, working in the wilderness. He then came back to the Sorbonne and passed all his courses in zoology with flying colours. Today he is a self-contained, rehabilitated human being, and that is what nature did for him. It gave him an identity of his own in nature; a natural experience. The boy was sick and tired of towns and cocktail parties and grand people. He needed the voice of nature to speak to him, and he became a different human being. And I think we all need that all over the world today. We are becoming increasingly industrialized.

And what do they do for the movement when they come back from wilderness trails?

We do not ask them to do anything, we haven't a bureaucracy ... we are all a group of individuals working individually.

It would be interesting to know how they are doing now. As you said, going back to the wilderness is to be reborn, it is a kind of religious experience. You get closer to cosmic forces, or to God. You yourself believe in God, but has your faith or your conception of God changed with time?

I do not think so. I have never had a definition of God but I just have a tremendous feeling and a sense of direction, of creation in that area, which I know is real, and this is the most important thing in me. I trust it completely. I have always known it somehow, and it has not got less with time; it has got stronger. So that in a sense one knows, one knows through experience: and I think it is just that people have this area in them but sometimes it gets cut off. Human beings know far more than they allow themselves to know: there is a kind of knowledge of life which they reject, although it is born into them: it is built into them. But in their rational selves they shy like frightened horses away from a God who is not the source of opium for people but a reawakening and renewal of creation and a transcending of the forces and nuclear energies in the human soul. The task of using creatively the nuclear power in the atom without, will never be complete without first containing and transcending the nuclear power within the heart and soul of the individual atom: these two discoveries, atom without and atom within, are aspects of one another in the sum of the same greater thing. To know this and assume individual responsibility for their effects in our own lives is to be modern; to know only one and not the other is to be partial and archaic and a danger to creation.

What do you feel about your roots? Do you feel rooted in this English soil?

Well, not particularly in the soil. I think one's roots have got to be inner roots and ultimately one's roots have to be in what you call God, otherwise they get washed away very quickly. But there are certain particular pieces of earth and country, especially where one is born, which evoke feelings like these more strongly than others; but it is not dependent on that.

I am quite sure you yourself believe in life after death. But what would you say to convince a friend of it?

It is very difficult. I would say, for instance, that people who were close to me and have died, come closer. I feel they are there, near, all the time. It is this clear and urgent feeling of nearness which I find so convincing. I do not think they could speak to me because I could not possibly understand the language of reality beyond death, they can only communicate this nearness, and I cherish it – though it is just a feeling.

Several times you mention in your books the presence within yourself of 'another person', 'another self', who is able to take command in case of emergency, or in matters of life and death. Have you ever identified this other person in you?

I cannot say that I could identify it precisely. Jung talks about how he discovered as a boy that he had a wise old man inside him with whom he could speak, and this wise old man became so clear an image to him that he painted him in time, and gave him a name; he called him 'Philemon', after the Philemon and Baucis of Greek mythology, the humble couple who took the gods in when they came to earth. But I have no name for my 'inner self'. I do not have one particular vision which covers all of my life.

I have had one valid dominant over a critical part of my life about which I still hope to write, but in general I just have a clear feeling of something significant. It is not in my case somebody as old as time so much as a child of all the life that has ever been, a newly born child of eternity. I prefer to think of it as something child-like which somehow takes over and speaks and seems to know far more about what I have not yet experienced than I do myself. And I can only tell you that on occasions when I am absolutely obedient to this voice, even when it tells me to do something which seems particularly suicidal and ridiculous, as happened in the war, I have had a feeling of happiness almost too keen to endure.

I remember, for instance, one particular occasion in the Japanese prisoner-of-war camp when it made me do something which normally would have meant instant death, which was deliberately to disobey the order of a Japanese '*gunzo*' or sergeant. I had been ordered away and was going, when this voice spoke without warning and said, 'Go back to him!'. I turned round on my heels and did so; and I know that thereby I prevented a man's killing on that day. But the happiness, in the midst of the danger and the pain that was inflicted on me, which I received from having been obedient to that voice, still remains indescribable.

This is the kind of thing, I believe, we come to when we try to live life religiously. I think to live the religious life wholly one must be obedient to one's greatest awareness. I emphasize awareness because it is not a purely conscious state, it is much more. Part of it, of course, is instinctive. Part of it is reason; but it is all sorts of other intangible and non-rational things and intimations. That is why I speak of one's greatest awareness. Modern human beings, particularly the rationalists, think that awareness is only what we can articulate, only what we can think consciously – but awareness is far more than that. It contains a great many non-rational elements, like intuition. Intuition is not a thought, and yet it tells you what is round the corner of time or round the corner of life, and if you follow the hunch it brings you into a new area of yourself. All the great scientists, the great religious teachers, the great prophets, are people who followed an intuition. Einstein's theory of relativity was formed nearly a hundred years before it could be proved. We are only now, when it is due to be replaced by something else,

144

evolving the instruments capable of proving what is true in it empirically; and yet it made sense and was a great cross-roads on our way to grasping the nature of physical reality. So what I do feel is that man's task is to become more and more aware, and more and more obedient to his own intimations of greater awareness.

In the temple of awareness there are merchants in plenty. Techniques of awareness are selling well.

There are probably as many techniques of awareness as there are human beings in the world. But awareness is not a prescription, a technique or recipe, and there are no short-cuts to it. I think the saving thing is to be aware of the fact that the great mystery of life is not the existence of an unconscious, but of consciousness, and what it is in the unconscious that perenially seeks greater consciousness. It is just a fact that consciousness constantly enlarges itself, and the problem for us is that the more consciousness is enlarged, the greater our responsibility to life and the universe becomes. That is why many people shrink from it; that is why many like to be lost in the crowd – mind, identity and all – because then they have not got to carry this burden of individual responsibility.

But there is something there that will not let us alone, and that is where the meaning of life comes from. A strangely neglected English poet, Francis Thompson, wrote a poem called 'The Hound of Heaven'. In it he flees the hound of heaven, he runs everywhere, he hides everywhere from it, 'down the labyrinthine ways' of his mind – he does not want 'the following feet' to overtake him. But the hound of heaven is the love of God, and in the end the hound seeks him out and gets him.

You know, listening to you, I am more and more convinced that the British as well as the Bretons in France are quite close to the Japanese. They share the same feelings, especially towards nature. The Japanese love ghosts and what is boiling in a witch's cauldron. Shakespeare, of course, is universal, but he sounds so sure, so real and so frightening in a Japanese context.

Well, I was only saying to a friend the other day that I think the two nations in the world who have been most influenced by nature are the English and the Japanese. English poetry is absolutely full of nature and a love of nature, a love of birds, grass and flowers, and even the common fly is 'gilded' as it 'lechers' in Shakespeare's sight. Wherever you go in London you see that everybody has a window-box with flowers in it; even if they cannot have a garden, they have a window-box at least.

So you do not belong to any church, you are white but know also the black, you are like a white Bushman and the earth is your hunting ground.

I do not know . . . but I think one's whole life is a search, is a matter of reunion as Dante sought it, with God, a reunion with one's origin. I always feel that origin and destination are one; they are the same thing in the human spirit, and the whole of life consists of making your way back to where you came from and becoming reunited with it in greater awareness than when you left it; by then adding to it your own awareness, you become part of the cosmic awareness.

It is a quest, like the quest for the Holy Grail, isn't it?

It is the same as the quest of the Grail, yes. Even the word 'grail' has this special meaning; it comes from the Provençal '*graille*', which means a great container. People ate out of a common soup container called a *graille*. It also has the same root as the Spanish word '*corral*', which means something round and containing, and is the word which in Africa, through the Portuguese, has become '*kraal*'; so this is now a Zulu word derived from *graille* and *corral* meaning an enclosure of huts and cattle which is round, forming the circle which has always been magical and an enclosure of life, sacred because it is an image of wholeness, something which contains all. It is the OK Corral too. This is more evidence that the search for a divine container, to be divinely contained, is African as well. It is most moving that even the words show how unending and universal is the quest for the spirit to be contained in wholeness. And there is yet more. When a Zulu in time becomes wise and resolved so that he becomes an *Induna* – a headman and adviser to the king – he wears a circle of metal or ivory around his head to indicate he is whole. It is an African substantiation of the sacred halo around the heads of saints and holy men which the western imagination demands there for the same reason.

T. S. Eliot became a good friend of yours. Do you know what was his own

146

definition of a poet? Did he think of himself as a poet in the first place?

Well, there was the famous case of Yevtushenko when he came over to Britain. He was regarded then as a sort of great, Russian, liberal poet – which was rather phoney. I did not think he was nearly such a good poet as many other Russian poets, and not the uncompromising spirit he and others made him out to be. He is near enough to the frontier to know what a radical poet really would be like, even if he has not got the courage to cross it completely; there is just this glimpse of it to dress his poetry up in the kind of stage uniform of a radical. When he came to England I myself happened to be in Russia, where I read about his experiences in England, in the Russian press for foreigners.

I talked to Eliot about these articles – there had been one about himself – and he said, 'Do you know, I just couldn't get on with him because he kept on saying to me: "What do you think, as a poet?" and "Where does a poet stand in this regard?" and "How do you, as a poet, feel about all this?" And in the end I had to tell him, "Look, I am not 'a poet', I don't really know what you mean. I'm just a man who sometimes happens to have a poem in him." ' This completely foxed Yevtushenko, but it tells one a great deal about Tom Eliot. He was very interesting in this way, because he did not feel that you had to do nothing all day but write poetry. He started by working in a bank, the most dreary job you can imagine, to earn a living, and when he discovered there was a poem in him, he wrote it. He did not feel that he had to write poetry all day long. The feeling that he had to share in the life of his time, in many of its dimensions, was natural to him. It was almost as if in his heart he shared Dante's sense of the importance of being 'a citizen'.

Dante seemed to have a magnetic influence on him. Was it so?

Yes, Dante meant an enormous amount to him. You will find in 'The Waste Land' just how much Dante figures, because a major part of Eliot had the same sense of the importance of the feminine to man as Dante had, and which was personified in Dante's love for Beatrice; not just the ordinary love of a man for a woman, but that and infinitely more, until it was something almost supernatural. They both had that same sense of feminine imagery, which is very beautiful. It is interesting that Eliot's second wife is very fair and if you look at her closely she has got something Florentine about her features. They were very, very close and happily married.

I found myself often talking Dante with T. S. Eliot, talking about the things in Dante that stayed with us most – for me there was Dante's encounter with Ulysses in hell and his moving exhortation to his crew to follow on and through and to look westward to 'that unpeopled world beyond the sun', because they were men and not made to live like beasts. Those sorts of things. I remember Tom Eliot saying, 'But you know, what really moved me most, I think, was Dante's passage through *Purgatorio* on the way to *Paradiso*. The people there in *Purgatorio* were inside their flames expurgating their errors and their sins. And there was one particular incident which isn't well known but which meant more to me than any other. That was when Dante was talking to a spirit, an unknown woman in her flame. And as she answered Dante's questions, like all the other spirits, she had to step out of her flame to talk to him, until at last this unknown feminine spirit was compelled to say to Dante; "Would you please hurry up with your questions so that I can get on with my burning?"'

And this to me is the essence of Eliot. All his life he was a man who hastened to get on with his burning.

That is the destiny and desire of every true poet.

And of every great artist really. One also should not forget that there is a sense in which Christ was an artist: Van Gogh, in one of his letters to his brother Theo, said something to the effect: 'All other forms of art pale into insignificance compared with the art of Christ. We paint on canvas but Christ was an artist in flesh and blood . . .' It comes back to what I have always felt, that it was not for nothing that for the Greeks and the Romans art was a divine process and the function of art was a religious function; that the true artist is following, whether he knows it or not, Christ's injunction to be guided by the guide he left behind, which was the Holy Ghost. Goethe made an interesting observation. He said, 'All art loses meaning and becomes merely repetitive when it loses contact with its religious motivation.'

Do you feel your life has a certain motivation, a certain meaning?

I feel this is a question I could not answer until after my death, because every day, as in that poem of Eliot's, one does not cease from

148

exploration, and it is also a great re-remembering, this exploration, it is making conscious, making alive what was unconscious in one before. When I was a boy, I read in the New Testament:

> 'Consider the lilies of the field, how they grow;
> They toil not, neither do they spin:
> And yet I say unto you, That even Solomon in all his glory
> was not arrayed like one of these.'

I have tried to take no heed of the morrow – not in an irresponsible way but as an act of trust in a life given in trust. In that sense I go from day to day, and although I love the instant I have a sense of immense distances and of great open horizons in front of me. It seems that the footsteps are extremely important and that if I look after the footsteps, the miles will take care of themselves. They are in better hands than my own. Sometimes it worries me and I feel perhaps I am too casual, not to live by more of a plan. But really, except within the limits of bread and butter, I do not know how to plan.

But when it comes to writing books, do you have a plan or do you build them up slowly and instinctively, as an oyster makes a pearl?

I feel that I do not write books, but grow them. Usually the title and the opening sentence and the last sentence come to me simultaneously, and the excitement in writing is in discovering the foreign land in between. If I knew it all in advance, I doubt if I would ever start.

━━━━

Today, which part of the world would you most like to explore?

I really feel that I do not want to do much more travelling in the physical world, although I get terribly, terribly homesick for Africa. In that sense I have a home. My eyes, my ears, my nose are tremendously, permanently overcome with nostalgia for the bush and the desert and the natural world of Africa – and the skies and the sunsets and the natural things. For me these have permanently possessed my senses.

But I feel I have so many books that I want to write, and I have written the opening chapters of one of them. Then with friends of mine I have made another television film* on the Bushmen of the Kalahari.

I would really like to lead a private life as much as possible, I like to work anonymously, and in a sense that is the reason why people in the world, and people in this country really know very little about my life. If I am asked to do things that seem really important I say 'yes', and only on condition that I do it anonymously. I think it gives one a great freedom as well as imposing a great discipline on one, because one could not abuse anonymity, not when one is accountable utterly to oneself. For instance, an anonymous critic could easily become what we call a 'poison pen'. So you must be more disciplined, more precise, more demanding in a sense, when you are anonymous. Yet it also gives you freedom, in that all the irrelevances of the world are cut out – you are just free to confine yourself to the meaning of what you are doing.

But you cannot really confine yourself to only one identity, one activity, one kind of book and one country. You always jump over walls and escape definition: journalist, writer, soldier, farmer, conservationist, explorer, wise man, political adviser.

Well, this is the 'yet being someone other' that I talk about. It was not my intention to be that, but it happens that I have become that. To me the Zen exhortation to do instantly with all your heart and mind what life presents you with, however enigmatic, is the beginning of the way.

A dialogue between poets, writers, philosophers, thinkers, scientists and artists is essential to our survival, but what about communicating with the so-called ordinary people and the so-called primitives? Mozart can do it. Do you remember the experience mentioned by Claude Lévi-Strauss in Tristes Tropiques? *The music the Amazon Indians liked best was by Mozart.*

Yes, that is a lovely illustration. I think that once one knows how powerful and how deeply shared in all races and cultures the symbols of meaning are, there is a possibility that this sort of communication can become primary and endless, and one gets this feeling of neighbourhood, which one day will lead to a true brotherhood of man, a union of all men strong in their infinite, individual diversities and not the dreary state of conformity we mentioned demanded by the totalitarianisms of society and the world.

*Testament to the Bushmen, directed by Paul Bellinger and produced by Jane Taylor. A book of the same title is published by Viking.

What moves me very deeply about primitive peoples is that they still attach an enormous importance to a certain kind of communication which we have lost; and that is that they allow the being of the person they are with to communicate with more than words. They seem to let the soul of the other person – or the animal – communicate by the way it expresses itself, in the look and in the bearing, in the tone and in the voice. They allow that part of communication to play an enormous role; whereas we in the West tend to let words play an excessive role. We forget to listen to the tone and the expression which are used, and these are vital because we tend to use words in a fraudulent manner. Words demand to be treated with great truth. We feel it is such a terrible crime in the West to counterfeit money; but it should be a worse crime to counterfeit words. We see it in the newspapers and we see it amongst politicians particularly, who say things they really do not mean, or things they do not even understand. The word was in the beginning, and, if it is to be at the end, exacts all we have of reverence and respect.

Can you imagine somebody being hanged because he or she was trafficking with words?

Well, as we will not even hang people for murder, I think that would be carrying it to the extreme. But I do feel that we should regard this as being as criminal as any other fraud. It is a counterfeit of the spirit that goes on daily, you see, made worse because it has been joined by the visual counterfeit possible in television. But primitive man guards himself against that by listening in to the being of the person who is uttering the words and by adding this to his evaluation of the words.

Some of those primitive men are so good at this that they can exactly imitate the different animals, and even other human beings. I am thinking particularly of one of the Bushmen you knew who was so good at imitating a professor.

Oh yes, the professor! That was a Bushman! After a while he became more the professor than the professor was himself – just by observing the distinguished man and taking his being into and upon himself . . . yes, I have never forgotten that.

I remember one occasion also when I was tracking an animal, a buffalo, with a Bushman. We were tracking it because we needed food very badly. The Bushman was following it, but suddenly he swerved aside and he went off in another direction and I followed him, although I could clearly see the buffalo hoofmarks leading off in the opposite way. And then he stopped behind a bush and beckoned me over, and there was an antelope standing ahead, which I shot. And I said to him, 'But how did you know an antelope was there?' He said, 'Suddenly, following the buffalo, my eyes were full of antelope; and I went where the fullness in my eyes came from, and there was the antelope.'

Do you think they have some psychic power unknown to us?

No, I think we all have it in us, but they take intuition much more seriously than we do. I remember an occasion, some years ago, when the front door bell rang here and I opened the door and it was my secretary coming for work in the morning. I looked at her face and she said to me, 'I've got something to tell you.' And I said to her, 'I know what you are going to say – you're going to tell me that the mother of X committed suicide.' I had not been thinking about him, I had not even seen him for months. And she said, 'How did you know?' But it just fell into me as I stood there with her. I do not regard myself as clairvoyant, but I think it shows that there are other ways of communicating that are important. This would not seem strange to primitive people at all.

While we are talking about other ways of communication, what was that story of the red pyjamas you once told me?

Oh yes, the red pyjamas. Dr Jung and I were talking one day about the experiments conducted at Duke University by Joseph Rhine on what is called parapsychic phenomena and Jung said: 'I had a very interesting experience once: I met William James in America. He was one of the most impressive people I met there and I also met a great friend of his called Professor Hyslop, who became a professor of psychology at one of the great American universities. James and Hyslop were very close friends. When they graduated from their universities their parents did what wealthy Americans did in those days, they sent them on a tour of Europe. These two young graduates arrived at Cherbourg and disembarked and took the train for Paris. When they arrived in Paris they found their baggage had not arrived. They had to spend a night at the hotel without their luggage, so Hyslop decided he would go out and buy some pyjamas, which he did. They both soon forgot all about this episode.

'Well, they stayed close friends, and later in life they made a pact that whoever died first would try and communicate with the other to try and give evidence that there was life after death. James died first, and Hyslop waited for a message and no message came. He waited a long time – seven or eight years – and concluded that there must be no possibility of communication, because if there had been James would surely have been in touch.

'Then, one day, he got a letter from somebody in Ireland – he did not know the person, he had never been to Ireland himself and had no Irish connection. The letter was to this effect: "Dear Professor Hyslop, Please forgive me if I am writing to you in vain and intruding on your time, but my wife and I have for many years practised very seriously with a planchette.* For the last six months our lives have really been made miserable by a certain William James who keeps on coming through, has given us your name and your address and insists that we should write to you. This William James has a question which may sound rather ridiculous. He wants to know if you remember the red pyjamas?" And Hyslop's first reaction was: this is absurd, is this all he's got to tell me from the afterlife? "Red pyjamas" meant nothing to him. And then suddenly one evening the penny dropped. He remembered the incident about the lost baggage and going out and buying pyjamas in Paris. He had only been able to buy a pair of very fancy red silk pyjamas and William James had teased him about it enormously. And to him that was absolute proof because only he and James had known about the red pyjamas, nobody else could have known about it, and he felt there could be no more objective evidence that somehow William James was still around.'

That was the story as Dr Jung told it to me.

Did Jung himself ever try to communicate with the dead?

He had a girl cousin who was a gifted medium – I believe she died rather young – and as a young man he was interested in spiritualist seances. But he came to feel that this was not the way, this was too archaic a method, and he did not pursue it any more himself, but he took it very seriously.

I remember him saying to me, 'One must always follow the thought

* A talking- or writing-board which is said to spell out messages from the spirits.

153

and feeling that give one the greatest sense of meaning: you must let the meaning be your guide.'

Now when Jung's wife died I wrote to him, and he wrote a very moving letter back to me in which he said: 'I am glad only of one thing; that my wife has been spared the knowledge of what it means to lose a lifelong partner and to be faced by a silence to which there can be no answer.' I really felt bad with a kind of despair because I wondered what had happened in him to abolish his precept of following the thing which had most meaning for him. But about six months later he unexpectedly came back to it and wrote to me – and I quote from memory: 'I would like you to know that I was wrong about the silence not having an answer. I have had a dream. I dreamt I was in a vast theatre which was dark and empty, and I walked down the aisle of the theatre until I came to the orchestra pit and it was like an abyss between me and the stage. But suddenly the stage was floodlit. There in the centre of the stage was my wife, beautifully dressed and looking lovelier than I had ever seen her. It was almost as if she was there to present me with a portrait which had been commissioned on the other side specially for me.' So, in other words, all was well.

He later told me too that he had realized that he had known in the dream that the beautiful dress his wife was wearing had been made for her by the girl who was the medium, who had in fact been a good seamstress and made fine dresses. This established for me the authenticity of the dream as a message from beyond the here and now. In this objective world of dreams to which we are subject, the portrait of his wife was an image; an objective witness of the existence of another form of life after death, and the dress made by someone who specialized in communicating with life beyond death was clearly included to remind him of an element of greater reality which was being overlooked. It was a very significant episode in the life of Jung and had great meaning for me.

Did he elaborate on this at all in his later years? Surely as he drew near his end he must have had more thoughts on this?

Jung told me to the end that in all his work he was terribly impressed with the way old people lived as if their end were not near. Without exception they seemed to have no sense of an end at all. In his work it was quite clearly established for him that the human soul, the individual soul, at the very least, in an important part of itself, was outside space and time and lived on – that there was no end to it. 'My advice to old people,' he told me just before he died, 'is to live on. Life will take as great care of death as it did of birth.' And I must add one shining element in Jung's make-up. No matter how gloomy the moment, how sombre the discussion or tragic the subject, I never recollect ever leaving him without a quickening of hope and heart, never, ever.

Jung himself enjoyed longevity, but Mozart, for instance, died young. It is strange how the fire of talent or genius burns. Who controls the flame?

Well, you know there is an old English saying – I think it is derived from a classical saying – that 'those whom the Gods love die young'. In writing about Jung I deal with the question of longevity and I say, although it may be true that those whom the Gods love die young, those whom the Gods love most live long. Of course, ages are relative; the lifespan of man today is so much longer. Probably people like Mozart, and Keats and Shelley, if they had had modern nutrition and modern medicine, could have been made to live much longer. Think of all the people who died of tuberculosis, and all the people who died because they did not know what we know now about diet and hygiene and all the other factors. We should not forget the enormous security that science has conferred on modern man physically.

But don't you think the briefer the burning-out the more intense the flame?

Or it could be that the people who are in much greater danger are the people with not enough intensity. On the other hand, intensity by itself is not enough; it too needs to grow and absorb all the other qualities that only time out of its own character can give. It is a very mysterious business that I would not pretend to have an answer to. I have often thought that people die when their work has been completed; they have been given enough time to do that. Shakespeare died in his early fifties, not very long after he had finished *The Tempest*, which really was the ultimate work of Shakespeare as an artist.

Didn't you once make a presentation of that play for the BBC?

Yes, I did, because Shakespeare means an enormous amount to me, and I think that I introduced perhaps a new concept in that programme. I said, whereas most people look at Shakespeare as having written different plays, Shakespeare really wrote one work in all. His plays are all sequels of one another and profoundly interconnected. The story they and his poems tell is only finished with *The Tempest*. Then you know there is nothing else beyond. In fact it says so at the end of *The Tempest* in that wonderful statement of Prospero. When he says he will drown his books, his writing self, deeper than any plummet could ever sound, he has arrived at the moment of which Eliot speaks as returning to the beginning, to what we started from, and recognizing it as home for the first time. He is returning all of himself, at the end of the long journey of differentiation which his writing has been, a long hard labour of making the divine, the creator in himself, flesh and blood, surrendering all of himself without demands to the collective unconscious which gave birth to the artist in himself, surrendering himself to God: 'My ending would be despair if it were not for prayer.' And he is free, before handing himself over to all that is symbolized by 'prayer', to see the world behind him at last:

> 'The cloud-capp'd towers, the gorgeous palaces,
> The solemn temples, the great globe itself . . .
> . . . shall dissolve
> . . . We are such stuff
> As dreams are made on . . .'

It is a deeply religious end, and this is where all art leads to, to that end. And his great breakthrough into his real poetic self, the discovery of the end to which he had been born, was in that magical experience of summer when he and all the world about him were young. Rightly *A Midsummer Night's Dream* is a dream at the beginning of one long season of growth and ripening. *The Tempest* is a dream for all seasons. No wonder Mozart wanted to make an opera about it; no wonder too that his *Magic Flute* was his own *Tempest* and that his *Requiem* so rightly was not finished on earth. In *The Tempest* Shakespeare had a dream not just for a season but for all seasons.

Because of the nature of your books and because of your own nature, do you sometimes feel you are a solitary man?

I do feel in some ways cut off from people by the nature of my work. Not because I do not love people – I love them very much – but because

156

as a writer I have to work with my imagination and my mind, and therefore I must lead a life that does not take my imagination away from my work – which means that I must go away from people at times. I find that the most important part of working is not the period when I am actually writing, but the periods when I stop writing between one day and the next morning. That period is terribly important, and though I cannot write in it, it is one in which my imagination should not be caught up with other things since it is my instrument of writing. That is the sort of incubation period, a time of vulnerable growth. Something goes on, and I like then to go for long walks in the country just by myself. I would love to write twenty-four hours a day, but words are so exacting, such hard work, that I cannot do more than three or, if I am lucky, four hours at a time, however much I long to push on. So, in between, I am anxious to get on to the next morning; I can hardly wait to get back to it. But at the same time there is a certain sadness that I am cut off from people whom I love in that time, not physically but in my own self. Solitude does not necessarily mean loneliness, because one has companionship of a different kind. Even so, I have always been aware of the fact, and I am afraid people may feel it and resent it, that there is a part of me that is not there, it is off somewhere else. I am, as the Bantu say, not in my body, not really at home, although physically there.

So you belong more to the Kalahari Desert than to the fashionable circles of London.

Oh, much more! I cannot tell you what sheer physical and spiritual contentment I have found in the desert and how my last night there has always been a very, very sad night, because I feel I am about to move back into prison. It was an enormous privilege I had, exploring that desert systematically, to come to know a country where you feel no human eye has ever been and to feel as if you have arrived in an undiscovered area of your own self. It is a very moving and life-giving experience.

I have come over a great big sand dune in the desert and on to what we call a 'pan', which is a hard, open area where perhaps four streams collected at one time in the rain, and found it covered with animals. I arrived with vehicles making a lot of noise, yet none of the animals ran away; they stood fast and looked on in astonishment. They had never been threatened by anything like that before. Even the jackals came out of their holes to look at us. It was an extraordinary kind of vision of what life was like in the beginning.

Does the Kalahari differ from the other deserts? Is it much more attractive to you?

The lovely thing is that I have known several kinds of deserts. I know the Sahara, and the Syrian desert – but the Kalahari Desert is marvellous because it is only a desert in the sense that there is no surface water. It has trees and grass and a fantastically rich animal and bird life, so that it proves that a desert can be fertile and beautiful in its own Cinderella way. When its prince, the rain, comes, there is an explosion of flowers and animal and bird-life. Desert fruit has a sweetness you do not find in country where it rains a lot, so when the rains fall the animals who live outside the desert smell it and come to eat the desert plums and all the other fruits. The elephants walk hundreds of miles into the Kalahari at these times because they have a very sweet tooth; and remember, it is a long tooth, so that the desire too is long. They enjoy the fruits of the desert with an abandonment that for me has been a special delight to watch. There was something entrancing about seeing the biggest animal on earth as if he were an undernourished boarding-school boy let loose in his larder at home at the end of term. And of course the greatest joy to me was discovering that the first person, the Bushman, still lived in the desert. That made it unique – a man who is still living in harmony with the desert and with the animals.

I had a dream: I wanted the whole of the Kalahari made into a 'world trust' area. I wanted it sealed off from outside intrusions, left just as it was, so that we could learn about it, and our arrogant, imperious culture would not intrude on it except very reverently, purely in the interests of the desert's preservation. But that was not possible because of this obsession of men in power to subordinate everything in life to political considerations. The Kalahari is not merely in Botswana, it is also in South-West Africa or Namibia, and it goes over into Angola right up to Mossamedes, so you can see how politically fragmented it was. I had wanted the whole area to be a 'world trust' area because economically the use it has is infinitesimal and transitory in comparison to the use it would have had to mankind as a witness of what nature was like in the beginning, and a reminder of what nature meant us to be.

Is it hopeless, do you think?

I think it is a Jacob and Esau problem. The man of the Kalahari is Esau and we are Jacob, and there is a great gulf between us. This sense of property, of possession that we have is utterly foreign to the Esaus of the world. We have, he is.

Shelley wrote a great poem on Prometheus which says, near the end, 'to hope till Hope creates from its own wreck the thing it contemplates'. We have a lot of wrecking of hope from which to create our new hope of the future, for the Bushman as well as ourselves.

Ingaret,* would you be kind enough to join us? It was, I know, through you that Laurens first met Jung. You yourself studied with Jung and Professor Meier in Zürich. And you were lucky enough to have made the first tape-recording ever of Jung. May I ask, under what circumstances did you go there?

INGARET: Well, extraordinary circumstances. I went alone, with only Laurens supporting my decision, to work at Zürich. I went out of a sense of compulsion. As I wrote to Laurens at the time, 'It seems to me that people's private and personal lives have never mattered as they do now. For me the whole of the future depends on the way people live their personal rather than their collective lives. It is a matter of extreme urgency. When we have all lived out our private and personal problems we can consider the next, the collective step. Then it will be easy but before it will not even be possible.'

Would you revise that opinion now? Or does it still hold true?

INGARET: No, at the end of the war that was the main thought that drove me to Jung: to find out all I could about myself and my own personal life in relation to what I had written. Then it so happened that there were a great number of students at the newly founded Jung Institute at Zürich. The moment inevitably came when we all had to write a thesis on dream analysis. At the end of this, out of all these people, my thesis was chosen as an example of a model analysis. Jung said it could not really be bettered. Well, this was terribly serious, almost a shattering pronouncement. It seemed to put a whole weight of responsibility round my neck, which I did not want. After all, I was a playwright and wanted to go on writing. So I went to Jung and said, 'Look, I'm not a doctor, I do not want to put up a brass plate. I've got my own life which is writing and the theatre and I love it. And I don't know what to do!' And Jung just said, very simply, 'When you are ready the people will come.' And I thought, That's marvellous! Obviously, nobody will come! I came back to London, opened my front door, and there was a letter on the mat

* The author's wife, whom he married in 1949 (see *Jung and the Story of Our Time*, p. 43).

from a woman I had worked with in the war, and it said, 'Ingaret, you have always been interested in psychology' – which was true of course. 'I have got a great problem. Would you see me?'

That was the beginning. I have never asked anybody to come, I have never said anything to promote this work which came to me. I have just allowed it to come as it comes; and when it does come I do not and cannot say 'no'.

But today you are supposed to be 'retired' and yet still you continue to see patients and help them.

INGARET: Exactly, I have said now I have earned the right to withdraw and to retire because I am going to write a book, which I am doing. That means in fact that the only real difference is that I say: Look, I never charged anybody. I am retired. If I see you now and can help you I do it not because it is my profession or because I am this or that, but because I would like to help if I can.

You are so active, with your writing, your patients, and looking after your flowers. You are taking care of people like flowers and flowers like people. I must confess that I have overheard your conversation with your flowers: you were calling them 'my little fellows'.

INGARET: Well, I do care very much about people and I have known something about people and the way they can go wrong. Consciously I have known since the age of ten, through the way I was able to help my mother. My mother was deeply, deeply wounded by her upbringing. She was in great fear all the time and I was able through some intuitive understanding to help her by sending her to the right people even long before I had been to Jung.

You have helped your mother, you are helping your patients, but did you help yourself? I mean, did you change somehow with this meeting of heart and mind with Jung?

INGARET: I do not think it made any difference in essence except that it orchestrated consciously the urge which sent me to Jung and made my cause, as it were, fulfilled.

And for yourself, were you able to find answers to your own questions?

INGARET: No, no . . . I do not think I had any sense of unanswerable problems. I just had this irresistible need to find out, and to do. But I had to have four years training, learning how to work in London and Zürich, before I could be satisfied that I really did have some understanding of it all. You would have to ask Laurens, but I think the great difference it made to me was feeling very, very honoured to be able to help people. Take a recent and classic example: three women alcoholics. Well, this is a dire disease and it is very difficult to cure. But I was able to free those people for their life again. This is something. Yes, I have been able to help a lot of people, so that is enough for me.

It is a whole life and a whole book. We are all waiting for this new book of yours. Will your patients be part of the book?

INGARET: No, not yet. This book is really an account of one's own wrestling with one's own values and one's own perception, and one's own meanings and meaninglessness. And I am a very strongly extro-verted person at the same time. I am not just a person who sits and dreams and contemplates and reads. I am out and doing. I've always been on the move – sometimes catastrophically.

I know something now of this creative, catastrophic movement of yours. You once told me that in your work with people what was called a 'nervous breakdown' to you was always a 'break-through', a disguised moment of opportunity and renewal.

May we now turn to Switzerland, which after all is where we all first met? I'd like you, if you would, Ingaret, to read the poems that you wrote in Switzerland, because I know the Swiss mountains and the snow have always been a fertile inspiration for you.

INGARET: Well, gladly, if you wish. But do please bear in mind that these poems are not really what I wanted them to be – I was in bed with a virus when I wrote them. We had had a most productive month of work and lovely skiing behind us last year – as you know, we always work in the mornings and ski in the afternoon and work again in the evenings – and then suddenly this rather serious virus infection assaulted me in London and in a strange way magnified my longing to get back to the mountains. Hence these poems.

I would like to begin with one about my favourite mountain, the Relleri:

The Relleri

'The 'Relleri' is revelry
For those who dare its slopes.
It stretches its six thousand feet
Skywards, with stalwart hopes:
So high that its strong shoulders
Are mantled by the clouds.

They brush it with a gentle kiss
Then wander on through life.
Their heavenly search is endless,
No mountain knows their strife.
Yet contact is unending
As in all natural life.

So man is brought to silence
By the beauty and the strength.
He pits his puny efforts
Against the soaring heights.
But above, the sky is watching
And only it can know
The ant-like helplessness of man
Struggling far below.

So to the sky we raise our eyes
And lift our hearts in prayer
Grateful for heaven above us
But glad we are not there . . .
For we need to make our journey
We need to know our goal . . .
To rise above the mountain
Who points us to our role.'

The Relleri seems in your poem to be more feminine than masculine . . .
INGARET: Ah yes, this is certainly a lady mountain to me – she's a woman, she's female.

And to you mountains are living, they have their own personalities. Could you read your second poem, please?

The Eggli

'The Eggli is of stalwart bulk
Which slows her to seeming sloth
So the trees cling round her petticoats
Struggling for higher growth . . .

Sublime in her natural form
She treats them with gentleness . . .
Yet the sky above is watching
Aware of her inner stress –

As humans, like ants, come pouring
All over her sweet, snow-face!
And at once their wrinkles of passage
Rob her of youth and grace.

But the sky above is helpful
(It, too, is a part of Space . . .)
So snow, inaudibly, ordered,
Soon covers that wrinkled face.

Then smiling, with joy and beauty
The Eggli is young once more,
Waiting, like us, for the answer
As to which is our Exit door?'

Wonderful! And you know something, it evokes for me some Hokusai or Hiroshige ukiyoe, or prints.

INGARET: You can see it, can you? Yes. I love these mountains, I am identified with them and their personalities. The third mountain was the last one to which my guide took me the last day before I left. He and I went together, and it was the first time I'd been to the Saanen Loch.

The Saanen Loch

'In Saanen there stands a mountain
That really is of two worlds.
Its slopes are steep and silent,
Yet open to all who come.

And come they do in haste most dire
To swarm, and ski, and race, and fall
Like dancing flames above a fire.

Yet cradled within that mountain
Is a deep, blue, nameless lake . . .
And silent it lies,
Facing the skies
Yet somehow most deeply awake.

So perhaps in our own inner being
There is also a great blue eye,
Which watching all, and knowing all
Says nothing itself to belie?

Nothing? Well, only in dreams . . .
For dreams are our real inner freedom,
Like the lake, they reflect the sky.
And they tell us the truth of our being,
But with faith, and unable to lie.'

The key word in this poem of course is 'dream'. But what about you, Ingaret? You have spent so much of your time and life taking care of other people's dreams. What are your own dreams? It seems you are not of this world — of this world only. You belong to many different worlds, you have been so many people, you have lived through so many different times. You have even fought like a soldier when Laurens was away in Africa and Java for ten years. In a sense you have fought your own war.

INGARET: I fought the physical war for four years by making bombs by day and being an air-raid warden at night, and I fought my own . . . I do not know the word — it was not despair. I think it could only be called wrestling with faith, trusting that, no matter what happened, all whom I loved would come through and we would be able to continue together again. Then came my work with Jung, and gradually the discovery that I could bring help to other people in their lives and dreams. That, for me, has been an absorbing and abiding challenge; yes, another kind of struggle, if you like, but one that has fulfilled many dreams of my own.

Laurens, you have such close connections with so many parts of the world, where do you feel you really belong? Who are you? Where is home to you?

In the sense that I have a home, it is where my wife makes a home for me, but if it were not for Ingaret I would have a tent. And I hope it is not arrogant, but I think it is true that wherever I have been in the world I have felt strangely at home; but home is not a particular place. It is extraordinary, but sometimes out in the desert or in the bush I have felt far more at home than I have felt in a house called 'home'. I am not evading your question, but it is a very difficult one to answer because I have not got a very conscious concept of what I am and what I am about. I have just got a feeling of finding out all the time. It is probably a great weakness in me, in my make-up. But I do know I do not belong to crowds, although I have had to work with crowds.

I do not really know what I am about because my whole life in that way has been so strange. All my origins have been strange and the only way in which I have tried to make out what I am is to decide whether I belong to Africa or to the rest of the world. In that book of mine, *Venture to the Interior*, you can see the extent to which I deal with it there and came to the conclusion that the spirit of man is nomad, his blood bedouin, and love is the aboriginal tracker on the faded desert spoor of his lost self; and so I came to live my life not by conscious plan or prearranged design but as someone following the flight of a bird.

Could I put the question in another way: where are you most at ease? You told me you felt at home in the desert or in the bush. What about the sea?

I feel very much at one with the sea, and many of the happiest moments of my life have been spent at sea in ships. I have always felt very much at home at sea. I love storms at sea; I think they are the most beautiful things I have ever seen. I think of a typhoon I went through with Captain Mori in the *Canada Maru* on my way to Japan – it was very, very beautiful.

How can you be at the same time in love with the sea and with the mountains?

166

Great natural phenomena – great mountains, the sea, deserts, forests – I feel a very great kinship with all these things. I feel very close to them; they have great meaning for me.

What about Switzerland, Jung's home?

Yes, I used to go to Switzerland long before I happened to know Jung. I love Switzerland – above all in the winter under the snow. The mountains underneath, and the snow itself, which is a miracle to me. These things, the natural things of life, mean an enormous amount to me. For me it is a great drama which I never get used to – to watch the day turn into night – it is marvellous, a very great experience. It means more to me than going to the theatre.

But I would not like you to think Switzerland has just super picture-postcard attractions for me. I have a very special feeling for the country and its people, and I have many friends there. It gives me something no other country does; it gives me the sense of living history and continuity I find as necessary as air. Its roots in European history are deep and intact. It is still without hubris, a country of city-states, with the balance in spirit of town and country still maintained. And it is a country of individuals and a nation with an integrated ethos. I have a Swiss friend who says, 'Our great contribution to life has been to prove that three races, three cultures who basically hate one another, can yet be a nation.' And he laughs as he says it, but he has a valid and exemplary point. And there it has given the world something indispensable; God knows what we would do without it. It has also given us the only positive form of neutrality that exists, neutrality which is not an evasion but a high moral commitment: some form of impartial ground of place and spirit, where a divided world, often at war, can still be kept in contact and meet; a neutrality which enables it to do for the world what nothing else can. The International Red Cross, for instance. There is a vast and vital difference between Swiss neutrality and, say, Swedish or Irish neutrality. The Swiss is a commitment, the others an evasion and, at best, a hope to keep out of trouble.

To go with it there is a national urge to look at life, science, art, trade, everything in the round, and whole. Jung could not have come out of any other culture than that of Switzerland, as Paracelsus did. It gives me a great encouraging feeling of the thrust of a history of meaning when I stay, as I do, in the old city of Zürich in the hotel built out of Paracelsus's house: or when, high up in the Engadine, I still hear Romansch, which was the Latin spoken by the Christian legions of Rome who invaded and conquered Switzerland.

And above all I respond to the self-reliance of mind and work which maintains an individual intact without diminution of his obligations to his country and people. The most ludicrous foreign conception of all is that the Swiss are unimaginative, solid, over-thrifty and dull. It just maddens me because, behind the tourist façade, it is true there is a self-respect, a sense of public law and order, decency, and an air of conventionalism, but at heart there also is great zest for life, a temperament that even the Latins could envy – courage, honesty, imagination, a lively fantasy and a great caringness and gift of companionship and friendship, as well as a concern for the material, not as an end, but as a means to something alive and beyond matter.

Above all, they are a true people. You may disagree with them, but they are not false.

———

One of your favourite authors, Joseph Conrad, was partly, like you, a foreigner, an outsider. But he so much enriched the English language and literature. I like the idea that the peripheral individual or nation comes often to the rescue of the centre.

It is also very interesting to me how, through America particularly, the people of central Europe are contributing to the English language, both to the writing and the speaking of the English language. Some of the most wonderful, picturesque, lively, witty words that we pick up over here come from Yiddish, especially New York Yiddish, and a lot of the humour too.

We are extremely lucky really, in the English language, that we had the whole of the Saxon vocabulary, reinforced by Celtic foundations; and then we were conquered by the Normans, who were French-speaking, so we acquired a great deal of the French vocabulary as well. We went on to draw widely on Latin and Greek, so that English is a language with the most incredible richness and wealth of expression and nuance.

Do you think that some people, like the Jews, are more gifted than others? Do you believe in chosen peoples?

I think that, one way or another, all people are chosen, but they are chosen in different ways. I think the Jews are definitely chosen in the sense that they have the most highly developed gift of religion, the most sustained, continuous and evolved intimation of religion in the Western idiom, a religion which is unifying and constantly reappraising and renewing man's relations with the God that cannot be named.

I have lots of Jewish friends. When I talk to them I am aware of the fact that I can talk to them in a way in which I cannot talk to other people, and they respond in kind. When you think of the history of the Jews, their suffering from their period of bondage onwards to their massacre in millions by Hitler, I find it most impressive how unsoured and unembittered on the whole they have been, how creative, what a source of art, fun and gaiety they have retained. Above all, they have proved what is of the greatest importance to the future: that you can remain a coherent and integrated people even when deprived of country, worldly power and native language, as long as you retain a common faith in your religion, God and his word. It puts those for whom self-determination is a political form of heroin, and who regard a prescribed terrain and political power as a precondition of nationhood, utterly in the outermost shade.

I always feel very close to them, and my people in Africa felt very close to them. For instance, my old grandfather, who could hardly read or write, was on his great farm one day when a man appeared with a donkey and asked if he could buy any skins and collect any bones lying about. My grandfather discovered that this man was a Russian Jew who could hardly speak any known language, and my grandfather asked him, 'What are you doing here, why have you come from Russia?' So he told my grandfather, 'I had to leave my family and come here and try and make a living so that I can get them out of Russia. We are being persecuted and killed in Russia, particularly in the Ukraine.' So my grandfather said, 'This is terrible – how can they do that to the people of the Book.' This man came every year: then one year my grandfather had a very good wool season when he sold a lot of wool – the grandchildren of this Jewish family still talk about it as the 'year of the miracle'. They told the story to a newspaper the other day, and described how my grandfather walked into a tiny little room in the interior of Africa, where this Jewish man lived and collected his skins and bones to be sold for barely a living, and he took out a little linen tobacco bag, opened it and poured the contents of it onto the table, and out came gold sovereign after gold sovereign. The man looked absolutely amazed and my grandfather explained, 'That is for you to get your people out of Russia.'

This story lived on in my family and remained a measure for us all of our instinctive feeling for the Jews and what they represented.

We do not see any end to the war in the Middle East between Israelis and Arabs. It seems to be a vicious circle. How can it be broken?

It is, and one must not forget that many Jews in the world are very opposed to much of what the Israelis are doing. You must not confuse Jew and Israeli. And remember, too, that all these issues are keenly fought over in the Israeli Parliament in a way in which they are never done in Arab countries. There are many Jews who feel it was a great mistake for the Jews ever to become identified with a particular piece of land. When they were identified with a search and a quest and a certain state of spirit, many Jews believe they were being truer to their destiny than when they became a nationalistic people. I myself was very much against the creation of a state of Israel because I felt you could not found a Jewish state on another act of injustice. Because it was, initially, an act of injustice to the Arabs who had been there for two thousand years.

I find that many of my Jewish friends were horrified by this too. But then, on the other hand, I do feel that if we try to undo it all now and go back to the beginning, we create another act of injustice. We have got to say, well, all right, this was wrong, we must now redeem this injustice in another way. We must all combine to redress a wrong, inflicted on people no longer alive, in another way. This is what is so wrong with people always hiding behind history, using suffering we never suffered, the wrongs inflicted on vanished generations, as ways to political power. We must say, there are no automatic historic claims and every generation has to earn its own rights.

So I feel that a tremendous act of redemption is called for, to redeem a great wrong which was done, in the interests of the Jews themselves above all. They should try in their way to do something to put it right. People get so hurt. We talked about the suffering in southern Africa. People get so hurt by their suffering that they become bitter and they will not be redeemed. This is where I think the Christian message of forgiveness, patience, endurance, persuasion, is of such great practical importance. All these things have got to come in our approach to the problem. They cannot be achieved by force because, if there is one thing you cannot do, it is that you cannot cut a Gordian knot – because as fast as you cut it, it grows again. Impossible as it sounds, you can only unravel it with patience, which is the wisdom of time. It always starts with ourselves; that is where it begins and ends.

———

In your books you often refer to the Bible, St Paul, King Arthur and the Knights of the Round Table, Dante, Shakespeare, Goethe, Conrad, Baudelaire, Apollinaire, Jung, T. S. Eliot, and so on . . . Which name, which book is the most important to you?

Well, 'literature' is not only written literature. Spoken literature – the stories I heard of Africa as a child, like the star-story I told you – are of tremendous importance to me. I remember them in every detail, and they still live inside me. Then, when I come to the written word, I think the first great stories that really had meaning for me were the stories in the Bible which my mother and others had told me when I was a boy. After dinner my grandfather never failed to read the 'Book of books' to his family and all the assembled servants of the house. In his day it was their textbook for everything. They had no other literature except the Bible.

Close to the Bible I would put Homer's *Iliad*, the *Odyssey*, and the *Aeneid* of Virgil, and then all the legends of Greece and Rome. Next would come Malory's *Morte d'Arthur*; the legend of the Holy Grail and the Knights of the Round Table is in a sense the document which made all that had been stirring in my imagination assume an active pattern, a dynamic model for doing, for all the seeking that is, for me, our quintessential quest.

In the course of your quest have you succeeded in identifying the Holy Grail, your Holy Grail?

No, I just feel its presence around and within me, without having a definite image of the Holy Grail. It became, as it were, the climate of my spirit, and what its imagery has always evoked in me is much more than the Grail. The idea of life as a quest goes very deep in me, because it seems to link up with the history of my family and my people, who had left Europe to look for a new country and a new way of life, and the quest, the Holy Grail, was an extension of this searching into another, spiritual, dimension. And the story is even more important to me now, when all the sense of wholeness – as represented by the Round Table – which nourished and compelled the human spirit, is scattered and fragmented by our specialized, partial and compartmentalized day.

Oh, I remember the scene where Arthur is killed, the last battle and how I cried and cried for days. I could not bear to think that this could be the end.

You could have tried to rewrite the ending . . .

No, I did not want to rewrite it – you cannot do that to a story. This is one of the problems for me: stories in a way are more completely real to me than life in the here and now. A really true story has a transcendent reality for me which is greater than the reality of life. It incorporates life but it goes beyond it.

Strangely enough, it was a book about another and perhaps more profound meaning of knighthood which also had a fateful impact on me. It was the last book my father gave me before he died: *Don Quixote* by Cervantes, abridged for boys and superbly illustrated, and from that moment on the elongated knight of La Mancha rode with me.

Dante came into my life very early by way of a painting. We had a book at home on the lives of the great poets, with illustrations, and in it I saw the illustration of Dante's first vision of Beatrice in the streets of Florence. My hair stood on end, and I thought, 'Well, that's me!' Because, young as I was, I had already had a similar experience in the dusty streets of my native village.

My father had a vast library with books in French, German, Dutch and, predominantly, English. He was a great lover of books, and people in our part of Africa used to come from far and wide to borrow books from him; he acted as a sort of lending library for the whole community. I loved reading; I loved history, I loved poetry, I loved literature and art, and above all English literature. Strangely enough, I found Dutch literature boring. It was for me inferior, too materialistic, too moralistic, almost too awful. There are fine things in Dutch literature too, but really it is on the whole not one of the great literatures in the world. Yet even to it I am indebted.

But I do not know what I would have become or done if it had not been for the literature of the spoken word, the poetry and the stories above all. They all, if true in the telling and truly read, are seeds of new awareness and, through increase of awareness, elements of increase in the quality of our being and sources of renewal and greater becoming. For me the greatest of these remained the stories told by the anonymous story-tellers of Africa. The people who influenced me most were the great people of my childhood whom the world will never know and whose record is only in the deep of my heart: the rag-and-tatter and despised Bushman, Griqua, Hottentot and Sotho story-tellers of my childhood. Were it not for them, I doubt if my imagination would ever have been as open as it was to Homer, Shakespeare, Dante, Cervantes and the rest who became my neighbours in a world of the imagination where there is no divide of time and space, but all is propinquity and now.

Graham Greene has always been a great traveller and a great hunter for meaning. Do you know him?

Yes, I knew him well in my own London beginnings. When I first came to London in the great world recession, I had an introduction which led to a Mrs Pawley, who had been a Miss Heinemann of the great publishing firm of Heinemann's. Mrs Pawley was a widow and a friend of Henry James. She lived in that lovely Queen Anne street in Hampstead, called Pond Street, and I took an enormous liking to her. She invited me to Sunday afternoon tea there whenever I wanted to go, and she always laid on Victorian afternoon teas with five or six different kinds of cakes, cucumber sandwiches, scones and crumpets – a lovely tea, with several friends in.

The very first afternoon I was there, a young woman with a baby had also been invited, and she turned out to be Mrs Graham Greene. Graham Greene had just come down from university and was working as a sub-editor on *The Times*. He finished work early on Sunday and came on to join us there, most Sundays. So I got to know him very well, and from those days on we have been friends.

Do you admire his prowess at dancing on the razor's edge?

Well, I have admired his courage at the same time as I feared the element in his nature which seemed to me half in love with danger, and loved gambling with his own – not with other people's – life, and at times even as if gambling with his own soul. I also felt deep sympathy for him as well as admiration, because I was aware of something desperately sad and unresolved in him, which at the same time made his laughter, his humour, his sense of enquiry and interest in the world all the braver and more honourable. He was never self-indulgent of whatever element haunted him but bravely used it as a dynamic to explore himself, and life and his time.

There is a lot more I would like to say, but Graham's story is not over yet. It is much too soon to sit in judgement on him. I would just like to raise my hat to someone who is on a brave if reckless journey and takes us to areas of ourselves we would not have reached otherwise, and be grateful for the feeling of companionship he and his work have given all these years.

And what about D. H. Lawrence? Where do you place him in your life in London? I ask because I believe there are two events you can be proud of in your early career as a journalist. First was the leader you wrote upon the death of Lawrence. You were probably among the very few who from the beginning recognized the significance of D. H. Lawrence and wrote about him and defended him.

I know that he is being 'rediscovered' now, but I do not think people in this generation can have any idea of what Lawrence meant to my generation. They take what he brought to literature for granted now but Lawrence was really what was called a 'breakthrough'. He was a 'breakthrough' in human awareness. He had the rare courage of his own imagination – to go where his own imagination took him without other models or guides. And the result was that he brought into consideration, into modern imagination, into literature, all sorts of areas of human reality and subjects that had been either totally forbidden or utterly suppressed in the Victorian era. The obvious example is sex. He brought sex in, it is true, in an extremely archaic way in the sense that almost all he says about it is physical, but nonetheless, he brought it into the light of active imagination. It is very much a man's idea of sex and lacks a woman's sensitivities. The woman's share in Lawrence is dominated by the mother-son relationship, which was so important because it was his own relationship and explains why he went off with Frieda von Richt-hofen, who was older than he was. The fineness, the subtleties, the sort of immense Dante-esque world to which woman is the guide was mostly absent – yet it was there, only in a somewhat primitive way. But then, nonetheless, it was a great act of enrichment to an impoverished British area of imagination.

I know that the Victorian view of sex, the pale, flowery, pre-Raphaelite view of women, needed some sort of act of compensation such as Lawrence's instinctively was. And it was perhaps the only way in which such profound inhibitions could be overcome, and it did open the door to an enlargement of our awareness and an enrichment to come. But it did leave Lawrence a prisoner of his act of discovery, or rediscovery. He was to smart against a feeling of reimprisonment for the rest of his days.

A woman friend who stayed with Lawrence and Frieda in New Mexico told me how they would walk out in couples, Lawrence and the other man in front. Lawrence, who would get lost in his own talk, would come to a halt, but when Frieda and my friend overtook them and went ahead, a strange fury overcame him. He would rush after Frieda, berate her for daring to walk in front of him, and even hit her across the back with his stick. It was clearly symbolic of his archaic concept of the proper place of woman.

And he was a very remarkable poet. I think his poetry is tremendous. I discovered it during my first journey to Japan and read it on my way back on captain Mori's ship, the *Canada Maru*.

Lawrence has a very special feeling for nature. I would say that he was also an African more than a European because of his unique sensitivity.

Very true. Yes, he had this capacity for *participation mystique* with nature which we talked about – his birds, beast and flower poems, the poem about the snake for instance, and the Etruscan cypresses. I think his vision for physical reality, the plants, animals, and earth, was great.

Among his outstanding qualities were his emotional and physical understanding of living things. In an age which tended to be extrovert and over-rational, he brought a whole range of instinctive reality, not only of sex but all instinctive and natural reality, back into modern man's spirit. And I think in that way he was unique and tremendous. But he did this, as pioneers do, in an archaic way, which came out in his thinking. When a man surrenders himself to these vast forces in the collective unconscious, the hero immediately becomes a kind of a dictator. He had this strange love of so-called 'he-men', dictatorial men. The man had to be in charge and dominate the woman, who was seen as longing for domination, often secretly.

But we are not doing an analysis, and must not overlook the enormous service he performed in his time. All sorts of things, things we take for granted now, he was the first to explore, and that takes immense courage. And what he did had the grace of an immense reverence for natural life. That was his greatest service to our time, when natural life was more and more under attack.

So I remember clearly and with emotion that night when I was in charge of the *Cape Times*. One of my tasks was to 'put the paper to bed', as we used to say, and particularly take care of the leader page. About midnight, it was getting late and it was about time to lock-up the leader page, when the chief editor, Bill Parsons, came up to me and threw a telegram on my desk and said, 'Young Laurie, I think that would interest you.' And I took the telegram and read, 'D. H. Lawrence, controversial poet and novelist, died of tuberculosis at Bandol, in the South of France this evening.' It was such a shock to me, because I felt it as an intimate personal loss. I felt I had known him personally and closely through his writing. So I went down below to the works and I told the father of the chapel, 'Hold the leader page, and take that leading article out' – my editor had written it, a long political leader article. I went upstairs and wrote a tribute to D. H. Lawrence. I remember ending it with a poem which I often thought about when I was a prisoner-of-war: it meant a great deal to me. It's a poem called 'Moonrise'. And I ended my leader with some lines from that poem:

'. . . and we are sure
That beauty is a thing beyond the grave,
That perfect, bright experience never falls
To nothingness . . .'

I put the leader at the head of the leader column. I came back at 2 o'clock the next day, thinking I'd probably get the sack from my editor. And as I got into my office I found a note on my desk saying, 'See the editor immediately.' I thought 'Well, this is it.' So I went down to his office, knocked on the door and went in. He was at his desk, turned around and I noticed that he'd been reading Jane Austen's *Emma* – that's the sort of editor he was – instead of looking at the cables. And he saw me and he smiled, a very nice smile. He took his pipe out of his mouth, and he said, 'I'm very glad you've come. I wanted to see you, and tell you what a joy it was this morning to see a civilized leader on a civilized subject in the paper.'

I discovered afterwards that we were the only newspaper in the world to take notice of D. H. Lawrence's death in that way. Even *The Times* in London did not carry an obituary. They just had a news item about his death, perhaps because not long before he died there'd been an enormous scandal – Lawrence had an exhibition of paintings in London at the Leicester Gallery. He was nearly arrested, the police raided the gallery and the exhibition was closed down. They said it was obscene. Well, the whole of the so-called 'obscene' area of life was brought back into civilized awareness by D. H. Lawrence.

Listening to you, I feel that you knew Lawrence intimately. It's strange how you talk about certain people who count for you . . . you are so close to them, they could be a brother, or part of the family. Did you have the same sort of feeling for Lawrence as you had for T. S. Eliot? Did you feel as close to him?

I did meet Lawrence once at the Café Royal. But I did not know him and also I did not particularly take to him then. He was a very slight man with his beard, and his shining, almost cold, piercing eyes, and had much of the compensatory energies and assertiveness small people often have, and was more egotistical than I thought he would be. And I suddenly realized that the instinct in command is not necessarily warm. It can be as cold as ice as well. But to be fair to us both, I did not really speak to him much. He was holding forth. I was there with Aldous Huxley and Gerald Heard and I was very much listening in; thinking perhaps that I had better stick to reading him. But I did feel, and I still do feel to this day, a very close bond with him.

With T. S. Eliot I felt it the moment I read him, and then I had the good luck to know him, and we became friends. And to be drawn as much to the man as his work, as I was then, is an incredible bonus.

The other event I believe you can be really proud of as a journalist was the campaign in the Cape Times *against racial discrimination, and a leader entitled 'White Justice', which brought about the most expensive libel actions in South Africa.*

That was the heading to a leading article Desmond Young and I wrote at the end of a long campaign against racial discrimination when a white jury gave a scandalous verdict of 'not guilty', in a case brought against the police for brutality and corruption. It led to perhaps the most celebrated libel case in South African history because the jury sued us and the *Cape Times* fought them right up to the highest court of appeal, losing purely because of a technicality. It was immensely expensive and uncomfortable but worth it in every way because it was the cornerstone of an honourable tradition in papers like the *Cape Times* and the *Rand Daily Mail*, to expose and denounce abuse of authority and power in these areas, with increasing acceleration from then on to this day.

One of the poets we have just touched on and it is obvious that he is perhaps closest to your heart is T. S. Eliot. Could you tell me more about him, and begin perhaps with one of your favourite poems, 'Little Gidding'. I think this poem is pure music and gives us a taste of what is waiting for us at the end of our quest . . . the idea that when we go back to where it all begins, we find that the beginning and the end are the same. It shows the way to 'satori', illumination. Would you be kind enough to read out the last part?

> 'What we call the beginning is often the end
> And to make an end is to make a beginning.
> The end is where we start from. And every phrase
> And sentence that is right (where every word is at home,
> Taking its place to support the others,

The word neither diffident nor ostentatious,
An easy commerce of the old and the new,
The common word exact without vulgarity,
The formal word precise but not pedantic,
The complete consort dancing together)
Every phrase and every sentence is an end and a beginning,
Every poem an epitaph. And any action
Is a step to the block, to the fire, down the sea's throat
Or to an illegible stone: and that is where we start.
We die with the dying:
See, they depart, and we go with them.
We are born with the dead:
See, they return, and bring us with them.
The moment of the rose and the moment of the yew-tree
Are of equal duration. A people without history
Is not redeemed from time, for history is a pattern
Of timeless moments. So, while the light fails
On a winter's afternoon, in a secluded chapel
History is now and England.

With the drawing of this Love and the voice of this Calling

We shall not cease from exploration
And the end of all our exploring
Will be to arrive where we started
And know the place for the first time.
Through the unknown, remembered gate
When the last of earth left to discover
Is that which was the beginning;
At the source of the longest river
The voice of the hidden waterfall
And the children in the apple-tree
Not known, because not looked for
But heard, half-heard, in the stillness
Between two weaves of the sea.
Quick now, here, now, always –
A condition of complete simplicity

(Costing not less than everything)
And all shall be well and
All manner of thing shall be well
When the tongues of flames are in-folded
Into the crowned knot of fire
And the fire and the rose are one.'

Don't you think there's a touch of Taoism and a touch of Zen in the spirit and the expression of a great many of T. S. Eliot's poems?

Yes, certain elements that have parallels in the ancient Indian view of life have always been natural to T. S. Eliot. For me, his poetry is a watershed in modern English literature. Take, for instance, his great poem 'The Waste Land', which was a watershed, if you can accept so paradoxical an image, in his own spirit and writing. 'The Waste Land' is an image of the desert where the spirit of man, the spirit of Eliot, as it were, had to go like the great people of all time – just as Christ had to go into the wilderness, into the wasteland, into the desert – before they could fulfil themselves. In this great poem he quotes things in Sanskrit and from Buddhist literature, and this is not all. There are traces of Dante in it, quotations from French poetry in it; he quotes that upside down, inside out, harlequin spirit, Gérard de Nerval, and you find yourself sailing into 'Le Prince d'Aquitaine à la tour abolie', the words Andrew Lang translated as 'that dark, dishonoured son of Aquitaine'. Then there is a moment in the poem when the rain is about to break and the thunder mutters – in Sanskrit. And one is shocked into realizing the tremendous synthesis of cultures taking place in Eliot, and that he is doing for us a reintegration similar to the one Dante accomplished for his day.

How did you come across T. S. Eliot's poetry for the first time?

I had an older brother who was at university in Europe and America and he came home and first told me about Eliot. Then I had a master at school who brought the first T. S. Eliot poems, up to 'The Waste Land', back with him from New College, Oxford, and he said to me, 'You can read it if you like, but I can't make head or tail of it.' I took it home to read during my school vacation, and I always had to work at home. On this vacation I was herding sheep, and I herded them very badly because the

moment I started reading him it was just like a bell ringing. I thought –
this is one of my special voices, this makes complete sense to me. This is
the voice of my hour, it keeps my time. It belongs to what I call 'my
neighbourhood', like Homer, Shakespeare, Jung, Dante and all. This is
the marvellous thing about the world of the spirit, and I think of art: the
extraordinary feeling in which, through them, time and space between
person and person are abolished, leaving this extraordinary feeling of
propinquity. It comes to one as a sudden illumination and produces this
feeling of relatedness, or of belonging to the same closely knit family.

Then when I had the good luck to get to know Tom Eliot and his
second wife, Valerie, and we became friends, I found a very affectionate
man behind that rather aloof New England exterior of his, a warm-
hearted and loving man. And a man of immense principles, too much for
his own good, almost; he had the Quaker, the puritan New England
sense of principle. So much so that he was in love with his wife for five
years, but because he was older he thought it was wrong of him and he
would not say a word to her about it. It was only when they were staying
together with some very old friends in the South of France that his
hostess realized, 'This girl is in love with Tom!', and she took him aside
and said, 'You've kept this girl waiting long enough! You must speak to
her!'

It is an illuminating story which tells one a great deal about the quality
of both Valerie and Tom Eliot.

*Your description of him, full of warmth and humanity, is in contrast to what
is written by certain critics about T. S. Eliot more or less abandoning his first
wife, isn't it?*

But he did not. He suffered very, very much with and for his first wife.
I knew her slightly and it was quite clear that she was alienated and
abnormal. And he suffered and endured it for years, and he just could
not do anything about it. It haunted him for the rest of his life. It would
haunt anybody, no matter how people comfort you and say, 'You did all
you could', one would think, 'I failed, I could have done better ...' I
know that he was haunted by that, and it comes out.

Through his poetry?

Through his plays particularly. It comes out in *The Family Reunion*
where the feminine spirit is lost at sea. That is what happens when

people lose their reason – it is a symbolic way of saying it – they drown. The conscious element, which is sanity, is drowned in the flood of the unconscious. One guessed that Eliot in his formative life was not emotionally cared for. It was as if he had been emotionally deprived and had been nourished on too much principle and not enough straightforward, uncomplicated, demonstrative animal affection. I have never read a biography about him because he did not want anybody to write his biography for fifty years after his death, so I think one should respect that, and wait, and not become an accessory after the fact. I think it is singularly unworthy to brush aside the wishes of the dead, who are without defences, and tell their story before it can be honestly told. Voltaire said something to the effect that one owed the living all possible compassion, but the dead nothing but the truth, and to write another's life before the whole truth can be told seems to me an indecent sort of peephole curiosity.

You saw him just before he died, didn't you?

Yes, a few days before he died. My wife Ingaret and I were talking to Tom and Valerie at our house in Cadogan Street a few days before they were due to sail for the Caribbean – his lungs were in such a state he could not take the English winter. Valerie and Ingaret were sitting apart on the sofa and Valerie was telling of the 'wasted' five years before she and Tom had married. He and I were talking about Dante, and what it had meant to us and to civilization that there had been a person like Dante. I think that even Shakespeare did not touch him in the way that Dante did. I think that Tom was so much a classical person that, in a sense, Shakespeare was perhaps too much of a romantic for him. His early essay on *Hamlet*, for instance, is singularly unilluminated and uncomprehending. He does not grasp what *Hamlet* is about really. But Dante, oh God, there he was at home and all of himself belonged and had fire and recognition.

Then the next day we were hit by the most extraordinary bad weather, and he caught a cold and had to go to hospital, and he never left it again. It was not long before Christmas – I have still kept the Christmas card he sent us from the hospital. And the handwriting is so clear and firm, there was no tremor, no hesitation, no indication of death in it; perhaps there was no death in his spirit, no end. What was significant was that Valerie, after so many years, chose this night to tell Ingaret something of her story, which ended with the cry, 'Oh! What a waste!', as though something in her perhaps knew the end was near.

———

Could we now talk about two of your first and oldest friends, William Plomer and the poet Roy Campbell? In a Tokyo bookstore I came upon an interesting little book which was a homage to Campbell by his friends from all over the world. It was published both in English and French.* And there were a lot of nice stories about Campbell being a super kind of friend, a kind of genius, with his great love of corridas, his flamboyant manner, his conviviality, and so on. In this book Campbell tells the story of how, with his little daughter of two and his wife in Spain, when everything was under fire in the Civil War, he saved a manuscript entrusted to him by the Carmelites, a manuscript of St John of the Cross. He managed to get through the lines with his family – through the raping and the burning and the killing on sight – and he made a vow that if he and his family escaped death he would translate this manuscript of St John of the Cross. And this is what happened – they were saved by a British destroyer, and he did his translation. Whatever his political ideas, he seemed to be a man of his word and a true poet with a true talent.

Yes, I met Roy when he had just made his reputation with an epic poem called 'The Flaming Terrapin'. He was born in Natal. After his schooling in Durban he was sent overseas to Oxford. I have never followed the details of Roy's life very closely, but I seem to remember that he could not stomach Oxford. He left and went away to the Mediterranean and worked in sailing ships – he told me lots of stories about sailing ships which may or may not be true. He had a tremendous imagination and was so driven by it that for him the imagined reality was greater than the non-imagined reality. That Mediterranean period became his mythological incubation, of which I remember only mysterious, impressionistic snatches, fragments as if painted by Turner, with sea-shanty music drifting on the phosphorescent air wherein these sea-shapes, sunsets, moon-rises, ships and weird encounters

---

* *Hommage à Roy Campbell*, Société Cévenole du Mercou, 'La Licorne', 1958.

appeared, and in particular a fragment of a collision with a four-master, coming with all sails set out of the swirl of moon mist, glancing Roy's ship and without a tremor disappearing into the fog and steam to the singing of, 'Oh Shenandoah, I hear you calling . . .' And of all that, only the 'I hear you calling . . .' one felt was real, was the rock in it all, for I am certain the calling was real and with him always and at the end.

I liked Roy's father very much. The Campbells were a Scottish family who had gone out to the Caribbean and learned how to grow sugar there, and had brought sugar to Zululand and Natal, making another fortune out of that. But Roy's father, Dr Sam, was different, and not the least interested in money. Instead of following the family fortune he went to Edinburgh, took a good medical degree and returned as a very good doctor. But Roy did not get on with his father at all. His father, I think, symbolized what Roy's spirit was at war with: the respectable, wealthy, bourgeois, colonial establishment of Natal and duty to the community and so on. Roy was born an individual, and that was not his idea of life. From the beginning he was in rebellion, particularly in rebellion against a community where there was really no art or appreciation of art at all. It was entirely a place for money-making, and he could not stand that. He was a born poet, a poet and nothing but a poet. Even at school he was writing poetry of extraordinary quality: for instance, his outstanding 'The Theology of Bongwi, the Baboon', which contains the lines

> ' 'Tis God who made me in His shape
> He is a great baboon'

Even as a fantasy, that was an outrageous thing to write at that time.

I think his voyage to England, alone at sea, was a decisive time. For the first time he was really alone and allowed to experience himself and respond to whatever came his way without anybody else present to determine how he should react. For the first time life could happen naturally to him and he could respond as his own volcanic nature disposed and, not surprisingly on such a great sea of history, the symbolism natural to him erupted in him and it says much for the poet in him, untried as yet, that he could shape and catch it all in 'The Flaming Terrapin'. Ostensibly it is about the sea, but what flows out like one stream of lava after the other, is Roy's Africanness. Africa – in spite of his Anglo-Saxon upbringing, in spite of his English schooling, in spite of his English breeding – bursts out of his imagination. It is really the first great African poem ever. It is a tremendous achievement in that sense, as well as in its own right. The images of zebras, buffalo, flamingo, the country and the savannahs, are magnetic and reborn, although the shape is classical and traditional. It is a tremendous, wild poem, and it completely caught the imagination of Britain. The poem was a bestseller – in itself a rare event – and Roy became a hero, even in South Africa.

Not long after, he came back to Port Natal with his wife Mary and little girl called Tessa. I think you should let me tell you the story of Roy and Mary because it has so much of the texture of dream and myth naturally woven into his life. Mary's sister, Kathy Garman, who ultimately married Epstein, the sculptor, told me that she and Mary were walking from Fitzroy Square in London to the Fitzroy Arms, which was very much a poets' and artists' pub in those days. They saw on the opposite side of the street a very tall young man, with a black cape thrown over broad shoulders and a wide black hat. The man looked sharply across the street, looked not at her but at her sister Mary. And Mary, as if electrified, looked instantly at the man. And Kathy remarked, with a voice still full of wonder, it was almost as if there had been an earthquake, and she knew something had happened between those two which was irrevocable, and that for neither of them would life ever be the same again. And even she herself, she told me, felt quite shaken by the speed and the violence of the mutual recognition. Somehow they walked on, but later that day they went back to their flat in Fitzroy Square. They had not been there long when there was a knock at the door. They opened it and a young man, who was a friend of theirs, said, 'I want you to meet my friend, Roy Campbell.' And from that moment he and Mary were joined. For Roy, I am certain, there was never another woman.

He reappeared in Durban society for a while with his beautiful Mary, until they went and lived on the coast, where a great friend of theirs and mine, Natalie Campbell, lent them a little cottage, Peace Cottage, right in the jungle by the sea. I first met him there and thought, 'What a marvellous, arresting face!' You should see the portrait painted by Augustus John of Roy. He had rather long, rather wide, antelope eyes that were blue-grey. He was still very thin, and one saw the fine bone in his face. He had rather an elongated face, very fine, sensitive features and a lovely high forehead, and was very tall, very slim but wide-shouldered. And he talked – and how he talked – he was a good talker, animated and driven with a tremendous sort of nervous energy.

But he very soon antagonized most people. He had a thing about Natal – they had all tried to make him something that he did not want to be. 'How do you earn any money just being a poet' – that sort of thing. Then there came this question of *Voorslag*. I had met William Plomer also, and William now joined up with Campbell in editing a magazine, *Voorslag*. I was asked to come down and see Roy and Mary again at the cottage, with William. We arrived late at night and soon Mary and William left Roy and myself to talk right through the night. And I realized we had really clicked, as we said at school. Then the next day, when I had to go back to work, Roy said to me, 'You must join us, you are one of us.' Now, that sounds a small phrase. But that 'one of us' is one of the most precious things that has ever been given to me, because it was the first time anybody had recognized the writer in me. It is a debt I can never repay Roy. I cannot tell you how I needed that act of confirmation, to get recognition from a poet, established as he was. It was just the thing I needed most of all in life.

And so then I joined with him on *Voorslag*.

Voorslag was perhaps the first serious literary and cultural magazine founded in South Africa. It was founded in 1926 by Roy, who persuaded William Plomer to join in with him, and it was after the first issue that he invited me as well, to be its Afrikaans Editor, with the idea of turning *Voorslag* into a bilingual magazine. The spirit in which it was founded and the intention is implicit in the name *Voorslag*. It is very evocative in South African folk mythology because literally it means the 'lash of the whip', and particularly the long, fine, searing lash tied to the end of the whips used by the pioneers to drive their huge spans of oxen and heavy covered wagons deeper into the interior. Its appearance from the start caused a sensation all over South Africa, largely because of Campbell's and Plomer's original, inspired and provocative contributions. Although we all three resigned after the publication of the third issue, it had altered the literary and political climate, not least of all because of its uncompromising attitude to all forms of racial and colour discrimination. In fact its impact has been acknowledged just recently by the University of Natal which has produced a book incorporating facsimile editions of those first three magazines as well as an account of the three founders.

It was after this period on *Voorslag* that I met Captain Mori and made my voyage to Japan with William.* And then, when I got back from Japan, Roy had gone to England and I joined up with him there and spent about three months with him in the loneliest period of his life. Mary asked me, 'Could you possibly come and keep Roy company? I have a sister who is very ill and my family needs me.' It was one of the coldest winters that I can remember; Roy was in rags, hardly eating and drinking too much. The house was cold, and all day he would sit in his unmade bed, a blanket round him, trying to write or read or talk endlessly while drinking a mixture of cider and gin. He hardly slept, and the moment he awoke he would be trying to write again. I got to know the rejected side of Roy very deeply and he was at times black with his dark night of the soul. How he endured I do not know.

I did not know at the time what precisely happened to Mary and could not tell, therefore, that a great deal of Roy's anguish was due to the fact that for the first time he was suspicious of Mary's absence. As it turned out, he had every reason to be. Mary had gone off with their hostess, Vita Sackville-West – or Nicolson – and had a lesbian affair with her. It did not last long. In fact Vita's own measure of what her relationship with Mary amounted to, in the sum of the many other relationships of a similar kind she had in her life, is made clear in her book published by her son. There Mary hardly merits a single sentence to herself. But Mary was the whole of Roy's life. I do not think that from the moment he first saw Mary until the end of his tragic days did she mean less than everything to him. When he forced the truth out of Mary on her return he was so angry that he struck her and loosened one of her teeth and then immediately, full of remorse and turmoil, took her off to live in the South of France, at Martigues.

One of the first things he did in France was to write his satire, *The Georgiad*, in which he has a scathing attack on the Nicolsons.

*Described in *Yet Being Someone Other*

Everyone in Bloomsbury said words to the effect of, 'How uncivilized!' 'How ungrateful to the Nicolsons, after all they did lend him a home!', and in fact no one in that world seemed to see that there was any civilized reason why they should ever not have anything in the way of sex if they wanted it, and explains perhaps a little how they created an atmosphere of life in which I felt I had no part myself.

I hardly saw Roy at all after that. I got a cable from Desmond Young, who had just been appointed Day Editor of the *Cape Times*: 'Come help me fight racial prejudice.' I went out to see what we could do, and it was at the end of this period that the 'White Justice' episode occurred. Meanwhile, one of the first things I did was to get him to publish once a week a poem of Roy's, which meant a steady income for Roy. I think it was £6 a poem, which was a lot of money in those days. And I got Plomer to write a column from London for which he too got £6 a week.

I did hear one more story about Roy. He fancied himself as a bullfighter – Martigues was not far from the Spanish border. Roy had gone out into the amphitheatre to tease the bull, and being slightly drunk he fell, dangerously. A gasp went up from the amphitheatre as the bull came charging down on Roy. But at the last moment the bull came to a stop with a snort and with dust kicking up from its heels, while it shook its head at this man lying beneath him. And then suddenly the bull lowered his head and gently licked Roy's face. Roy stood up slowly and walked away with the tears streaming down his face, and never entered the ring again.

That's very moving.

Yes, because Roy was not a killer. There was this great and tender capacity for love in him, so great that I suspect he was always afraid it would unman him, and it made him pose a character he did not possess.

You know, there is a period in the lives of all artists, particularly poets, when just to be their poetical, lyrical self is enough. It gives them everything they want. But then there comes the mature moment when they have got to put their art and themselves at the service of something in life that is greater than art. And how do you do that? That is the great challenge. And Roy could not do it. All the years of drinking and wandering and posturing was Roy evading this challenge. But he could do it vicariously. People who cannot do it by themselves can do it by proxy. Roy did it by translating *St John of the Cross*. He found a vehicle which took him into a dimension he could not attain for himself, and the translation is precisely so great because it was Roy himself who was translated in translating the poem.

I would like to go back for a final image of Roy Campbell to the time when you went to visit him at the cottage at Sezela in southern Zululand and he was taking care of his baby girl.

Well, that was little Anna's night, the night I have never forgotten. I used to take a very late train on a Saturday night which stopped about ten miles away from the cottage, and I had to walk the rest of the way along the railway line, through the jungle, which was still quite wild in those days. I got there at about two o'clock in the morning. William and Mary had already gone to sleep but Roy was sitting with Anna, who was the new baby. He was tender and concerned and tense. She had been crying all the time – I think perhaps her teeth were hurting or something – and Roy was looking very thin, with very dark shadows under his eyes. And he said to me, 'You know, I have been sitting here all the time waiting for you.' I knew then how he wanted to get out and away. So we quickly had great mugs of tea. He had a great swig of brandy as well and said, 'Let's go out.' We went and walked from the house down to the beach. There is always a heavy swell in the Indian Ocean, and this swell was coming out of the dark, rising up in the moonlight to a vast phosphorescent crest before crashing down on the beach and rolling up almost to our feet. The sands were wet and full of stars and we trod Orion and the belted constellation under our feet.

Roy said, 'I have just finished "Tristan da Cunha".' I knew he had been working on it and said, 'Oh, how marvellous!' He asked if I would like to hear it and I said, 'I'd love it.' And then there were the waves crashing, the moon shining and the baby had gone to sleep. We walked along the beach and I listened to Roy, who had a beautiful voice, reciting it – more to the night and the sea than me – from the beginning: 'Snore in the foam; the night is vast and blind . . .' to where he says goodbye to the island: 'Slip the long cables of the failing light', and then to the last verse:

'We shall not meet again; over the wave
Our ways divide, and yours is straight and endless,
But mine is short and crooked to the grave . . .'

And that is the end of perhaps his most personal poem, a poem which was to mean a great deal to T. S. Eliot as well. Suddenly the island, as it is for Odysseus in the *Odyssey*, is a symbol of the self. This storm-battered, rocky island is Roy's self.

It was an extraordinary night, which I remember not without pain because it is still with me and real, and yet it is gone. It seemed to me that in the reciting the whole of the universe took part, because the stars were not only up there, they were at our feet, dancing on the earth as they did in the sky.

I think we should leave him there, on that beach by the sea.

Yes. That is an image of Roy that always walks with me, of the eternal poet and that poem. And with it the feminine, caring for the little feminine self in his arms.

———

Your relationship with William Plomer was a much more complex one.

Yes, well, Plomer is a much more difficult person to describe. For one thing, I know consciously so many more facts about William's life. I was in continuous contact with him. I had known him directly over a much longer period than Roy. That alone makes it difficult, when you know so much about yourself or about someone else. But he was a totally, totally different character. I always drew a distinction between William and Roy. I said William tended to be Apollonian, Roy Dionysian. William tended to be more the classical, containing type, Roy much more of the romantic. And so there was a great divide between them. And what was interesting was seeing two such opposite characters coming together, at a brief moment – and, out of their oppositeness, as it were, being of immense value to one another. A sort of cross-pollination of the imagination between them took place, and made them both write some of their best work at that period. Roy wrote 'Tristan da Cunha', 'A Zulu Girl', and 'The Serf', amongst various other poems, beautiful poems, during that period. Roy also became much more aware at that brief moment, which comes up in 'The Zulu Girl', of his Africanness. His feminine Africanness. The Africa in himself. And the Africa round about him. I do not think he had given much thought to it beforehand.

And William was very conscious of this. William came to Roy very much as I did, through 'The Flaming Terrapin'. Roy came to William through *Turbott Wolfe*. He had just written *Turbott Wolfe*, which had created as great a sensation, a greater sensation even, but a less favourable one in Africa, than 'The Flaming Terrapin' had done. And when I met William I had actually known his family before. I knew his young brother and mother slightly. I knew William's father later as well. But William's mother was most important to him. She was born in England, was very English, and, like many English people who came to Africa, had become even more English, because in that context their Englishness seemed under threat. And in the way she spoke, the way she dressed, she behaved as if she also had to be an ambassador of England under attack, as it were. And the fact that I met his mother first is rather significant, because in a sense, in William, one met the mother first. She was the great, the really great influence on his life. He was very much his mother's son. He did not like his father. Roy also had this thing about his father. But William had it in a more intense form. He could not get on with his father, although to their credit they never ceased trying. William did his duty by his father to the end of his days. And I often felt very sad about it because they were so trapped in something: William not free to like his father because his mother at heart was against her husband.

The father also had come out to Africa from England. He had fallen in love with Africa. And I think William's mother had married William's father rather romantically. She did not really know him before, but she was of a great period of the Empire and all that, and met this young man serving the Empire, in the Cape Mounted Rifles. She married him there and then, and then discovered that they really hadn't very much in common. He adored Africa and she loathed it from the start. She really hated it. She did not like anybody in Africa much that I could make out. She was a very soft, sensitive, highly intelligent, perceptive but withdrawn sort of person. William valued greatly his family's aristocratic connections. But his mother was upper middle class in the best sense of the words, and had a kind of withdrawnness about her which was increased in him. Since she did not like Africa, did not really love her husband, and did not like the way of life imposed on her, she was deeply frustrated and rather cynical for a woman; and yet had the courage and the spirit to endure it all with great dignity and without loss of her sense of humour. Her children certainly helped. She had a very nice younger son in Peter Plomer, who calls himself James now, and subsequently became an Admiral in the Canadian navy; a very remarkable person in his own right. And first of all, of course, William who was born in the Northern Transvaal at a place called Louis Trichardt. He spent the first three years of his life there – and in my reckoning three years of one's life is quite a long time: long enough to make a very, very deep impression. And something of the impression that Louis Trichardt made on William comes out in a poem he wrote called 'Wild Doves at Louis Trichardt'.

Wherever you go in Africa you hear the turtle-doves, from the Cape to Abyssinia, and from the desert to deep in the bush. People do not associate it with that continent, but it's one of the abiding sounds of Africa. From the Cape to those Red Sea hills, wherever I have walked, always, night and day, there is the sound of those turtle-doves calling, forever calling, hunting the noon as they startle the nightlight. God knows what they are calling but they are calling, as if to proclaim that everything is a-calling in Africa . . . you know it as well as I do. The sound went deep into William, and their power of recall as expressed in this poem suggests that Africa went deeper than William allowed himself to know.

When fairly young, the Plomers went back to England, and for a short while William was at school at Rugby. Short as the time was, Rugby had a very great influence on him, and became the only school that William talked about later – I think because of its importance to this Englishness of his. He always maintained that he was not African – that he was English. His standard joke was, 'If kittens are born in an oven, they're not necessarily biscuits.' I felt that I was in a sense the keeper of William's Africanness. As long as I believed in it, I hoped he would recover it one day. But although there were from time to time signs in his writing that this volcanic underworld of Africa might erupt again, he denied it a permanent expression by a sustained and deliberate act of conscious choice and the most sustained determination. How great the denial was is clear from his autobiographies. Various people he had known in Africa after Rugby, who were at school with him in Johannesburg, or had influence on him, like Enslin du Plessis and Teddy Wolfe the painter, are hardly mentioned. The people he mentions are people who cut a figure in the world, people who are considered important in the Establishment of the day; but not the people who really influenced him.

I cannot conceive, for instance, if I had to write my life, how I could avoid beginning with scores of unknown African and other anonymous, so-called unimportant people whom I love, whom I miss every day of my life, and animals – dogs and so on, who had a tremendous influence on my life. But they do not appear in those pages. And then, as if he needed an antidote to his African self, he took an enormous interest in his ancestors. And another significant thing, William told me that at the age of about seven or eight he realized he had a gift for drawing and painting as well as writing. And he felt he could not do both, which I thought was very interesting. He had to choose, and there and then decided what he was going to do. 'I'll stop the painting – I'll just be a writer.'

Why this self-mutilation? A tree is a tree and should grow branches in all directions!

Absolutely, yes. But this is what he consciously did. That is the key to his success in this almost superhuman suppression of his African self. William was an inspired creation of himself, a conscious creation of himself. And the damage he did to his instinctive self I suspect was great. All in all, he had hellishly complicated and paradoxical raw material to work on. And yet he was contained, ultimately, through enormous belief, this almost religious trust in his Englishness, in his family. He loved writing and literature. He made his choice, he had the gift, and there was no doubt he was going his chosen way. So that prevented chaos from ever overwhelming him in the way that old Roy was overwhelmed from time to time. Roy was again and again going into chaos, and coming out of it, hanging on by his nails to a minimum of order. But William never wavered seriously and carried steadily on. It shows in his handwriting, a young, rather vulnerable, painstaking sort of handwriting, regular enough but curiously poignant. If you compared William's handwriting to Roy's, William's handwriting – which I knew from the time William was twenty to the time when he died – never changed. It was beautifully regular. A lovely handwriting. He wrote *Turbott Wolfe*, for instance, in pencil on coarse trading-store notebooks, sent it off like that to The Hogarth Press, and they sent it on just like that to the printers. Roy's, on the other hand, got bigger as he got older, as all our handwritings do.

I always thought that the character of *Turbott Wolfe* was much influenced by William's friend Teddy Wolfe, the painter. Yet at the moment when William was coming of age and his Englishness was apparently entrenched, though he was physically still in Africa, there came this strange period of *Turbott Wolfe*, and 'Ula Masondo'. There came this eruption, this violent underground upheaval against the consciously imposed pattern. Perhaps I should begin with the title and with the character called 'Wolfe' in it. Mind you, I never discussed this with William: I felt keenly that it was something done and not to be raised in that fashion or any except that of an objective reality. Teddy Wolfe, who had been to England, had a distinct gift as a painter and was highly regarded by the intelligentsia of the earlier Twenties. For instance, he was a friend of Arnold Bennett. He had been to Morocco, which was the fashionable thing to do, and he rented a flat in Fez, where he painted a lot. And then he returned for a while to his home and brought a tremendous new breath of culture into Johannesburg, where William was still at school. And he also painted black people as if he found them beautiful in their own right. One of the loveliest paintings Teddy Wolfe ever painted was the back of a black miner. I do not know what has happened to that now but it was, I think, one of the most significant painted in South Africa, and certainly in William's life, making him aware of something that was already waking up in him too. It, too, is not mentioned in William's autobiography. But having known both Teddy Wolfe and William, I have no doubt that the William who had longed to be a painter, was set aglow by Teddy's uninhibited artist's approach to black subjects, and this was too much. He could not overlook this Africa any longer while he was in Africa, the conscious pattern was not yet set enough. It broke in *Turbott Wolfe*, with an explosion that was colossal. Structurally it may not be a great work but it's just this red-hot lava, hot from a volcano that has overslept. It is a pure force of history breaking out in one solitary sensitive soul, and the writing, the vividness of it, the fire of it, even if William does not know what he is saying, and what it is about, is tremendous. And then there is this scorn that he has for colonial life, the people that he picks, the merciless light in which he shows white colonials and the anger they arouse, as against his beautiful descriptions of the black people; and above all, that black girl. And they stand still on fire in one's memory. And that sad end, when Turbott Wolfe, the aesthete for whom Africa is too much, is deported from Africa, and he is on the train and leaving Africa for ever. I think that is something prophetic, an aspect of William which is prophetic and foretells his own future. He could not reconcile this Africa thing, which startled him and exploded in him, with his Englishness.

He would have to change into something which he was determined not to be. What, he did not know; but he had neither the heart nor courage for it and took cover in his Englishness. It was his fortress and keep, and a valid choice for him if not for his art. He wrote one of his greatest things, which is a short story called 'Ula Masondo', about a Zulu boy – a miner who's buried in a fall of earth in a gold mine.

To me, there's a profound symbolism in this; because a half of William was buried deep down, entombed. And the earth is feminine. The natural man is buried deep in this archaic mother earth, as William was buried, in a sense, in his own maternal earth. And buried thus, Ula Masondo has a dream. As the description of the dream gets nearer and nearer the crisis deep down in the earth, William's prose becomes much more tense, much more like poetry, until suddenly it switches over and becomes poetry of a supreme tense lyricism. Only William had the capacity in his day to write a story which naturally becomes a poem. And right through the crisis this beautiful poem, this long poem, is sustained until the crisis passes, and then again becomes inspired prose before it dissolves to its tragic end, when the rescued miner returns and does not recognize his own mother. The symbolic meaning is obvious. The point is, how could he not acknowledge now the element which so entrenched him? It is a marvellous story. And that was written at that period when he knew Roy and worked with 'The Zulu Girl'. He also wrote some short pieces he kept in a diary called 'Portraits in the Nude', which have lovely moments but are coals of a dying fire. And then came Japan. And the fact that he went to Japan, left Africa as Turbott Wolfe did, was echoed as the goodbye to Africa in the novel. I think Japan was a bridge that was a stage back to his civilized conscious concept of himself and his role, and the dismissal of all this primitive stuff. He wrote about Africa afterwards again, but from a great, imaginatively safe distance in his short-story collection, *The Child of Queen Victoria*. There too are those lovely perceptive things, but the fire is gone. It is almost like an older man remembering.

Did Japan count for him so much?

Oh, Japan counted for a lot, as you can measure by *Sado*, his major book about Japan and his account of his first relationship with a foreign country. But William was always in command of himself, knew exactly how and when to end this relationship, to leave Japan when his Englishness was threatened and in case Japan conquered him. So he chose in good time to go back to England; again, a perfectly valid choice as William's always were, rationally. But was it the only alternative? What of this other Louis Trichardt self, forever listening to the calling of those doves? What did it think of the choice? Did it wish for all these good and excellent reasons for its rejection in hell again?

I said earlier how I felt, in a strange way, that I was a keeper of William's Africanness. We had met in Africa, we were both of Africa. We felt very strongly, both of us, about creating a non-racial world in Africa. The great influences in my life as a child had been the black and coloured people of the country. And I loved them very much, as I loved other people, freely, not in an abstract manner but individually, free of colour prejudice. So I felt very much joined with him, and recognized the power of this Africanness in him and me. And then, I had had this experience of going to Japan with him. In fact I took him to Japan. And after I left I wondered, and was anxious for him. We did not have much correspondence: we only exchanged a few letters and I was on the move all the time. So, when he suddenly turned up in London, he had done the journey by way of the Trans-Siberian railway, overland, because he was a bad sailor. I could not imagine him facing a voyage like that, or for that matter any voyage, again.

I arrived home at my flat one night to find a great friend of mine, the

Frenchman René Janin to whom I dedicated my first book,* waiting at the door. He said, 'I've got a great surprise for you, Laurens!' And I don't know how, or remember why René knew first. I must have told William about René in some of my letters. Anyway, I went upstairs and there was William hiding behind the door, and it was an evening of more joyful meeting than I could have imagined. Part of me was inclined to feel anxiously that he was already a slightly different William from the one I had known. He had put on weight, yet he was very alive and he was obviously overjoyed to be back in England and we had a very happy meeting. And although we had the past in Africa we shared and nothing could take it away, I was aware that something new had moved into position, which I thought was Japan, of course. But it was not really Japan in any profound sense. William had a much more, what you might call, balanced view of Japan. In a sense, Japan for me, from the word go, was an affair of the heart. But for William it was much more an affair of the intellect. I do not know how deeply his emotions were joined in the experience.

He revised his autobiography, the first section of which was called 'Double Lives', some three times. And I find by deed and omission odd things about it. For instance, I have already mentioned the omission of persons whom I thought had been important to him. And a personal example. Why did it take him three revisions of the book to mention that he owed the voyage to Japan to me? The question puzzled me almost as much as the discovery after his death that he had written on *Voorslag* for the *London Magazine* without mentioning my role in it. But the main point here is that with each revision he is less and less angular and more rounded about Japan. The meeting with Teruha at the Geisha party† got a very dismissive description in the first version where he speaks of the Geisha 'with their red lips and their red little tongues darting out like serpents' fangs'. Then also, he had a poem about Mori, which is very, very stringent. He amended the poem later on in several other versions. You have to go back to very early versions of 'Captain Maru' to see what he wrote about him, and I just hope that Mori never sees it; because Mori adored William – it would have hurt him very much, and also I am

* *In a Province* (1934).
† Cf. *Yet Being Someone Other.*

not certain Plomer meant it quite like that. He wrote it at the time of the Japanese invasion of Manchuria and all that, and made Mori the peg for a generalized reaction to a new chauvinist Japan.

Even as a poet? As a lover of the moon and insects? Surely there was food in Japan for that part of him as well?

Yes, of course. The poet and the lover of nature in him never lost contact, and then above all he adored his Japanese students. When he met them on a specific level there was no barrier at all. As a nation, as a whole, he tended to think of them a little bit in the conventional collectivized way. His own Englishness implied a certain collectivization of himself and impelled him sometimes into collective judgements. I am simplifying it. But he was very sensitive and very perceptive and Japan could not fail to give him a great deal. But generally not on the deepest level. With me it became a very deep part of my life, but if you refer to *Sado* you will realize that when he decides to leave Japan he will leave it for ever. There was, in fact, never any looking back. And it is very moving, in a way, his goodbye to Japan, because one knows that he will never return.

He didn't go back with Benjamin Britten for the adaptation of the Noh play Sumidagawa *from which he made* Curlew River?

No, I often asked him to come back with me, but he never wanted to go back again. This was William. He never went back to Africa either, except once, which was a non-event. I'll tell you about that. But, as you can see in *Paper Houses*, the country visually made an enormous impression upon William, Japanese visual arts made an impression upon him, and certain aspects of Japanese culture like Noh moved him deeply. All these things were great original experiences, but none was deep enough to become a commitment.

He was more of a spectator – a sympathetic spectator.

Yes, he was provisional. Wholly so; it was a stage, after all. Although, for instance, he saw Mori's qualities and respected him greatly, there was just a side of himself that would not go beyond Mori and his immediate friends. So, I should have seen at once what this immense excitement about getting back to England really meant: that it really overlaid the Japanese interlude. He was as excited as a young boy to be in England.

198

And so we went about a great deal to see the England he loved. I was doing freelancing, and writing in London on my own, so I had my own time. We had a lot of time to go to places together. And he went first of all to look up churches with which his family had been associated, and various places connected with his family story. I should have recognized the decisive significance of it all, for he was doing a 'return to the ancestors'. It had a very deep metaphoric meaning for him. I knew that, of course, on one level, but I really did not realize it was far more important than anything that had happened in Africa – this coming back. Also he immediately started writing poetry again, and the first was a long poem called 'The Family Tree'. The title really says all that I have tried to say. The poem ends with these lines:

> 'The old camellia drops a red rosette
> Down on the clean-swept path again to-day –
> What is the meaning of the word "regret"
> When so much grace accompanies decay?'

I naturally hastened to introduce William to my friends in London. He had immediately taken a great liking to René Janin, which made me very happy, and moved in among my circle of friends as if he had always been there. But soon after, I got this fateful cable from Desmond Young, when I felt I had to go back to South Africa to help but did so most reluctantly. And from that time on, William and I corresponded regularly. I think I must have thousands of letters from him somewhere. We always wrote to each other from then on. That period in Africa was one of the hardest of my life. I knew at once that I did not want to do newspaper work as a career, that I wanted to go on writing, and finish a long historical novel I had begun. But on the other hand I had a feeling of obligation towards Desmond Young who was a friend and a chivalrous spirit after my own heart. At the drop of a hat he helped me to make it possible for William to go to Japan with me by appointing him special correspondent.

For a special feature on Japan?

Yes. And then also I felt very deeply about the way things were going in South Africa. In the ruling government they were already talking about segregation, which is the English word for apartheid. They were beginning to pass industrial anti-black legislation. The old humanistic traditions of the Cape were being abolished. And they were starting on an evil road, which I still hope may be near its enigmatic end. I have never in my life worked so hard. I felt the least I could do was to stay a year – because Desmond had incurred great expense to bring me out to the Cape. I stayed eighteen months in the end, and then I was physically and spiritually – in spite of great physical strength – utterly exhausted. Those eighteen months were so painful that I myself did not realize how painful it all was in my life and the life of my country. It took me ten years before I could talk to anybody else about it.

It was like a disease?

It was just the hurt of it and the pain of it, and the misery of it, you know. And the work – I was exhausted by the sheer weight and urgency of the work. I came back as soon as I decently could. And of course had a wonderful meeting with René Janin, and William, who was then entrenched with my friends, and who came with two others to meet my ship at Tilbury. Also Tony Butts had joined them and was a great source of interest and fun, and made a unique, selfless, original though eccentric contribution to the atmosphere of our little world. And William on his own began to draw all sorts of celebrities to him, like Walpole, who became a great friend of his and was very helpful to him. One of William's many qualities was a great capacity for friends. He was the best possible company that you could have, and in a way was at his best in company. He was very witty. He was original. He had all his own sorts of perceptions, an eye for the bizarre and the oddities in life. If you went for a walk in the country with William it was always something special. He was tremendously interested in life itself and no mean botanist. And this visual quality of his made him an inspired observer. And to me what was interesting too, he began to do a lot of drawing, and one thought: 'Ah! That choice between writing and painting! Was it so final?' And there something showed, which I think is English: when they have a gift it makes them uncomfortable, or – to use their favourite word – embarrasses, that archetypal English understatement.

They feel embarrassed because of their social obligations or their image?

No, it embarrasses the rest of the English personality, it is an inner thing. They laugh it off. They make a joke out of it. They pretend not to take it seriously. To be accused of taking oneself seriously would be the end. So William made a joke of it. For instance, he drew the most savage caricatures of the Queen – the image of the highest feminine value – consciously and deliberately, or just doodled them, which was even more interesting, and I suspected it showed how much he resented his archaic tie to the feminine – his bondage to his mother. He had to mock it, as if he could only keep it in its place by pretending it did not matter. And William made a joke out of his urge to draw and used it rather satirically or just to be funny – drew really only funny things. It struck me forcibly at the time there was more to it than met the eye: it had a sort of symbolic significance.

But what about his Englishness? He was rejecting through the Queen also part of his Englishness?

Of course, he rejected it, not literally but as a reflection of something in his own nature. It was a form of projection you know. This is what happens with the Royal symbol all the time. People project onto it. They project their hatreds or their loves or their aspirations – whether negative or positive, happily for the British mostly positively. And obviously there was a negative streak in William's relationship with the feminine. You see, in a sense, he was not emotionally grown up, and the child in him had to mock people of the law: people such as judges, lord chancellors. People who resent authority also love to make fun of policemen and see them slipping on banana skins. And so his was that sort of thing. And I wondered, where does this savage thing come from? Because the royal caricatures were violent and brutal at times. I think William was moving in a world where practically all his friends, all my friends, were communists, fellow-travellers, or left-wing, far, far left – so archbishops, popes, priests, captains and kings were automatic targets for attack. William was for the moment in two worlds, and his imagination reeling under the shock of unemployment and a world in recession. Intellectually, consciously, in so far as he had a political attitude, it inclined way out to the left. He was not a communist but he was near and among them. People still had this naïve trust in Russia as a genuine exercise in Utopia, and it was a problem for me because almost all my friends were even more that way than William. René was a notable exception because as a boy with his father, the General, and Military

Attaché in Petrograd, he saw something of the Revolution, even saw his young friends shot. But to return to William, here, I think, certain external factors played a part. This extra emphasis came from the intellectual climate in which we lived.

Do you suppose they would have been conservative if the régime were liberal or leftist?

After the war there could have been no greater admirer of royalty than William. He wrote poems about Queen Mary, very good poems. That was quite genuine, but was out of the genuine instinctive English William. By then he also had friends among the royal family.

But he had to experience the war first . . .

That is true and profound. Something happened to him, all of us, in the war. William through the war experienced his own Englishness on a non-intellectual level, in a deep, natural, instinctive dimension. The war went deep down, we were so near the end of ourselves in that war. And I think it put him in touch perhaps with a totally unknown aspect of himself. I think what happened to William in the war happened to millions of people, and explains what has always been to me such a very strange phenomenon: I believe that the human spirit at times really needed wars. And that is why it has had so many of them. It needed the war, because it was the only way in which life could put people right with themselves. I have always thought of war and disaster as terrible healers who are called in by life to put right something which is wrong and could not be put right any other way. And I think this last war in which we fought, which was really on such a desperate scale, was the nearest to a completely black and white war that there has ever been. It really was a war which was not only inwardly but externally about good and evil; because really, a tremendous evil was threatening the Western spirit. And confronted, as it were, with this horror drama, this *grand guignol* of the human spirit, William and I, like everyone else, were really vitally touched and profoundly changed. And I think therefore that the highest symbol of human values, the symbol of royalty – and, in this case the very important Queen – reflected this profound change in himself.

I would like to say much more about the war. But I think this says it all symbolically. Although it is a story of an individual, in the case of William, it is also the story of a civilization. And so much of the last war was a lethal threat to the feminine values of life in danger of being eliminated by a purely archaic masculine eruption that was totally out of control in Western Europe. All the feelings, all the caring, the loving values of life suddenly were under attack – under the totalitarian and Nazi phenomena – and became very nearly extinguished. So this little symbol, the story of what happened to William, in a sense is symbolic of what happened to all of us in that period, that these values were very much heightened in us and the element of caricature and embarrassment went. But even so, typical of old William was that he retained something of his old self unrepentant. When the Queen of Holland escaped from Holland and landed in this country – she was a very large woman, Queen Wilhelmina – I remember William could not help drawing her – it was the last time I was to see him draw a queen – in a rather smiling caricaturish way. Kindlier by far than any he had drawn previously. In this drawing the monumental Queen of Orange was standing almost like a statue of herself at the foot of the gangway of a British destroyer. And he'd written underneath: 'Every ounce a queen.'

It was kind and rather civilized.

Yes. And after that he drew different sorts of things, you saw that clearly in his postwar work. For instance, somebody had shown him a photograph of a corner of Hiroshima shattered by the atom bomb. And there in the midst of all the rubble was a delicate little porcelain cup. He made a drawing and called it the 'Phoenix cup'. This beautiful little teacup had survived intact, and that to him was the meaning. Even ultimately, atom bombs may come, earthquakes may come, and disasters may come, but still there is the cup – this little grail of Japan – to hold the inner, the New Testament to abiding creation.

And what is more the tiny can redeem and renew life.

A tiny, tiny thing. One of the loveliest poems he ever wrote is about the death of a sparrow. Ah, you remember the ancient reference to 'the fall of a sparrow'. So that was the new William. But already on my return from Africa before the war I noticed there had been another very profound change in William. He had always had rather a bold, smiling, confident exterior, which he presented to the world. But I felt that on this occasion he was profoundly sad. He had written to me in Africa from the island of Corfu, which touched him very deeply. Corfu, of course, was Nausicaa's island: the island where Odysseus meets his feminine soul in its purest form and is refreshed and renewed by it. And it is also the island where Odysseus in the *Odyssey*, after years of trials and tribulations, was launched on his final journey to the meeting of meetings, for fulfilment of his selfhood, Penelope and the perfect marriage of masculine and feminine. This is the most extraordinary piece of literature that mankind has ever known, this marvellous matching of the masculine and the feminine, this complete equality in their infinite diversity and opposition. And yet, only through being so utterly different, could they be one. And William wrote to me, from this very island, some of the most feeling of letters which showed that something profound and possibly tragic had happened to him. And then much later I noticed one night after dinner with René and Tony that he was very sad. He could not go to bed and we decided to talk, walking up and down the streets. And to my horror he was nearly suicidal. He told me that for the first time in his life, he had really deeply and utterly fallen in love with someone who was everything that he thought beautiful and true. And then he discovered that he had been betrayed and exploited in the most cynical way.

Happily I think this long talk – we walked for hours – had a therapeutic effect on him because slowly, very slowly in the days that followed his spirit seemed to lift. Slowly be began to write some very beautiful poems about that period in Greece, and of course, that was the most healing of all. It was a great turning point for William, this confrontation with his own capacity to be humanly, not intellectually, hurt.

Did the meeting with Benjamin Britten take place at that time?

No. All this was a long time before the war. What had happened was that while I was in Africa he had gone to Greece with Tony Butts. Tony was a descendent of the Butts who appears in Shakespeare's play *Henry VIII*, and who was responsible for the line all schoolmasters use, 'But me no Butts!' Tony Butts and his mother, though very rich, had looked after their money very badly. I can remember Tony opening a letter at breakfast and saying to me, 'Oh, there's another quarter of a million gone.' They'd lost a quarter of a million in some glass factory in Germany and he just laughed about it. In the end they were actually

204

reduced to living on a mortgage of a Holbein painting of his famous Tudor ancestor, the 'But me no Butts'. This superb Holbein was kept in a bank. They had a mortgage on it which provided their income. And every year the value of the painting went up, and then they merely raised the mortgage and had more for the next year. This was their income, and this is how they lived in an expensive flat in Buckingham Gate. It was bizarre, and it was like William to pick out somebody like that in life. He had a strange thing in him which drew bizarre things to him, and it came out very much in his later postwar ballads. In fact, there was something a little disproportionate in someone so balanced having this attraction to the bizarre. For instance, he went to stay in a boarding house in Maida Vale, and soon after, his landlady was murdered. This gave him material for his novel, *The Case is Altered*, which became a Book Society choice. When he met Anthony Butts, who really was that rare phenomenon, a genuine and inspired eccentric, he liked him so much that they set up house together in London.

William has portrayed the quintessence of Tony so well, made him live again, in *Museum Pieces* and *Strange Relations*, that I need not, nor indeed cannot, add much to the portrait. But he was a gift to life. Impulsive, reckless, over-generous, undisciplined, talented, wild, funny, without any preconceived notion of himself, others or anything, he was near to being a purely natural phenomenon, though centuries of good breeding and intense Englishness came in between. As he became precipitously poorer, the more generous, uncomplaining and full of fun he became. I remember how once, after struggling in vain with that uninhibited, infectious laugh of his, William tried to be stern with Tony and said, 'If you go on like this you will end up in the gutter.' Unabashed – it was impossible to insult Tony – he went silent and gave the prospect serious consideration before smiling and exclaiming, 'You must admit, I will make it considerably more decorative!'

And then in the war his own history raised him high to meet the challenge in his own way: dying of cancer in hospital during the Blitz, he killed himself by jumping out of a window, having left word that he thought there were others more useful to Britain who might need his bed.

For years we had made a habit of it that Tony Butts, William, René and I, every Sunday night, had dinner together in Soho in a tiny little Greek restaurant, which was owned by an old retired Greek sea-captain called Stelios. One just went down into the basement where there were mostly sea-captains and sailors in the restaurant, and no menu. Always Old Stelios seemed to be there, talking and telling sea-stories instead of minding his pots. The first time I went down there he was saying with great drama to his clientele, 'Well, Gentlemen, I can tell you: it was at ten past three on the 5th of November, 1897, in latitude so and so, longitude so and so, that I saw my first sea serpent.' He was a character ready-made for William and Tony, and while he talked we would go into the kitchen where all sorts of tasty things were cooking. We would just lift the lids, sniff at the saucepans and choose what we wanted. So there we were every Sunday night. It was our regular meeting. And I saw this new William coming into being. But it was a William in transition, not the *Turbott Wolfe* William, or even *Sado*, but one more and more adapting with great success to this prescribable, conscious English pattern of his. At the same time he wrote poetry; and some Japanese stories such as those in *Paper Houses*, which he had started in Japan. They were stories told to William. For William was not really a story-teller in the orchestrated sense of novels, which did not come naturally to him. All the stories that he told were either things that had happened to him, or disguised autobiography, or other people's stories. And he told them extremely well. But they lack that depth and fantasy and richness a story has when really created from within one's self. The real explanation is, I believe, that he was most of all a poet. He really was a fine poet, and the last and best of his poems will endure.

But once, suddenly, he wrote something which brought him into some dispute with a lot of his friends, particularly with Tony Butts. It was already the fashion, the high intellectual fashion, to be anti-colonial anti-Empire. It annoyed me always how compulsively people had to be anti-colonial and ashamed of the Empire. And William wrote some rather sardonic stories about it, interesting stories of Africa in the childhood of Queen Victoria. But then he did what really was the unforgivable intellectual thing. The arch-villain of Empire in Britain and in Africa was Cecil Rhodes, and William wrote a short, eminently readable life of Cecil Rhodes. He did it really for money. He was very hard up but he did not do it indecently, his crime was purely his subject, and it was very much held against him by Tony Butts. I have got some of Tony's letters which express how angry he was about this. In the main, however, I saw William in this tremendous turning-over period before the war becoming more and more a man of letters, compelled by the need to make a living to join Cape as a literary adviser. He remained there to the end of his days, every now and then breaking out into poetry. And all he did, he did extremely well, with balance and style, but I could not avoid comparison with Africa, and wondering where was the lava? What had happened to the earthquake? Where were all these subterranean fires – where had they gone? I could not see any of those elemental forces being enlisted in this distinguished man of letters that he was becoming. But I thought I must go on being Africa to him. Stand fast, and one day it would return. By the time the war came he had a very select readership – small, perhaps, because he was never a popular writer, but one of quality: he was very highly thought of. His broadcasts on radio were superb – people loved them. And he brought something uniquely his own to whatever he did, something alive, something humorous – and something which gave great pleasure.

Then one day he was sent a suitcase, a cheap cardboard case full of diaries, the diaries of a nineteenth-century country parson called Kilvert. He edited those diaries with great imagination, skill and fastidiousness and had them published. And they were immediately successful, and today there is a Kilvert Society. People who know about diaries and Kilvert regard these as among the great diaries of history, and this illustrated William's most moving qualities: he took a real delight in discovering and producing unknown talent; it was part of his truly dedicated love of his chosen art, and he put himself again and again at the service of other writers, sometimes rather mediocre ones. People would write to him and he would advise them. He took great trouble about his correspondence. And then it was almost as if he found a vicarious expression in an unemployed family self: he would take great pleasure in the families of his friends. And he was generous in mind. He never said anything destructive about manuscripts to their writers.

Then came the war, and years later I came back to a world I barely recognized. And William had then started writing his autobiographies in a way which made me very sad for more reasons than I mentioned before, but mainly because I do not believe one can write an autobiography truthfully even when you include nothing in it which in itself is not true. By this time he had an enormous circle of friends, a very busy social life, and he worked hard. We met regularly, we enjoyed meeting regularly, yet it was almost as if it had been decided that if there was one thing we must not be it was to be too serious about anything. We must just laugh and be together and enjoy each other's company. Yet occasionally something would happen to Africa, and it would draw a spark out of him. For instance, the suicide of a very fine Afrikaans young poet – one of the most gifted and wonderful girls I've ever met in South Africa, who was a great friend of mine called Ingrid Jonker. I introduced William to her when she was in England and they took to each other, and I had never seen her so happy as over here in his company and that of some of my friends. He helped to translate a small anthology of her best poems into English and got them published. She had not written much and most of it is great, and it is only sad that the language, the idiom, is so of Africa, and so full of the images of Africa still in travail of rebirth, that it is really not translatable.

She went back – which was quite a different story. She had already tried to commit suicide many times – all those who loved her had a tremendous battle to keep her alive. Her letters were increasingly desperate with phrases in them like: 'My people [the Afrikaners] have rotted utterly away from me.' 'How I long to be back in London where people still treated me like a little young lady.' 'For the Dearest Lord's sake, come and see me soon: I am dying of human famine and thirst.' 'My love to Old William: I still see him coming in to the Ivy.' I wrote back and cabled and promised I would be out soon and promised to take her to the Namib desert where she longed to go, but something in her could no longer wait. She was found drowned between great grey boulders in the South Atlantic on a Cape beach after having called at a police station earlier for help. A young African poet called Nat Nakasa, whom I was trying help, committed suicide in America almost at the same time. And I wrote to William at once and said the timing of the two suicides seems to me too mysterious for misunderstanding: there was something, a message in it for us. I begged him, 'Only you can write about this. It is as if these two were born Siamese twins in fate. Neither the creative feminine nor the masculine is allowed to live in our country. There is something there I am certain that you will see and only you could express.' And William wrote a very beautiful poem about it, with lovely African images in it, and the African fire flared up and helped to prevent the two suicides from just being a 'No'.

He was a many-sided person, and it was not surprising that in the second half of his life his most important statements were poems. I am certain they will always stand. And there was no laughter in these: I think of 'The Chosen Way' and especially 'Bamboo'. For 'Bamboo' is like a veil drawn from his eyes and he suddenly realizes what his life in Japan had given him unconsciously, in spite of the highly conscious and mangled relationship he had allowed himself. It is a marvellous poem, original in form and charged with the pain of a nostalgia one only feels for the loss of an experience which meant far more to one at the time than one was prepared to admit to oneself. There at last you have William's own answer out of the deeps of his unconscious poetic self, answering those who might think his experience of Japan perfunctory. Japan did not let him off the hook. It stayed with him to surface naturally and most eloquently in 'Bamboo'. That was the old William, his primeval ancient imagination in flower of flame again. Once he was asked to go out to lecture in Africa. He wanted me to go with him and I said, 'No, I will go back to Africa with you but not to lecture.' He replied, rather sadly and helplessly, 'I can't – it's not my sort of Africa.' So he went off to the University in Johannesburg, after all those years. He also did a very brief visit to the place where he wrote *Turbott Wolfe*, The Entumeni, or The Place of Thorns where his father had a trading-stall. He came back silent and rather upset and would say little about his journey except that he would never go back. I think he had been back without going back. Or it frightened him again and he knew he never wanted to do it.

I do not know if his real development even as a poet ended there as well. He went on writing, because nothing except death would stop him, and the ballads, the black ballads, the impressionistic pieces, came out of him steadily and were remarkable and enjoyable, but to me something was lost for good on the way. The ballads were witty, funny – it was a legitimate side of him – but it was to me very sad that I cannot remember ever having a serious conversation with William again.

He was escaping?

No, I do not think so. He was not running away. He had not closed up shop: was still decidedly in business. Benjamin Britten, when he discovered that William was a great friend of mine, asked to meet him. He came to stay with us in Aldeburgh and we introduced him to Ben, who had always been a great admirer of William. Ben was thinking of doing an opera on the Beatrix Potter story-books. But just at that moment the late King died. Our beautiful young Queen, who was on tour, came hurriedly back to England and the Coronation was being arranged. And everybody had a feeling, a very strong feeling in England, that a new age was going to begin with this new Queen. One of the great ages in British history, Britain's own personal and private Renaissance, was the Elizabethan Age. And we all felt we could start a second Elizabethan Age. We thought then the Coronation must be special and splendid in every way, and let it have a special opera written for it as well. The idea caught on immediately. Yes, let there also be an opera specially written for the Coronation! And so Ben and William wrote an opera, called *Gloriana*, based on an episode in the life of Queen Elizabeth I.

Ingaret and I went to the first night. It was probably the last great Coronation night of its kind that the world will ever see. There can never be a Coronation like it again, because alas! there are not enough kings and queens left in the world. Unemployment and redundancy among the working classes, proportionately, is nothing compared to unemployment among royalty. Apart from Great Britain, the Scandinavian countries, Holland and Spain, royalty is singularly diminished. I remember the late King's Coronation before the war, which I think was perhaps the greatest Coronation there has ever been. At that moment the British Empire was still intact and the whole Empire was drawn to London for that Coronation. Well, this Coronation in many ways was almost on that colossal scale. The opera house in Covent Garden itself looked like a fairy-tale. Row upon row of all the crowned heads and princes and the aristocracy of the world in silks and satins, tiaras and uniforms, adorned with pearls, sequins, sapphires, rubies, medals, orders, so that from the inside it looked like a treasure-house of some great antique civilization rediscovered; even its velvet furnishings and gilt charged with visual symbols of royalty and emblems of a vanished chivalry.

And then came the opera. It was based on the story of the relationship of Queen Elizabeth I with the Earl of Essex, which ended with her having Essex beheaded after his discovery that under her wig the Queen possessed but a scanty head of hair. Well, you can imagine, to offer this story to a beautiful young Queen who was just starting out, nothing could have been, to say the least, more tactless. It was almost as if, from the start, an icy draught had hit the audience. And it was no passing sulk on the part of the audience; the atmosphere became even colder, more withdrawn, until it verged on the hostile. Ingaret and I sat through it sick at heart. We saw Ben and William sitting in the box watching the performance, and Peter Pears, their great friend and ours, struggling with the part of Essex. And hardly a hand lifted in the intervals in applause. At the end, it was all that the composer's friends in the audience could do to keep the curtain up so that the composer and the librettist, William, could come on the stage to take their bows. Then the curtain came down, and I think there were few people in the audience who did not leave troubled and sad. It showed again this strange, fragmented view of royalty in William, and it seemed as if he and Ben were unconsciously mocking the symbol. What made it worse for them and their friends was that nobody gave the music a thought or made any effort at understanding the composer and his librettist. Immediately there were all sorts of stories doing the rounds of intellectual and artistic London, the cruellest of all perhaps coming from Ernest Newman, no doubt spurred on by his long battle to defend Wagner against the sort of musical taste which Ben represented in such an inspired way.

Could you give an example?

No! I would rather not – I know all concerned are dead but they were my friends and I cannot pass on something I would have preferred not to hear and remember. But I mention this aspect of the event because it is another illustration of the insensitivity and ruthlessness of the aesthete, who would condone a rape, I feel sometimes, rather than forgive a false note.

Fortunately there were lovely musical passages and moments in the opera and no doubt they will be revived and live, and the opera itself, when it has no special, no great historic occasion to serve, will be free to be judged just as music. But out of this came the fruitful collaboration between Ben and William. Ben and Peter went to Japan and Ben, prompted both by William and myself, got hooked on Noh and, as a result of seeing *Sumidagawa*, he wrote *Curlew River*. We have a river at Aldeburgh, a haunted river of a lost world of marshes, fireflies and birds, called the Alde. It is the 'Curlew River' of the opera, the first of three of Ben's purest religious explorations. In *Curlew River* he explores the deep, instinctive, pagan religious root in himself – the natural religion as yet undogmatized, unclouded by preconceived ideas, the true pre-Christian and the ancient natural dimension in himself. That was followed by *The Burning Fiery Furnace*, which is a marvellous story: the one about three men cast in a Babylonian furnace. People look inside, and are amazed to see that the men are not destroyed. And wonder why? Suddenly they see there is a fourth being – a mysterious fourth – and it is full of a sense of discovery, not least of the Old Testament grace in Ben himself. I won't go into the symbolism of that, but it was beautiful. And then came the last of the three, *The Prodigal Son*. This is singularly Ben's interpretation of the parable, and in a sense William's as well. For me the interpretation is too literal and conventional and taken purely as a story of the reconciliation of the son and the father; a theme always alive in the Ben and William who needed reconciliation to the father in themselves. It has, however, lovely music in it of the magnetic quality that art of finality has. I do not know whether, but for that meeting with William, Ben would have found the deep, independent religious strain in himself, which he followed up in these three operas. It is even more interesting that Ben found this deep vein when his own life was increasingly bound for the dark; and it was most interesting of all that through William, and in part myself, Japan had contributed to the final resolution.

Then came the day Ingaret answered the telephone at lunchtime at Aldeburgh and exclaimed, 'Oh my God, I'd better tell Laurens at once. Or will you tell him?' It was Ben who said, 'They've been trying to get you on the telephone all morning – William's dead. He died in the night.' I think we need not go into the question of how he died. Only that morning I had a book from him, *The Butterfly Ball* – ironically the only real financial and popular success he was now not allowed to enjoy – and a letter in which he wrote, I am certain with a laugh, 'I am in bed after a heart attack but you should see the cardiograph – it's like a seismograph of a Mexican earthquake.' The fact was William died in the night and it was just as though one had been sitting in a room, a brightly lit room, and a wall had fallen down and let in the darkness. Because so much of our life we'd shared, fifty years of it since we had first seen, 'Heraldic in the sunlight, A scorpion on a stone,' as he describes the moment in a poem dedicated to me in 'The Five Fold Screen'.

Was he much older than you?

No, he was three years and three days older than I was. But I called him 'old' William as a term of affection, for 'old' is indeed the highest form of endearment among friends in my native country. Consider how different we were, so utterly, utterly different. We had hardly anything in common, except life.

And except Africa.

And Africa. And in a sense I couldn't give William as much of Africa as I would have wished; and perhaps, in rejecting the Africa in himself, William inevitably had to reject a great deal of me. But the fact that our friendship lasted in the way that it did, that we contributed to each other, has something triumphant about it. I am deeply grateful to life that William was a part of it. And I never forget those tremendously English qualities he sought, cultivated and served; he was brave, sensitive, fastidious, and in the midst of an unreal turmoil of complex and paradoxical elements, never lost his balance and contained himself, and stood fast.

And he had style.

And he had a great heart. He had a great gift for friendship. Also in a way which was unforeseen, in avoiding the kind of suffering that serving his vision of Africa might have inflicted on him, he suffered very profoundly through his individual relationships. He never knew, I believe, what it was to have a total human relationship, which so many of us could not get by without, but he lived with great dignity and without complaint, and he was never soured or deprived of his gift of laughter. For the moment he may be overlooked and not remembered, but he will be back, I know, because already he is near.

In Yet Being Someone Other *you tell how Captain Mori travelled all the way to England after the death of William Plomer. He felt it was an obligation, a moral obligation.*

Yes, at his age – he was close on ninety – it was an incredible journey. He joined a package tour – not because he wanted to travel – he had seen enough of the world as a ship's captain; he simply wanted to pay his respects to the ashes of his friend. I think that was very moving, and it gives you an idea of the first things in the Japanese spirit as well as an illustration of why I find them such a people of quality. He did not hesitate at the place where William's ashes were scattered to ask for permission to take some of the flowers planted there in William's memory back with him to plant in Japan, and with great difficulty we got him a cutting to take. But the cutting would not grow and he pressed me all the time to bring him another one. I could not send it because it is prohibited. I thought that, in spite of the Japanese Embassy telling me it is impossible, somehow I must do it. So finally I went to Japan and took the white lilac plant in a Harrods shopping bag and when I arrived in Tokyo at the Narita airport, and looked across the hall and saw 'Plant Quarantine' and Customs, I thought I should never succeed.

I went over and presented this flower and told the Japanese officers why I had brought it with me. They listened very carefully and they said they were terribly sorry, but it was against the law. Then I said to them, did they realize that this plant was above the law? They were immediately interested and asked how a plant could be above the law. So I told them the whole story. I could see they were passionately interested. Then one looked at the other, and he took his rubber stamp and stamped the shopping bag in which I was carrying the plant, saying, 'We shall be honoured to receive this plant in Japan.'

We planted it in Captain Mori's garden and every year in the spring I know that it is flowering, and I get photographs from him of his whole family grouped around the plant, and I know that the memory of old William is still young and alive among them.

There are many problems with Japan today on the economic front. The Japanese can be hard to deal with and they seem to understand us better than we understand them. So it is surprising to find that they can be sentimental.

I agree with you. I think our whole approach is based on European rational values that we should throw aside. We should look at the authentic symbolism of meaning which motivates us all. I am certain that if we direct ourselves to the Japanese in that area, we would get a very interesting and overwhelming response. However skilful they are technologically, in building trains, wireless sets, cars and so on, their personalities contain an area of doubting. One of my most acute reminders of how deep this unconscious – and sometimes conscious – sense of doubt among the Japanese, particularly young Japanese, could go, was through my friendship with Yukio Mishima.

I met Yukio Mishima in the United States. He and I went to the University of California and a series of colleges where we talked about Japan together, and I was amazed to find he was a wonderful companion, with a great sense of humour. He spoke beautiful English. He was a connoisseur of European wine and food, and he was in a sense westernized, just as some of us feel that the Japanese civilization is for us a valid alternative civilization. We could, if pushed out of Europe, feel there was a civilization with which we could identify. I think Yukio felt this about western civilization, that in some way it was an alternative, but nevertheless he was horrified that Japan was picking up all that was negative and materialistic in European civilization, that it was losing something of its honour, of its self-respect and the spirit of the Japan that mattered to him above all else. We talked about it a great deal. He was extraordinarily worried about the obsession with radio sets and motor cars and this whole way of living, although he enjoyed those things himself.

I think ultimately his death was of a special significance and truly Japanese. I saw him here in Europe not long before his death and I noticed the change in him since I'd last seen him in the United States of America. He looked to me not discouraged but very sombre. Later, after his death, I met a Japanese lady who's married to an eminent English theatrical producer. She is a friend of Mishima's wife and she told me that in Mishima's diaries after his death they found that, two years before he committed his form of *seppuku*, the date for it had already been set down. He knew that he was entering the last two years of his life and that ultimately the Japanese would not accept his message unless he could prove to them it mattered so much to him that he would die for it. He believed very profoundly in this thing that one picks up over and over again in Japan – that when life fails you, the only way to resurrect life and give it another chance was by giving up your own life and dying. He took death very seriously – not in a negative sense, but in a positive sense. This is one of the very difficult things that Europeans have to learn to understand about Japan: the extreme seriousness with which death is treated. In Japan, it is not treated as something which is purely an end or purely negative. It is something for which one needs almost as much preparation, ceremonial, devotion and love as for marriage. I have always been deeply stirred by the great Feast of the Dead – Japan's All Saints' Day – when everyday life stops and minds and houses are opened wide to welcome the dead. This is one of the most joyful acts of remembrance I have ever encountered.

Yes, the Japanese seem to have a feeling almost of the 'romance of death'. What experience of that did you have among the Japanese soldiers in the war?

We had very little contact with the Japanese soldiers, so we did not really know what happened outside the prison camp. They very often said to me in moments of rage when they got drunk: 'We like you, but how can we like you – you are disgraced in being still alive. We would like you much better if you were dead!' I have seen them do extraordinary things – for instance, execute somebody in prison and then after the execution they would say, 'We will now show you Japanese morality towards the dead', and all the troops were paraded and made to present arms to the decapitated body lying there. Then they would blow their bugles and truly honour the life they had despised when living.

You see, there are always so many different ways of approaching life, and I think that there is something valid in their approach to death. We no longer take it seriously enough in western civilization. The subject is avoided for as long as possible. People are sent off to die in hospitals; they are not with their own families and friends when they die. Animals are killed out of sight, so that nobody should see this unpleasant thing called death. We try to live as though death did not exist. I have often wondered if the very great extension of the years of life of the average

European has not had a profound effect on the European spirit, because in the Elizabethan age a person was old at fifty. People did not expect to live much beyond fifty. Charles the Great at the age of fifty was rehearsing his own funeral in Paris, by lying in his coffin. Death was much more of an imminent reality. Michelangelo said that it is true that death destroyed all men, but that the thought of death made the man.

But it is true the Japanese have a romantic affair with death: it is as if death really holds the romance for them that life lacks.

Quite often, for the Japanese, suicide means fulfilment and may have an erotic undertone. But could it not also be a form of escapism? For a Westerner it is odd to imagine that a Japanese prefers to commit suicide instead of speaking out, instead of attempting a dialogue.

Yes, there is something mysterious about that. I think it is the shadow side of the Japanese, and if they were to look into it very deeply they could make this compulsion contemporary, because it is an outmoded way of behaving. It is an archaic, built-in reaction, not an illuminated compulsion but a collective one, which the individual should face up to and break free from.

Other nations do resent the great success of the Japanese. How should they approach Japan and have a fair and balanced view of them?

I think there are two aspects to this question. There is the defensive reaction which says this is the Japanese way of continuing the war they lost, only now they are making war on our economy. I think that is the wrong reflex. On the other hand, the Japanese see this kind of hostility to their economic and technological success as the revival of the ancient forces that hemmed them in and would not let them expand into the modern world. This would be a very dangerous repeat performance of history in another dimension. My own feeling about it has been that somehow, in a non-rational more than a rational way, we have got an enormous area of sympathy for each other, the Japanese and ourselves. We ought to try and explore this through friendships. My Japanese friendships have been amongst the most meaningful ones in my life. Through our Japanese friends we must sit down and explore it together and find where we can bring each other closer to understanding one another. I think there is a great readiness for it. Of all the variations of the western spirit I think the United States of America, to the Japanese, is a country with which their relationship is still more technological and commercial than warm and spontaneous like the feeling they have for, say, the culture of France. They really seem to appreciate the ancient values of Europe as much as we do.

And look at the way they have taken European music into themselves. Through culture, through art, through religion, through studying the language, we can foster these bridges. I think it is most encouraging that the various Japanese firms who have started small enterprises here in Britain, with Japanese managing British workmen, have been eminently successful. People like them and they get on. Japan has got an enormous contribution of its own to make which we value and we want to take along with us.

———

Since the publication in 1955 of your book, The Dark Eye in Africa, *do you think that the 'dark eye' has got bigger in Africa as well as in the rest of the world?*

Well, I was using the dark eye there as an image of what I think is a universal phenomenon. I once made a film called *A Region of Shadow* in which the region of shadow is the black, symbolized by the dark eye. It is the problem of how nations and cultures which do not observe the proportions of their culture, always tend to go over into their opposites. Until now they have done this through acts of violence. It is not a conscious process. And a nation is not aware of its opposite. It simply builds up underneath as a volcano does in Japan or in Java.

But for what reason?

The reason for it, or rather the source, which paradoxically often is an excess of reason, is simply that all human beings, who consist of both light and dark, do not allow the light to pay sufficient attention to what is dark. It tends to think that the dark is negligible or that it is despicable and that it is something which has to be rejected and not talked about or known. But the dark side of humanity is a valid part of the human spirit with its own immense energies available to the human spirit, and these energies build up within us because they are never allowed any conscious expression or any conscious say in our individual lives. These

218

energies accumulate and in the end grow angry. As we will not let them in by the front door, they break in at the back.

The illustration that I use to explain this phenomenon is the 'dark eye' – *mata kelap*, as it is called in Indonesia. There you have constant examples of the man who leads his life in an exemplary manner for forty years. He is a good father, a good husband, a good worker, he pays his taxes, he does everything that society demands of him, he behaves beautifully. Then suddenly one day he is overwhelmed and grabs his dagger and murders everybody living round about him – his wife, his children, everything within reach. Then the dreaded cry, 'Amok!' goes up; in Java they say, *mata kelap* – the eye has darkened in him. He has, in a sense, been too good collectively, and has not sufficiently paid heed to his individual expression.

This, then, is an image of what happens to individuals and nations everywhere who go collective and stay undifferentiated. We have had two world wars which have been a form of darkening of the eye; they were on a collective scale. People are too collective at their peril, and the result is that their denied, individual self rises in rebellion against the established, partial self masquerading as a whole, and asserts itself in that catastrophic way.

And a whole nation can run amok.

Yes, you can see it building up in nations. For instance, what happened with the Nazis and Hitler was a collective darkening of the German eye. Cool, rational, scientific, industrious Germany suddenly ran amok and tried to destroy everything within sight. I am certain that the eye of whole civilizations has darkened over and over again. Even here in Britain, from the left-wing and the centre, we are threatened with a darkening of eye, with the rule of the collective denying the individual and specific. And that is the area in which prejudice arises, this area which I call the area of the shadow, the region of shadow where we are not sufficiently aware. Consciousness imposes upon the individual a choice, and this is the point. You come to a moment in life when what you have chosen consciously and worked at consciously has lost its power of increase – and perhaps all of the rest of your life should be spent in working on what you did not choose before, for what has been sacrificed has returned, dagger in hand, to sacrifice the sacrificer. That is where the darkness lives, and you must bring it up into consciousness as well and as fastidiously as you can. Then you achieve what Jung called 'wholeness'. A whole individual is an individual who has explored not just half his possibilities but all of his possibilities, as it were. That is the highest and most urgent task of the individual, his truly religious challenge – the wholeness which, we should never forget, is synonymous with 'holiness': to be whole is to be holy. And that is why Christ was the great healer, because he made what was partial in the life and spirit of man, whole.

Unfortunately, the age we live in has not learnt its lesson. It is tending to go back to a purely rationalistic, not rational but rationalistic extreme. We are living in an age where inhuman theories, based on abstract statistics, are imposed upon human beings – who do not even want them and are not at all suited to living by them – as the 'ideal way in which they should live'. We are going back to this cold, ice age of reason, which is what collective man does. If he is in the grip of compulsive, unconscious motivation, then he turns to an authoritarian concept of reason to bring it under control. We are far from having seen the end of the process in the European spirit, of which the French Revolution was the first major expression. One must not forget that in France itself the forces that produced the Revolution to a certain extent were addressed in the French spirit by the romantic revival. With the romanticism of the nineteenth century, the non-rational elements in France were brought back to life to create a new balance in the culture, thereby achieving a kind of stability. One does not feel that France would ever go through that again. I feel the reason why French culture and French civilization is so important to us is because at its highest point it was complete, it honoured both poles – it had its Descartes and it had its Pascal – two poles and infinite variations in between, and for a nation to be really complete it needs both these approaches to life.

But there seems to be a religious revival throughout the world. Isn't youth everywhere showing us new directions, opening our eyes?

Yes, but unfortunately even the young are doing it on a collective basis, and that is no good. You cannot do it in gangs. Take the pop phenomenon, where you have hundreds of thousands of young people saying we all feel we are one together – but that is archaic, that is not contemporary. Pop music is collective music; it is as archaic as tribal music without the innocence of tribal music in its non-tribal context: it is frighteningly undifferentiated music, and as impregnated with warning and somnambulism as Wagner at his worst. Then look at Women's Lib, where after centuries of a male-dominated culture the rejected, the suppressed feminine in the woman and its valid aspiration to be recognized and active, has been perverted into a form of Amazonian gang warfare. And the answer, of course, can only be in seeking and making pre-eminent the transcendent wholeness which Christ made flesh and blood. The real message of Christianity is the fully integrated individual who takes the sorrows of the universe and his community upon him in the service of the community. That is the deepest thing, it is our safeguard. You can even see it coming out of Russia: look at people like Solzhenitsyn. Life is on the side of this thing. What we have to watch are these vast cities we are creating, these vast multinational corporations, because what we forget is that we have an economic totalitarianism in the West which creates a collective man just as much as the political totalitarianisms do behind the Iron Curtain. We are in great peril and that is why returning to our own tradition of the individual is so tremendously important.

But people prefer social security, on both sides of the Iron Curtain.

It seems natural. But if you read about what is going on behind the Iron Curtain, man has never been so insecure. In the West too, where man's security of livelihood has never been greater, his inner sense of insecurity and of being lost, is overwhelming.

What are your feelings about Solzhenitsyn: can he speak for Russia now that he is outside Russia?

As you know, he did not want to leave. He was forced into exile, he was thrown out. And he says exactly the same thing about Russia as I say in a small way, and as Jung says. He says, I do not want you to attack Russia, I do not want you to come into Russia to help us. Leave Russia to us, Russia will evolve its own answers to its own suffering. But what we ask you to do is defend yourselves against Russia. Do not give in, do not be deceived by Russia. Above all, be true to yourselves. You are helping Russia to strangle us in Russia by being deceived by Russia and being false to yourselves.

To me, Solzhenitsyn is proof of what Jung says; that the only carrier of renewal and new life is the individual. And Solzhenitsyn proves it because when he was born he did not know Czarist Russia: he knew nothing but the Revolution. He was brought up on lies, on a collective illusion and his own instinctive life. He is an immense vindication of the power in life to produce, no matter what the odds are against it, the right individual at the right moment. It is one of the most important events of this century. The greatest urge in the collective unconscious is to produce this kind of individual, the individuated man. This is what life is about, this is what the religious quest of man is about.

So I think, although he has left Russia, Solzhenitsyn still speaks as somebody who is inside Russia. He still speaks with that authentic Russian voice. And for me, everything Solzhenitsyn says has the eternal mark of truth, because for almost four years I lived a Solzhenitsyn kind of existence as a prisoner-of-war, lived in the same area of uncertainty between life and death from day to day that he lived in. The individual was totally denied, and when you have lived in that same area you recognize a true voice, because you realize you have only one armour: you have got no arms, you are starved, people are dying around you, you never get up in the morning certain that you shall see the sunset again; all is unpredictable, cruel and inhuman and you know somehow only the truth and nothing but the truth matters any more.

When you went to the Soviet Union you brought back a painting representing the face of a man which is, for me, symbolic of the suffering endured by the people there. And one only has to look at Pasternak's or Solzhenitsyn's face to see how much suffering has been accumulating in the soul of the peoples of the USSR.

Yes, the painting you are talking about is a self-portrait. It represents the battle of the painter to maintain his individual self amongst all the collective pressures – that is why I love it. In Russian paintings traditionally there are no self-portraits, but this is one, a man fighting for his own identity. I think this is our great safeguard: this is the truly divine element in the human being when the individual is rededicating himself to truth by serving his own truth.

Who is in the best position to awaken our consciousnesses and promote truth do you think? Parents, teachers, scientists, wise men, artists, gurus, bringers of fire or bringers of darkness?

Well, I think everyone must be responsible, and the movement has already started; but above all the one who listens in to his dreaming self most, and lives it. For it is through our dreams that the new vision and energies we need will come, not through our heads. That is one of the reasons why I find Jung such an important phenomenon. He has performed an enormous service to the culture of his time, and at the centre of this meaning for our time is the axiom that man has to stand fast in the good while working hard to understand the nature of evil, without becoming part of it, that is the only way of making evil see light. Understanding is the essence of metamorphosis. One need not attack evil necessarily, but it is most important that one should not become part of it. And that is difficult.

One of the great problems of our time, which is totally neglected by the churches, is how we have to resist evil without becoming another form of evil in the process, which is what we are doing all the time. You see, I feel very much as Solzhenitsyn does – for instance, in the last war we allied ourselves out of desperation with the very evil we were opposed to when we joined forces with Russia. It was terrible, but people like Roosevelt, and to a certain extent Churchill, did not see in this desperate fight for survival that we were really allying ourselves with something which was evil. We are paying the consequences of it today with this terrible split between Eastern Europe and Western Europe . . . It is a split in spirit, and it runs very deep . . . a cataclysmic split in the spirit of Western man.

Have you ever had a direct, personal experience of evil?

I think one has it all one's life. Every day of one's life one has experiences of evil. I have had many experiences of it which have haunted me ever since. They are not very dramatic, and they involve me not only by what I did but by what I failed to do. For instance, I can remember a thing which was a very great turning point in my life.

Once, when I was quite young, I went on a great tour with some friends of ours, and we camped out by a river in Africa where we could fish and hunt. The family we were with had taken all their black servants with them. My particular friend was an only son and he was the heir to the estate of this very famous South African family, and he was spoilt. We came back at the end of a day from a rather fruitless hunting and fishing expedition, very tired. One of the black people there annoyed him and he suddenly started hitting him all over the place. All the white people immediately gathered round, and shouted, 'Beat him up, beat him up, that's right – you beat him up!' urging my friend on. And I felt there was something profoundly wrong. I felt I should do something about it, because this was evil, but I could not find the courage in myself to do anything. But I had a sister with me who was only eighteen months older than I was, my sister Emma, a wonderful feminine spirit. She blazed with fury and she immediately jumped in and pushed them apart and slapped my friend in the face and said, 'It's very unfair what you're doing!' She stopped it at once. But the next day the whole family felt we had betrayed them and we were sent away.

It is those sorts of experiences. I am just giving you one example which goes back very far, but it was a turning point in my life. It showed me how I had not chosen between good and evil at that moment, and there was something I could have done but I did not do. Yet on the other hand, it gave me a certain weapon, because it taught me the nature of that particular evil. In the world as I came to know it, I was amazed by the role, for instance, that unconscious envy and jealousy play, not only in human, in private relationships, but in matters of life and death. While I was in the war I saw, in the midst of battles, generals and admirals and field-marshals intriguing against one another so that they should have more power, persuading themselves that the fate of the war lay in their own advancement.

This gives me a clear idea of the sort of In a Province *material you brought with you to London. Who were the poets and writers and artists you met when you arrived?*

Well, I met a great many of them during that period. As you know, Bloomsbury was dominating the aesthetic world in Great Britain. It was the world of E. M. Forster, Lytton Strachey, Maynard Keynes, Vanessa and Duncan Grant, Clive Bell and Roger Fry. One person who became a close friend of mine was Arthur Waley, with his companion Beryl de Zoete. The link between Arthur Waley and myself was Japan. He translated brilliantly from Japanese and from Chinese, although he could speak neither. He just knew the writing, the characters. But we three had dinner once a week for a while, talking Japan and skiing, and I had some strange adventures with Beryl and was made to aid and abet her uninvited intrusions into exalted university rooms like those of Goldie Dickinson and Steven Runciman.

And then there were Virginia and Leonard Woolf, who meant most of all. I have to admit that I was not drawn to Virginia really. I was interested in her, of course. I saw how beautifully and sensitively she wrote. But her writing did not speak to me in depth. The first time I ever met her I had a clash with her about Charles Dickens, and I fear that made me fail my entrance examination. She said that if you saw Dickens coming down the street, you would shoot quickly down a side alley so as not to have to greet him, he was that kind of man. And to me, that she could dismiss this volcanic eruption called Dickens just like that, seemed to carry this kind of prissy aesthetics they called art much too far. Many of them were fanatical aesthetes, you know. As I had just come from Japan they seemed to me a curiously Japanese phenomenon. They could have been Murasaki's and Sei Shonagon's contemporaries: even if the world were burning to hell they would go on with their fine thoughts about Life and Art, and find life not quite good enough.

And few of those people really seemed to me to be interesting in the sense of being on course with life and their own natures. Leonard, of course, was the exception and the heroic factor among them. I do not know how to put it quite properly and precisely, but it was as if I found myself in a world of aberration; there was hardly a relationship there which seemed to me what I would call accurate. Everybody was inaccurate in what they were. The idea that somehow they had to fit into themselves as nature had disposed, never occurred to them. They seemed to live at least one or two removes from nature, in a world that was contrived. It was as if they were playing a game with themselves rather than living full out. They seemed to create a kind of 'ersatz' life which tried to bypass tradition and the more serious business of life. Aesthetics became almost their religion. They tended, in a sense, to sneer and laugh at what had gone before and to reject as superstitious the more instinctive approaches to creation and to life, and to substitute their sorts of sensitivities and their forms of self-expression for it.

These are some of the reasons. But really, basically, it was much simpler: there was not really anything there that I liked or found of lasting interest. I was on a different course and using a different map. But Leonard Woolf was a person I felt very drawn to and liked very much. He was my publisher, of course, it was he who gave me my first chance. I felt very deeply for him because he seemed to me to be rather a trapped man in two ways. He had a very good brain. He was a Cambridge rationalist and would have been trapped in his rationalism as so many of his brilliant contemporaries were, but was saved by his intuition. He was a most intuitive person. That and an objective interest in people made him such a good publisher. He would have been very good on a race course, he would always have picked winners. He did not publish a single bad book. And he was really the driving spirit in the place.

And then I found in Virginia a hard, unforgiving streak. There was something ruthless, almost cruel in her personality. This great sensitivity that one heard about was sensitivity about herself and her emotions, and her feelings – and not about others. It was never an objective sensitivity. It was a very profoundly subjective sensitivity. She was preoccupied with her reactions, her emotions. And they never really took in lesser humanity – with the result that I felt very uncomfortable with her. And the few times I opened my mouth in her presence, I found we were contradicting each other, as about Charles Dickens. And then at the same time I felt that she was not giving Leonard a chance, was almost eating him up, because Leonard, who had a warm heart as well as a cool head, put his whole life into making her creative and serving her. Leonard had started in the Colonial Service, and spent three or four years in a remote part of Ceylon as a District Officer. He did a marvellous job, and came back to write a very good book about it called *The Village in the Jungle*. He had a writer in him. And then he met Virginia. He left the Colonial Service and he stopped writing, apart from political pamphlets – again, he was drawn to the Left, in the high intellectual fashion. He sat for years on the Colonial Commission of the Labour Party, preparing the Labour Party to take over the Empire when they came into office. He published a political quarterly, and of course books. And as well as all that he was keeping Virginia whole and alive. Virginia took his whole life – and I do not know how much she gave him back. Yet only a fool would deny that she wrote beautifully and perceptively and I remember how, to the end of his days, Leonard would find great comfort in one of his women friends, who could read beautifully, such as Peggy Ashcroft or Ingaret, reading favourite passages aloud to him out of something like *The Waves*.

But my whole instinct was to get away from it all in London.

You decided to go back to nature?

Yes, I went and farmed in the West Country.

But from time to time you would come back up to London?

I knew a lot of painters in London, most of my friends were painters and they were the people I really got on best with: Enslin du Plessis and his friends, Bill Coldstream, Pasmore, Henry Moore, and many others. It was later on that I got to know more writers: the Huxleys, Eliot, and as the war grew nearer, through René Janin, Stephen Spender, Cecil Day Lewis and Rosamond Lehmann became very much part of my immediate world. I was always, and remain, very fond of Stephen Spender and admire him greatly. I did not take to Auden but was friends with Stephen Spender from the beginning. And in many ways Stephen was the most natural and gifted poet of the threesome: Spender, Day Lewis and Auden. But Stephen, with his family tradition and upbringing, felt that he had to do other things as well as write poetry. And he had this open quality of not minding being made a fool of by life and events, which I found both brave and endearing. He was also loyal and generous to his friends and, for instance, has done more for Auden than he would dream of doing for himself. He did not do what Auden did when the war broke out and go to America in order to preserve his art. He joined the London Fire Brigade and served in it throughout the war in London. He may be remembered for not paying enough attention to the poet he was. But he has served it in a broader sense and in depth by travelling far and wide to arouse interest in literature. No one can present poetry better than a person who is a born poet himself and the English-speaking world owes Stephen a great deal for a long, devoted and selfless service.

Cecil Day Lewis was another close friend, perhaps the most English of the three. He was throughout a poet and a fine writer, creative as a critic, gifted with unique insights and special perceptions. His essays are classics, and his translation of Virgil is an immediate rendering in a remarkable modern idiom of the original. He was, with it all, one of the most lovable and chivalrous of people and left one at his death conscious of his absence every day. I was grateful to life for such friends. There were others too who might have become friends but then I withdrew and became obsessed with the coming war.

Was it during this period that you started a book, the manuscript of which was destroyed in the war?

Yes. It was then. Also I became intensely absorbed with the rising horror in Germany. My whole sense of history was perturbed, all the alarm bells were ringing in me.

Were you a journalist at that time?

Oh, yes. Because of the danger I went back to it. And also I began a book of warning, *The Rainbow Bridge*, since nobody would listen to me, and I wrote it as if the devil were behind me. It was then that I discovered, through this threat, that world carnage had always brought new things alive in people and the threat of this war took me into a new area of myself. I discovered that everything the war was stirring in me was in a way mythological. It was a deep, profound, mythological warning. It was a *Götterdämmerung* that was upon us. I started reading German mythology and found that it was a blueprint of the war and what was happening in Germany. I realized that Germany had been taken over by collective forces – ancient mythological forces. So I was warning people: you can't stop this, except by force, because these people, the Germans, do not know what they are doing.

I was trying to farm and also to be a diplomatic correspondent, hoping in that way to do what I could to warn. But to me it was so extraordinary. I was obsessed by an inner certainty of disaster unless we acted. I could think of nothing else and was deeply afraid for the world. It was like watching an enormous storm coming towards you – blackening out the sky – thunder and lightning flashing. And yet people were behaving as if they were in for a nice spring day, the sun shining and the dew on the grass.

But what is your feeling about this lost book? It must have been quite awful to put oneself fully into a book, and such an important book, warning others – and then this typescript is destroyed in a bombing.

I was already caught up in the war by then. I was not in the country. And in a sense it was not so disastrous to me because my book had been overtaken by events. Everything I had written in the book was happening, so there was no point in writing on. But it had this tremendous personal impact on me, that I must heed this early warning system, be obedient to it, and take it far more seriously than I had in the past. It was a tremendous lesson to me, first of all of my own unawareness and the unawareness of the time in which I was living, and then the overwhelming realization that the great enemy of life was unawareness; and that the task of the writer, and the artist and the priest and the seer, was to diminish unawareness, to increase and enlarge human awareness, and continually work at the health and well-being of consciousness.

This became for me, from the moment I realized this, the most important task in life, and this is really what literature is – getting the heart and imagination involved in a drama of heart, mind and spirit. All stories heighten human perceptions, and so add something to human awareness, pushing unawareness and unconsciousness further back. This is the most important thing in life – the universe is a pilgrimage, a cavalcade, towards light, to diminish darkness and illuminate shadow. The stars, everything, are involved in creating greater forms of awareness, and by creating greater forms of awareness continue the fundamental task of creation. This would really be leading a religious life: working to diminish unawareness. That's how I saw it. This was the lesson for me of the destruction of that *Rainbow Bridge*, because the German one was the only mythology that I knew, where the forces of light, where the gods themselves, are vanquished by the forces of evil pouring over their rainbow bridge and destroying them in their own keep. And this still remains the threat that we face now, not as a German one but as a world one: we face it not only in the new totalitarianisms such as Russia but more in the proliferation of collective thinking, a narrowing of awareness and the decline of the individual and the apotheosis of the collective. This happens within and without our own cultures; this is the same psychological reversion that produced Nazism and Fascism and will do so again unless we are aware of its origins in each of us and deal with it there so that we can disperse the peril without.

We need to look closely into the nature of modern consciousness because that, as the myth shows, was the means by which the Gods were destroyed by the hubris of a consciousness that thinks it is greater than the unconscious which gave it birth and being. This is what the myth described: psychological matricide. This rainbow, which is a natural image of awareness, a covenant set by God in the skies over the flood-soaked earth in the beginning, so that no such flood would be released again, is abused and trampled on and the pledge of consciousness to protect life once again from being overwhelmed by unconsciousness is forgotten. For in this *Götterdämmerung* phase a new, and more disturbing possibility is created by a hubris of man's archaic, collective urges. This protective consciousness can be infiltrated and become an instrument of the evil it was created to prevent; it can be turned against creation, if it is raised too high and its base too narrow, and it is too far removed from its natural earth, its roots in the unconsciousness, to allow the free flow between consciousness and the unconscious which man needs to make his awareness whole. And it is far from over yet. This is why the rainbow is so compelling an image of consciousness and why mythology warns that man in his seeking may pass humbly, as it were, underneath it but never arrogate to himself a right to walk over it.

The decline in the quality and range of consciousness, the erosion of its many-sidedness, and limitation more and more to a purely rational and partial state, as well as its instant subordination to sweeping collective assumptions and abstractions, are the most disturbing characteristics of our time, and a sign that all these sinister hordes which massed in the 1939 unconscious of Germany are massing in many other cultures as well, and are not only not dispersed but in a state of general mobilization.

But whenever I think back to the beginning of that cataclysmic war, I think of two friends I have hardly mentioned who were almost the most important friendships in my life ...

Yes, I would love to hear about them.

I am thinking of Lilian Bowes Lyon and René Janin. Lilian's is such a strange story, which ought to be told in full. But one can't. There are things in her life that prevent one from telling it properly, yet. And the other person I was thinking of was a close friend of hers, to whom we all owed a great debt: my French friend René Janin. He was such an upright, brave person who belonged to a condemned and dying world but lived in it as if he liked it.

Perhaps I should begin with him, and how he found himself forced to go into commerce in London – something for which he had not been trained at all, and disliked intensely. Yet he undertook it with great style. He never complained, and did it as if it were some princely function that he was performing. He was of that world in France which outsiders do not know nearly enough about: a world that has the tone, the quality and finesse of France in its trust, and keeps it alive not by preaching, raging and forming political parties but by living their trust: the *petite noblesse* who survived the revolutions and generations of official rejection and mistrust, and in every sphere of life were an example of an abiding France.

Through his own family, René belonged naturally to this sort of French squirearchy. His father, for instance, had been a great friend of Pétain. They were in the same class at St Cyr and they both passed their final exams on the same day. Both were intensely Catholic, and neither was to find that very helpful in their chosen career, in which only 'men of the people' were marked out for high promotion. But it was typical that this impediment did not interfere with their choice of a profession. People of their level were naturally Catholic and naturally served France through its army, so there was no hesitation. I remember General Janin telling how he was given just about as bad a posting as he could get, and he thought he must not say anything about it to Pétain as Pétain would get most upset that his friend had been so badly treated after such a brilliant career at St Cyr. It was only many years afterwards that he discovered that Pétain had received an even worse posting, and had never mentioned it to General Janin for the same reason. It is a sweet story because it shows so delicately the kind of people they were in René's world. And these were the people, too, who were always called upon when France was really in a state of extreme crisis. The people of the Revolution always called on their despised *petite noblesse*, and their traditions, to come to the rescue of France. Ever since the Revolution it had been mandatory that the heads of the army had to be men of the people. And yet there was this aristocratic Roman Catholic element which was really the heart and essence of France at its best, and which, unrecognized and unrewarded, kept its spirit and will and élan.

And René, though not a soldier, was typical of those people who although socially and in terms of power were underdogs, through what they were in themselves were the topdogs. They were really European civilization at its best. René Janin's father, who studied and spoke Russian fluently, quietly and uncomplainingly progressed until he just had to be appointed military attaché at Petrograd, which was from the French point of view the most important military attachéship in the world. France was Russia's ally. France had an enormous cultural and commercial influence in Russia, and had built the trans-Siberian railway. Britain too had its own wide influence on Russia, but it was more political, economic and social. France had it culturally to an extraordinary degree.

René soon had a vast world of acquaintances in Russia. He was a very attractive person, interested in everything, spoke German as fluently as he spoke Russian and English, and seemed to me already the first totally integrated European – a forerunner of a united Europe. His English was so good that I teased him and said: 'It is indecent for a Frenchman to speak English as well as you do. But, thank heaven, there are two mistakes you make, and these must go uncorrected so that people should always know what you are!' One mistake was idiomatic, a punctilious 'What are your news?' The other his pronunciation of 'finger' as with a soft 'g'. He begged me to tell him, and I refused because we had such fun playing it over as a game, but now that he is dead I rather wish I had. Somehow he brought a kind of flavour into our foursome – William Plomer, Tony Butts and the two of us – that nobody else could, with lots of colour and nuance that we would never otherwise have had.

He was in touch with people and things one does not normally meet in the art world in London. We used to have the most uproarious parties through René at the D'Erlanger's large house in Piccadilly, which used to be Byron's house, and where Catherine D'Erlanger, whom we saw sitting there for De Laszlo, claimed that she met Byron's ghost on the stairs regularly, and there was dear old Baron Emile, head of the tunnel project at that time. We had the most uproarious discussions about it.

All sorts of people from all over the world popped in, and sometimes on Sundays Catherine drove us down to The Royal Albion at Brighton for lunch, where the owner, Harry Preston, I think, still presided over his own world. He was a friend of the Prince of Wales and the sporting aristocracy and had his own special Brighton roots going back to the Regency, and was a friend of Carpentier, Dempsey and so on.

One of the people whom René met in that world, I don't know how, turned out to be the cousin of the Duchess of York, who then subsequently became Queen Elizabeth the Queen Mother, as she is today. She was a young woman called Lilian Bowes Lyon and she very quickly became a member of our foursome. She was born near the Roman wall in Northumberland, and loved Northumberland very dearly. Her mother was a Lindsay, a daughter of the famous Lord Crawford of Balcarres, a great scientist and a kinsman of the Lady Anne Lindsay, who came to the Cape as Lady Anne Barnard, wrote *Auld Robin Gray*, and started English literature in South Africa with her famous letters. Her father, Francis Bowes Lyon, was rather a recluse and an eccentric, who did not like coming down to London at all. He lived in seclusion in a place called Bardon Mill in Northumberland. And if he did come to London for the season for the sake of his daughters, he would hire a whole floor of the Paddington Hotel – the railway hotels were the most fashionable hotels in London in those days. Yes! He refused to have a house in London and thought a floor of the Paddington Hotel enough to bring out his daughters. Now, of the three daughters that I knew, Lilian found the life suffocating. She always had a longing to write. She had written one or two poems for *Punch* which were printed and which I thought were very good. But she also tried to write novels. She wrote two novels under the name of D. J. Cotman, which make beautiful reading.

It was at this stage in her life that she was being pressed very hard to go back to her family and one night when I was taking her home, she told me all about it. She was a very sweet, self-possessed, sensitive, and brave Scottish girl, but suddenly she started crying. I managed to get her to talk on and she told me why she did not want to go back. And, I in my impulsive African way, said at once: 'By God, you won't go back! There must be no question of your going back. It would be absolutely wrong.' I added, 'I think you are a born poet and a writer, and you must just stick it out. You have earned the right to a life of your own. You are one of us, and you stay with us.' And that decided her to stay permanently in London. She became one of our little group, and Lilian and William liked each other enormously. They used to write to each other. I believe William gave her a Red Indian name, 'Red Feather' or something. She had a name for him too, they kept up an enchanting correspondence throughout the war. They were very close and liked each other in that gifted way in which the best of homosexuals can have very good relationships with women. Women feel that they can just be themselves with them, and no problem about sex ever arises. And yet there is a natural sort of sharing of interests at the same time. She was very good to and for William, as she was to all of us. I think it was William's first close relationship with an exceptional woman, and Lilian enriched his life, so much so that he came to me one day, after his latest affair had ended, and wondered whether I thought that perhaps he ought to get married. He had thought perhaps Lilian was the person to ask. They were such good friends and had so much in common. She understood about him, she was well-born and had all the tastes that he had. What did I think?

My heart sank when I heard this, because I knew that Lilian would not settle for a relationship like that. And I am afraid she did not. I think it hurt William very much because some of the hurt rubbed off on to me, yet a deep part of himself was relieved. It hurt his vulnerabilities, leaving a strange paradox of hurt and not-hurt in their relationship. They did remain close friends, although friends with unspoken reservations. All the time, however, it seemed to me that of the whole lot of us, the person who was really worth the most, outstanding and unique, was Lilian. It was not just that I thought her poetry really first-rate and original, it was the quality of her being, the texture, the integrity and courage against the unknown and unpredictable. But she was a born poet and I begged her, 'Drop this novel writing, because you are poet.' So, in 1934, she brought out an anthology of her first poems, called, *The White Hare and Other Poems*, which was instantly recognized for its very great qualities. She had a very close feeling for the country and nature, which shone like starlight in these poems. They are evocative of Gerard Manley Hopkins,

234

whom she admired enormously. It was not that she picked up his manner, but that she had a great deal of Gerard Manley Hopkins in herself. She was a naturally devout and deeply committed person. From then on she wrote nothing but poetry, and she became one of the greatest woman friends I have ever had. I learned from her what an immensely rewarding thing it is to be friends with women. It was a period in my life when I was very much alone, and I could not have got by without her.

As always in times of personal crisis and heightened stress, I longed to write poetry, and Lilian's example and the fact that she sent me her poems as they were completed, warm from her dedicated and caring spirit, fired the longing in me so that I would try it out. But then to my horror I discovered that I never could write it at any sustained level. The trouble is, one can only write poetry in one's first and most immediate language, and I had only a smattering of a first language ever. It is true that almost all the white world around me spoke Afrikaans or English, but in my own world from the start I stumbled onto the foreshore of the ocean of words where flotsam and jetsam of the languages of unrealized cultures were tossed by the swell and surf of an Indian Ocean of time and tide, and bits of Bushman, Griqua, garbled Malay, Sotho and even a piece or two of Malagash from Madagascar, and more coherently some French, much more Dutch, Afrikaans and English increasingly intact, were all left stranded around me. What was I to pick up? Certainly not a first language. To make matters worse, we had a tradition of formidable Dutch governesses. We were taught in Dutch in kindergarten, our Bible was in Dutch, our church services and all official services were conducted in Dutch. My father himself spoke impeccable Dutch, although he wrote two novels with all the dialogue in what was his idea of the vernacular. And then in my reading I soon developed a preference for English. So I never had a first language, and poetry of my own was lost, a loss that hurts to this day.

But at this period a sense of no longer belonging made me struggle towards this ancient home of the word. And I remember on the day King George V died I came up to London to see Lilian, and everywhere – on the trains at Paddington, in the underground, in the streets – there was this atmosphere, like the lowering of the sky and the moaning of the air and sea which I had experienced before a typhoon. It was an unmistakable token of the death of a King, and I remember being moved that Great Britain still had the heart and the depth of spirit to grieve and to realize how important an event this was for a nation; more important at that moment because of the faint-hearted noises coming out of Parliament, despite the shadow of Hitler looming like another Adamastor over a new Cape of Storms. So important was this to me that in the train, to my astonishment, I had nearly completed a poem. I remember only the first lines:

‘When Kings die,
and like peasants,
Coffin-small
they lie . . .’

I thought I would show it to Lilian. But when I arrived there she had visitors. Her aunt, I think it was Lady Jane Lindsay, was there, with two small girls: one was the Queen and the other Princess Margaret, and what followed is not something I would normally write or talk about, but it is all of fifty years and more ago and my ration of life is running out. This little story seems to me born not to be forgotten as it will be if I do not tell it to someone, because I am the only witness left who could possibly remember it. I had found, of course, that ‘the-King-is-dead’ sentiment of the nation had preceded me, but the ‘long-live-the-King’ sentiment, which is its twin, had not entered yet. Princess Margaret, who was one of the loveliest and most magical of children, suddenly said to Lilian, ‘These are trying times in which we live, are they not Cousin Lil?’ and Lilian, smiling and, as always, wonderful with children, asked, ‘What do you mean by trying times, darling?’

‘Well, don’t you see, Cousin Lil, trying times are times in which you have just got to go on trying and trying.’

And somehow afterwards, although I showed my poem to Lilian and she liked it and helped to make it scan, I did not finish it, I think partly because of my lack of a first language and partly because the story I have just told said it all. And I went back to the country late that night, staring out of the window of the Cheltenham Flyer, a great train at the end of the line of an age when trains and much else were thenceforth to decline, and was full of foreboding. I think already the night was darker because of what was soon to come.

I was farming in the West Country and my circle of friends thought I was 'bonkers', having come so far to be in London, then running away from it – all except René, and suddenly he was sent away for good to Costa Rica because of his business undertakings. He went to a coffee estate called San Vincente, which, typical of René, would grow the best coffee in the world. Two coffees claimed the title – Blue Mountain and San Vincente – they commanded the highest prices in the German and Austrian markets where the real coffee was bought, but we all thought René's had to be the best. But for me it was a sad and irretrievable loss. I saw very little of him thereafter, and our correspondence gradually dropped away. But I saw more of Lilian and she remained a constant and steadfast friend. All the time, too, she grew as a poet. She brought just the kind of feminine element into that world which it grievously lacked. When the war broke out, and we all had to decide what we were going to do in the war, she went and lived in the East End of London, in Stepney, where the worst of the German bombing took place. She lived there right through the bombing and was a great centre for the community.

I did not see her again until about three years after the war, when I came back. She was in hospital then, because, after all the hardship and deprivation she had suffered, her circulation had gone wrong. Doctors had had to amputate a foot, and then a lower leg, and then above the knee, and then started on the other foot. But she was still writing marvellous poetry. She was helpless but had a wonderful collection of friends who came to see her, and a wonderful woman looked after her and made it possible for her to go on writing to the end. One of the people who visited her regularly was Walter de la Mare, a remarkable man and a strangely underrated poet. And he said to her, 'Miss Bowes Lyon, gravity is such a bore. It always pushes one down. I get so tired of things always falling down. I wish that occasionally things would fall up!' She had been feeling depressed and he tried to cheer her up, then said goodbye and went away. But a few minutes later there was a knock on the door and Walter de la Mare put his head through and he said, 'Miss Bowes Lyon, I just wanted to assure you, that if ever I see a teacup falling upwards I will send you a telegram!' And then he went away.

The war and her own congenital frailty had taken a great toll of her, but her spirit was undimmed and still she wrote, sometimes not being able to finish what she had started, and sometimes just a few lines that went like a shooting star through her imagination in flashes. For instance, this flash, the last time I saw her alive:

'Oh Pegasus, my Dazzler, bend your knees
So that I may mount you with ease . . .'

The lines would have stayed with me always because of their innate beauty and originality, but at that moment they overwhelmed me as an example of poetic courage, the sort of courage which made Mozart draw his *Requiem* to an end when he was literally dying. Lilian herself, though not dying there and then, was nearing her end, had already had both her legs amputated above the knees and was threatened with the amputation of her right arm. And yet she still wanted to travel on with her 'Dazzler', her poetic image of transport from the earth and its prose to heaven and its song, confessing her inability to do this unless the image could help her, unless her Pegasus could bend his knees so that her mutilated self could travel on.

I knew that she had not long to live and I would see her as often as possible, but I had to start almost at once another kind of life and was often away. I was sent on an expedition to Central Africa that was to prove very important to me, and an extraordinary thing happened. One afternoon I was going across a very high plateau, a remote and unexplored plateau. Did I tell you about it?

No. But do you mean the Nyika plateau and your expedition to Nyasaland that you described in Venture to the Interior?

Yes. I remember I had a dream the night before about a poem Lilian wrote on 'Duchess', a cart-horse of mine. And suddenly I had a very strong feeling, I must write to Lilian at once, without a second's delay, and I took out my military despatch book and I wrote her a letter. I put some flowers, which I had pressed between the leaves, in an envelope with the letter. About seventy miles away there was a great mission station with a post office, on the top of the escarpment on Lake Nyasa. I gave the letter to one of my bearers and he went off with it on a forked stick to post it for me to Lilian, and I thought how she would have relished the sight. Weeks later, on my way back to England, I was travelling in a flying boat. We landed in the Bouches du Rhône, which was one of the formal stages of the flight. Some English newspapers were put on board. I saw the words, 'QUEEN'S COUSIN WHO LIVED IN EAST END DURING WAR...' and I thought, 'Oh, how wonderful! Lilian has been recognized for what she is. People are finding out about her quality, her bravery and her poetry.' And then I took out the paper and I saw that she had died the night before. I was too shaken for tears, and heartbroken, I had so counted on seeing her again, and later thought, 'How cruel! Not even my letter would have got to her.' But when I got to London, Keith Miller-Jones, a lawyer and a great friend of mine who was very much part of our circle of friends, and also Lilian's lawyer, came to see me and handed me a letter from her written before she died. It was a letter of farewell, and characteristically timed to make me at peace with life and full of the most healing and caring concern, and it was hardly about herself except a cry to understand myself and accept that she just had to 'absent herself for a while'.

That finished me, and hurt all the more because my letter had not reached her. I could only think this letter was permanently lost. But two months later, from Nyasaland, I received a letter from Lilian which had been following me around. In it she wrote that my letter, flowers and all, had arrived and it had been wonderful, but she had to write quickly because she knew that she had only a few hours to live. And I thought it was miraculous that she had got this letter and could send me a message which sustains and upholds me still and tells me how near and clear she remains. But wasn't it strange, on this plateau, having this feeling, 'I've just got to write to her!' And it reached her just in time.

She was such a very gifted, talented woman, with immense courage. All I have done really today is to raise my hat to a great and great-hearted woman as a sign and a hope that the time may come when it will be possible to write of her in the round and to the full. And I wanted a world which has forgotten to remember her and her poetry.

Would you think Lilian Bowes-Lyon, Carl Jung and all the friends and all the people who have counted in your life are part of this small group of individuals who carry a little spark of fire, a little spark of truth, and who are helping us on our way?

Yes, in the sense that they all opened doors and pointed a way, and they did so because they were just themselves and they believed in friendship and personal relationships, and doing whatever they felt they had to do, as well as possible. It did not go beyond that. And I think that was tremendously important at that time. In coteries such as Bloomsbury, people got together because of a talent. 'He must be one of us because he's so talented.' Or, 'You must meet him, he's going to be a great writer!' But with us, our group was more, 'Oh, you'd like so and so!' Not because of talent – it was the quality of the person. Think, if only Virginia Woolf had been surrounded with people who thought of her more as a woman than a talent, treated her as a woman rather than a great, gifted brain, I am certain she would have been a different and more complete person. But so many of her closest friends thought of her primarily as an artist and her searching, lost humanity was left out in the cold. I still shudder at the cold of the half-this and half-that world where the woman in her lived as a ghost. It made our group of friends very important in that darkening, colder world where the human values were diminished and diminishing, where people were just being valued for their talent or for the importance of the functions they performed in life. We were just there together because we liked one another, and felt as though we belonged. And Lilian was a very important element in this; as far as I was concerned, the most important.

There are so many others I wish I could tell you about: Keith Miller-Jones, for one, who lived just for friendship; and Julian Lezard – but they are truly legion and I am overcome with gratitude to life that has privileged me to be so befriended from the moment I was born. I do not go past a graveyard, by train, car or on foot, without a rush of gratitude coming over me towards those unknown dead for having lived: a great thank-you rises like a chorale in me because they made it possible for us to be here, and I know that in the deeps each person is unique and wonderful and that it is only our refusal to know ourselves, light and dark, fire and shadow, all, and our failure to understand people and things and God as we can understand them and wish to be understood ourselves, that prevents us from achieving now, rather than later, the brotherhood that awaits us. It is all there ready and only addicts of power and ambition, greed and self-love, exploit the trust and love that is natural to us, and retard the happy ending that is built into our long-suffering creation.

I remember Jung saying how he found the effort he put into understanding people and their problems one of the most exciting experiences on earth, and that, having understood, he was humbled and exalted how all the apparent stupidity and meaninglessness was abstracted from life and it revealed itself suddenly as great-hearted and full of grace.

I know that you met quite a number of the war leaders and I would like you to tell me something about them. I wonder, perhaps because of my own involvement with Japan, if we could begin with some of the great leaders you served in South-East Asia and Indonesia, in particular, Mountbatten. But first there is something I have always wanted to ask you about what happened when you were hastening on your way from Java to see Mountbatten at his headquarters in Colombo. You told me the story about how you had done the journey without money and you had to ask an officer to pay for your food – your first good meal, I imagine, for days – in the NAAFI at Colombo, and you promised to buy him a dinner at Claridge's when you got home. Did you have an opportunity to keep your promise?

Yes. I took his card. And I kept it. And nearly three years later I wrote to him and said I was in London for a period, and should he be in London I would love to buy him the meal at Claridge's that I had promised him. He was working in heavy industry in the Midlands, and he had become completely civilian, but he remembered the occasion. He said, 'You know, you needn't have bothered about this – any of us would have bought you a meal – because, you know, you looked so desperately ill and starving!' To which I replied that I *had* been starving. So it was very nice seeing him. I would have felt awful if I had not met him again.

Can you sketch a portrait of Mountbatten?

My first meeting with him took place in Kandy, Ceylon, at his headquarters in the hills – a beautiful and sacred place of water and temples. What struck me first was the splendour. All the uniforms were shining; his staff looked like film heroes. When I went in to see him, he was sitting behind his desk and looked the part of a soldier. He was in his prime, and extremely good-looking. He had a great and immediate personality. I walked up to the desk and prepared to come to attention, as military etiquette demanded, but before I could even do that he stood up and said, 'You know, I've heard all about you from my wife. Delighted to meet you.'

242

Then he said, 'Come on now, what the hell is going on? Did you send that signal?' We laughed and I confessed I had drafted a signal for the Admiral. What had happened was that we were bombarded by signals and even messages from Mountbatten. Our limited system of communications could not cope, and in any case events were changing so fast that signals and their answers were out of date before they were sent. So Admiral Patterson, his flag officer, and I concocted a most immediate signal, to be sent in clear: 'We can continue to rock the baby to sleep only if you people outside the house would not make so much noise.' But I meanwhile realized that it was important to have something in writing as well, so I had written out a standard military appreciation of the situation in Java. I had written it on the plane on the way. But he waved it away saying, 'Well, never mind that for the moment. Let's talk about it.'

Then I told him how serious the situation in Java really was; that the Dutch were totally unprepared; that those of them who were coming to the island were expecting that they could just walk in and take up again where they had left off before the invasion, and nothing could be more mistaken and dangerous now that the islands were all in revolt. But I begged him to take into consideration that everybody on the islands – not only the Dutch but the Javanese as well – had suffered terribly under the Japanese. They had been cut off from the outside world for years. No one knew what had really been going on. I said that the last thing we should do was what the Dutch wanted us to do – start immediately imposing a military solution on such a hurt and bewildered world. I suggested instead that we should try to win a period of at least six months' grace in which people could find their balance, in which the new postwar world could receive them.

We had a long and very understanding talk about it. He brought in his Director of Intelligence, General Penny, and 'Boy' Browning, the General who commanded the Arnhem operation, and finally the man whom I found the most impressive of all, General Slim – always to us the 'Bill Slim' of the Forgotten Army. We had a long conference, at the end of which Mountbatten said, 'Look, gentlemen, General Penny is going to London tomorrow morning. I propose that we send Colonel van der Post with him to let him talk to the War Cabinet as he's been talking to us today.' So that was agreed.

243

The next morning I was in a plane and on my way to London. General Penny fell ill and went straight to hospital on our arrival, so the whole burden fell on me.

As you already knew Churchill, I expect you could turn to him for help?

No. I met him later, and in any case he was no longer in charge. A Labour Government, under Attlee, had taken over and I had to meet a completely new set of people, but fortunately I had known Stafford Cripps, and I knew how important he could be to us because of his sustained interest in India and everything connected with that part of the world. I had a hunch that I should see him first before I talked to anybody else. This was a source of comfort that I needed because, throughout the journey, I had been getting more and more depressed. Although, thanks largely to Mountbatten, I had left with a good feeling about the future of the area under his command, I could not help, from past experience, being worried about what could await me in London. I remembered once in the Western Desert when I went up to Divisional Headquarters to report on the condition on our front and they seemed to me already to have the picture wrong in certain essentials. Then I went to Cairo and I was truly dismayed when I talked to the Director of Intelligence and his staff because they semed to me even more to have lost the feel, let alone the facts, of the matter. Having experienced this, I found myself increasingly worried about what I would find in London.

I can't tell you how glad I was that I had met so intuitive and open a mind as Mountbatten's, interested only in the truth, and that I had left him with a detailed appreciation of the situation in Indonesia. I felt that he, at any rate, would have a good idea of the depth and extent of the nationalistic movement in that part of the world. I remember how in the beginning I had to get him to realize that this nationalistic movement could not just be passed off as the result of Japanese encouragement. I quoted my Indonesian liaison officer who had been sent to me by the Dutch Government, the remarkable and gifted Javanese nobleman who became a great friend and, thank heaven, is still alive: Raden Abdul Kadir Widjoyoatmodjo, always 'Dul' to me and my staff. He had also tried to leave the Dutch Government in no doubt about what was going on and warned them, in this regard in particular, 'The Japanese may have been the midwives but the baby is purely Indonesian.' And still they had not been convinced, or worse, in truly Machiavellian fashion, were determined not to be convinced. As a result, I arrived in England worried. I arrived somewhere in the West Country by air. There was a car from the War Office waiting for me, and I was taken straight up to London and went first to see Stafford Cripps. He grasped the seriousness of the situation at once, partly no doubt because his knowledge of that area predisposed him to accept nationalism as a natural outcome of imperial history, and he said to me, 'Yes, you must see the Prime Minister as soon as possible; I'll arrange it at once.'

That evening I saw Attlee in his private room at the House of Commons. But that is another story, because Attlee there and then sent me on to Holland to talk to the first post-war Government in the Hague. I spent nearly a week there with the Dutch Prime Minister and his Cabinet, and was already alarmed by the signs of a split opening up between the Dutch and Java and ourselves, between the Dutch themselves in The Hague and their representatives in Java, and between both sections of the Dutch and our Government in Britain.

But the only point of this elaboration has been to illustrate the speed with which Mountbatten could respond to events.

To continue the portrait of Mountbatten, if he had really understood the situation rightly in Indonesia, he must also have understood the Indian situation from the beginning?

Well, I for one had quite a lot to do with the preparatory stages of his education, as it were, in the political realities of South-East Asia and the great impact the Indonesian part of his career had on the man that was to become the last Viceroy of India.

So he was prepared?

Yes, he was indirectly prepared, in one sense at least, because not only had he to deal with Java and the old Dutch East Indies but also with Indo-China, Malaya and Burma, and he realized fully the extent of these violent eruptions of change that the war had released in South-East Asia. He realized that all the sleeping volcanoes of nationalism were in full eruption, and that was the reality that one had to accept and somehow prevent from causing immense destruction. He started off, as I did, with the belief that the destruction could be avoided, or at least contained, and that some new relationship could be established between that part of the world and Europe, which for centuries had ruled it. Also he knew before he finally left Indonesia that he was going to India, and one should remember, too, that he was commanding an essentially Indian army. Since the Mutiny every brigade in the Indian army had three battalions, one from Britain and the other two Indian. It was one of the finest armies, I believe, that Britain ever raised.

Incidentally, having left the fighting armies in 1942, to see them again after the Japanese capitulation was a revelation. My first thought was, there is no one there who did not get there by merit. They have learned their job! There were brigadiers who were all so young – twenty-three and twenty-five years old – they used to be forty or fifty and over – and all there on sheer merit.

It is rare to see generals on the battlefield with their men.

Yes, it was a remarkable army. But they had to keep count of Indian public opinion. India knew it was going to become independent. And Nehru sent Mountbatten a liaison officer, a Mr Punjabi, who was a fine man and kept his commanders in the Dutch East Indies informed of Indian attitudes and Indian susceptibilities about their soldiers. I worked closely with Mr Punjabi, especially when Mountbatten knew he was going to India. It was Mr Punjabi who was sent to ask Nehru, among other things, for some sort of message to help us in our efforts to reconcile Dutch and Indonesians. Nehru sent that message we spoke of before, to Sukarno: that the British were leaving India with a non-political and incorruptible civil service, judiciary and army, that Sukarno had none of those things, and without them a modern democracy and government were not possible.

You knew Mountbatten through all these events. How did he grow? Do you think he was a great statesman?

He had it in him, he had all the intuition, the sense of a wider plan, but he lacked experience. But, being an extraordinarily intuitive person, for instance, it made sense to him to let me tell the Dutch, 'If you have to give, give quickly and give even more than you have been asked for.' 'Try and think of what necessity will demand of you one day,' I had urged them on his behalf, 'things that even the Indonesians haven't thought of yet, and you will recover your lost initiatives.' And I remember adding something to this effect, 'History tells us that all these great changes in

246

life are let down because people let change force change out of them. They are not partners of change. They give little by little, reluctantly, and in the end they are forced to give far more than was originally asked of them. And even that far more, is no longer enough. And this is what we must prevent.'

Now Mountbatten interpreted that, quite rightly, as a prescription also for the sort of change demanded for India – for us to give quickly and give handsomely. But I think they all over-simplified what the giving really meant. I do not think he realized what a complex country India was and how profound its history. He interpreted events in Java to mean that Britain should get out of India quickly too, and not stay to see the change-over through.

You think this was a mistake?

Well, it seems to me that this is where Mountbatten might have lacked a sense of history, in the sense that Churchill had it. He had a great sense of tradition, service, of sympathy for the underdogs of life and power, but not this extra dimension of a sense of history which enables power in moments of change to call on the energies and values of history to contain them. He did not have the same inner personal measure of history to acquire 'an emotion' of history. The intuitive in him saw the future more clearly than the past, active in the now.

You see, Mountbatten had a very good naval officer's training which was perhaps the best in the world. Yet one wonders what more he would have done had he had Churchill's training, or lack of training. It is almost as if from childhood Churchill was preparing himself for a meeting with destiny. He could hardly pass through school, or into the army. But when, in India, with a hurt foot and being unable to play polo, he started to read Greek history, the penny dropped. From that moment on until the day of his death, Churchill was educating himself. He was reading, and re-reading, history. He also had an interest in the evolution of science and its applications, and in every way instinctively was preparing himself for something unique. Mountbatten was absolutely fine for war, but I cannot see Churchill agreeing to the partition of India.

Mountbatten consented, despite his own initial convictions against, for India to be partitioned, and the partitioning meant that vast populations had to move away from areas where they had been settled for centuries. I think someone should have told him – and I do not think they did – that this was going to be disastrous. So, in a sense, I think the haste with which the British forces got out of India was a tragic error. And the error was not just Mountbatten's; the London Government and advisers all came into it, and I think they failed him. We should have said to Nehru and to Jinna, 'We want to give you independence. But we are not giving it at the price of dividing India. You have got to make up your differences, and then you can have it.' I think that is what Wavell wanted but, dear heaven, Wavell had already had so much asked of him that I do not know for certain how much more he could have taken on.

Would Wavell have done better if he had been given the chance?

He was very, very tired, but I still think he could have done a lot, working for a government who believed in him as they did in Mountbatten. Do not forget that the basic error was in London, in the heart of generations of Labour socialist philosophies. They were the villains of the piece, as their intellectual heirs and successors still are.

Mountbatten had a marvellous presence, and he had unfailing courage, and he did all he could always with all of himself, and was a great servant. However, I did have some odd moments with him myself. For instance, I would always accompany my own general from Java to his staff conferences in Singapore. One particular general, Robert Mansergh, and the officers with him, were very much opposed to me and what they thought I represented. They were at heart really on the side of the Dutch and wanted to fight it out with the Indonesians. So I was very unpopular with my general. We did have two generals before him, however, who were different: first, General Christison, who was superb, and then General Stopford who was admirable, but did not stay long enough. Then we had Mansergh, this brave, able, 'bella figura' general. I remember Bill Slim, after a visit to a 14th Army Brigade Front which was hard-pressed and critical, and commanded by the then Brigadier Mansergh, writing among other things; 'Mansergh as usual looked as if he were just going off for a duck shoot.' Mansergh and most of his staff were all for the Dutch way of life in Indonesia and could not understand what this 'nonsense' was all about – giving independence to the Indonesians. I had to sit there at staff conferences and listen to him giving slanted interpretations of events in Java to Mountbatten. And

248

Mountbatten certainly picked it up at once, although I did not say a word. He would listen to all the various commanders giving their news and intelligence and then say casually, 'Is that all, gentlemen? Now I would just like to hear what Colonel van der Post thinks about it.' And then I had to speak, and speak the truth. There was hell for me to pay afterwards, with my own general and staff.

Of course.

And then Mountbatten once very nearly sacked a general because he gave an interpretation that could have ended in disaster. I should perhaps enlarge on this specific illustration, because it is so illuminating. A divisional general, a Gurkha deputizing for Bob Mansergh, had given Mountbatten Bob Mansergh's version of our intelligence which I had already fought against in Java and knew to be wrong. Again Mountbatten picked up this concealed difference between us. When at last he asked me for my comments he realized that there was something more serious than usual at stake and ordered this general and myself to see him alone after the meeting. I thought the matter so important that I asked the British Minister in Batavia, Gilbert MacKereth, to come with me to the meeting. I was Mountbatten's link in Java, through Gilbert MacKereth, with the Foreign Office under Ernest Bevin, in London.

I wish I could tell you more about MacKereth, who I think was a great British ambassador. He and his wife Muriel had become great friends of mine in Java, at one time perhaps the only real friends I had there, and I do not know how, without them, I would have got through those terrible months when I was, as it were, 'sent to Coventry' both by the Dutch and by my own general and his staff. MacKereth was a person of exceptional experience and vision and also knew what it was to be a soldier because he had ended up in the 1914–18 war as one of the youngest brigadiers in the British Army. He had a great capacity for seeing things in the round and somehow I knew that Mountbatten should speak to him directly as well.

This meeting between the four of us was perhaps the most uncomfortable of many uncomfortable ones. Mountbatten was relentless in his pursuit of the truth and very soon realized how he had been misled. His anger, which was Olympian, then turned on this very gallant little Gurkha general who was fundamentally innocent and merely carrying out his instructions. By the time Mountbatten was satisfied that at last he had an accurate and complete picture of the situation, the general was, I suspect, as near to collapse as he had ever been. So much so that when we emerged into the sunlight again, MacKereth, who knew how unfair a task had been imposed on the general, hastened to comfort him saying, with that infectious laugh of his, 'General, I can tell you that only one thing sustained me in this conference we have just had: I remembered when I was a boy at school how I helped to duck the Supreme Commander – Mountbatten – in our swimming-pool.'

A more dramatic illustration occurred during Mountbatten's visit to his Army Headquarters in Batavia. After years of such cruel and unbelievably dreary occupation by a ruthless and unpredictable enemy, the occasion was turned into a royal event, a coronation almost of liberation and peace. The streets were crowded with people in their best clothes and smartest uniforms, buzzing with anticipation and excitement long before Mountbatten arrived. And, of course, there was something else. This was the closest they had ever come to seeing a royal visitor. It was an ominous fact that although Indonesia had been part of the vast Dutch Empire for some 350 years, Dutch royalty had never paid it a visit. So you can imagine how numinous an element there was in Mountbatten's princely appearance among them.

I was not there myself. I had been firmly told by my general that I was not wanted for the day, and I was given work to do to keep me out of Mountbatten's way. For the first time I was not invited to any of the celebrations in his honour and was excluded from the staff conference after the official lunch, on the grounds that it was to be confined to a meeting of minds between the general, his staff brigadier, and Mountbatten. Two of my officers and two of our secretaries who were there in the streets, said the reception was sensational and that the crowds gave Mountbatten a rapturous welcome. His good looks, his bearing, his medals, immaculate uniform, and the electrifying effect of his confident, ardent, unafraid, uninhibited and direct personality intoxicated everyone who saw him. By nightfall, there were few of those women and girls, so deprived of colour and normal relationships with people of their kind all those long random years of war and isolation, who were not in love with him. The girls on my own staff certainly were.

But meanwhile I had been to see the Indonesian Prime Minister, Soetan Sjahrir, and asked him and his colleagues to stand by, because I could not believe that Mountbatten would not somehow demand to see him, despite the obvious desire of the Dutch and our own High Command to keep them apart. I had done all I could to persuade my general how desirable such a meeting was, and indeed how destructive the consequences if it did not take place. At the very least it would be discourteous, as well as a violation of Mountbatten's sense of the decencies of the occasion, not to mention how hurtful to Sjahrir and his people. But I was overruled and put into purdah for the day.

Between three and four in the afternoon, when I was in my mess practising a new piece on the piano, which kept me sane, one of my officers came running in with a shout, 'Quick, Colonel, you are wanted.'

I jumped up, grabbed my hat and came out on the verandah as the jeeps, with Mountbatten at the wheel of the first, pulled up below. I knew at once that he was both angry and in a hurry.

'And where have you been all day?' he demanded in a brisk, taut voice I knew could snap at any moment.

'Forgive me, sir,' I answered quickly, 'but I was given immediate work to do here.'

And at that I could not help glancing at the staff brigadier who had given me my orders rather brutally the night before, and who had jumped out of the second jeep, and was standing to attention, rather self-consciously, beside Mountbatten's jeep. The meaning of that involuntary glance seemed plain to Mountbatten and I believe prevented an explosion of frustration, unbelief and anger that had been gathering in him. The anger indeed remained; but as he was one of the few men I ever knew in whom anger increased clarity of vision rather than confused the senses, as it did with me, he saw at once what had happened.

'Whatever it is,' he ordered, 'stop doing it. I want to see Sjahrir. How are we going to arrange it?'

'That's easy, sir,' I told him. 'He has been standing by all day hoping that you would be able to see him. But I would only suggest that we go in my car. It will be safer.'

It was ironic that of all those there, the staff brigadier looked most relieved, and for the first and last time almost grateful to me, although there was no room in my car to take him along as well to what was an immensely constructive meeting.

But surely Mountbatten must have done something about such a set-up afterwards. Surely there were repercussions of some kind?

He left Sjahrir late and had to rush out to the airport and had no time, but even if he had, I do not think he would or should have done anything. There is an old and wise English legal saying, that the law does not concern itself with trifles. In the law of supreme command this was a trifle, this was how human beings are and at such a level they must be left to contain and dissolve these tensions for themselves. We had already had three changes of generals but these tensions, which this dichotomy of policy and time continually produced, did not vanish but became worse with each change. I think by then Mountbatten believed I could handle my ambivalent end of the situation and he left me to do it.

But, Laurens, it must have been pretty awful. You did not have that sort of authority of rank.

No, I never did. Some of my friends felt concerned for me and in the most sensitive way suggested that I had earned the right to leave, and promised to see that I went with honour and dignity. For instance, Admiral Sir Wilfred Patterson, my first boss, wanted me to go, and believed that things would only get worse for me. We had several long talks about it but when I explained why I could not go unless I was sacked, he understood. He understood that my contract with Indonesia was a contract with my own inner self and its own imperatives of doing and being at the moment. That was my authority ultimately for what I did, and I was lucky in that, so far, this authority had full worldly support from Lord Mountbatten and the Foreign Office in the shape of its ambassador, Gilbert MacKereth.

But, Laurens, it was still an impossible situation. You had come straight out of prison into all this. You were not well and were always at the centre of some storm, and on top of that you were humiliated by your own general and his staff. It was too much surely. Did you not even feel you ought to resign?

No, I never did. I was only worried sometimes that I might not be up to it physically. I never doubted I had to serve on until I dropped or was sacked. This inner thing that had to be obeyed of which I told you, a profound sense of being answerable only to life in what I did, insisted that I served on. I never felt humiliated, or insulted. I remembered a family saying, 'only cooks can be insulted'. Nobody, I knew for a fact, had the special experience to do what I was doing, and when one is the only one there is no choice. But it was hard and would perhaps have been unendurable if it had not been for the support first of something inside me, then that of the MacKereths, Mountbatten, and at home, Bevin and Attlee. And then there was the increasing trust of Indonesians like Sjahrir, Amir S. Sjharifuddin and my own 'Dul', Abdul Kadir, and many other remarkable Indonesians.

Yes, I see all that, but you are human, and humanly there must have been moments when rejection by the command of an army, especially an army to which you felt so committed, must have been intolerable?

After more than three years at this 'inward-bound' school which imprisonment under the Japanese had been, one had, I believe, a different measure of what was humanly tolerable and acceptable. That helped enormously and was probably decisive. But I was helped also by the feeling that I understood this antagonism. I was not surprised by it. I could see why the Dutch felt bitter, and why an Indian Army establishment which loved its role and loved India, knowing it was already on its way out of Burma and would soon follow suit in an India that had a new life and future, could identify with the Dutch.

But I will just describe the kind of incident that happened all the time. When our army finally pulled out towards the end of 1946, it left behind two brigadiers with a small rear-party, and me, with an indefinite sort of long-stop role in the field from which we were withdrawing totally. The night before the brigadiers left, they stayed in my mess. They stayed up all night, drinking and talking and ignoring me. In the morning early I took them to the airport in my car. When we arrived, a Dutch military delegation was already there, under their Chief-of-Staff, Admiral Pinke, for the official farewell. When the moment came to board the aircraft, all the Dutch officers shook hands with the brigadiers and saluted smartly. The salutes were punctiliously returned. The senior brigadier then turned to me. I came to attention and saluted in my turn. He stood there for a full minute, staring at me as if he could hit me. Then, without acknowledging my salute, turned his back on me and boarded the aircraft, I thought somewhat unsteadily. The Dutch farewell party could not conceal their satisfaction. But studied as the insult was, to use an inimitable cliché, it did not work. I felt terribly sad for the brigadier. He was the most decent of men, a Scot, brave and great-hearted, and I felt all the sadder when my second-in-command, who met the plane in Singapore, later told me he had 'to be poured out of it'.

Then there was my own departure, almost a year later. I wanted to go without saying goodbye officially, because it seemed such hypocrisy to me. However, I was persuaded to change my mind by 'Dul', the Colonel Raden Abdul Kadir who was the Governor-General's official liaison officer with me, and already a sort of 'assistant Governor-General'. He had never wavered in his support and trust in me. He had stayed in my mess all along and his wife Sri did all our housekeeping and catering. It was he who insisted, 'Laurie, you must not fail us now. For the honour of the house you must call on Dr van Mook and say goodbye officially.'

So I went at 11.30 the next morning and was received in the Governor's library. He did not return my 'Good morning, sir', but just said, 'Drink!' When I said, 'No, thank you', he turned his back on me, went to a cupboard and filled a large, cut-glass tumbler full of gin and drank it down like water, to call again over his shoulder, 'Drink!'

I said, 'No, thank you' again, marvelling at the unfailing talent of fate for introducing elements of farce as relief to its predetermined design. Thereupon he filled another glass, drank it down, filled a third, turned and came to face me across his desk, uttering as a peremptory command and not as an invitation, 'Sit!'

I declined, saying, 'I won't stay. I have just come to say goodbye. I am sorry that I should have to leave you like this.'

He said nothing and merely began sipping his third gin, looking somewhere above my head. I just said, 'Goodbye, sir', turned about and made my way out of the room, out of the palace and into the sun, as if I had gone from night, the dark night of the imperial spirit, into another day. And I could have wept.

But while we are still with Mountbatten, it was remarkable how extreme people were in their reactions about him. When you are an uncompromising character as he was, what René Janin and I used to call *jusqu'au-boutiste*, others tend to be extreme about you. And I think the officers who understood him best were naval ones. They had a far more relaxed approach to him: he liked people, I felt, to be natural and open with him.

Admiral Patterson was superb with him and behaved at times as if he could not take him seriously, which, if you are a secure person yourself, is rather nice. An example is that cable he and I sent about 'rocking the baby to sleep', and Mountbatten loved it. And then there was another dispatch. A rather elderly colonel, who I think had spent most of his life on staff duty, arrived in a panic from Mountbatten to take back a detailed report on the situation in Java, and Patterson gave him a large, fat Olympian-looking folder and said, 'I would like you to read it first to see if I have left anything important out.' The colonel opened the document rather officiously and then went pale because this is what he found on page one: 'The following is the considered appreciation of Rear-Admiral Sir Wilfred Patterson, C.S.5. of the situation in Indonesia.' On page two: 'I believe there are three towns of importance in Java; Batavia, Bandung and Surabaya.' Then there followed scores of blank pages, and on the last page of all, this conclusion: 'I regret that owing to the complexities of the situation this despatch could not be shorter.'

The colonel wanted to drop the dispatch like a live snake but was ordered to deliver it to Mountbatten just like that, and in a way it was not as frivolous as it looked. Any report was out of date by the time it arrived by hand, so fast did events evolve. Besides, a great deal of Dutch-inspired hysteria was being constantly thrown at Mountbatten and his staff at the time. And somehow this sort of response now and then brought things back into proportion. We sent him lots of serious in-depth signals, of course, that at first were, alas, not sufficiently believed.

Mountbatten's courage in battle, of course, was legendary but it was matched by his own kind of moral courage and sense of truth. He would quickly grasp if there was anything phoney in the air. He knew it at once; just like a good captain looking over his ship he would survey a conference and know at once if something was wrong. He was a very loyal friend. But he was, or tried to be, as ruthless with himself as others in what his job demanded of him.

I remember, for instance, what he said to General Christison who was the first British commander appointed to take over Indonesia to become in fact a soldier-statesman in that area. He said, 'Christie, I'm giving you probably the most difficult command that a soldier can have. I can't tell how it's going to turn out and how it has to be run. You will be out there entirely on your own and I'll try to help, but if it does go wrong it's going to be all your responsibility. You'll have to carry the can.'

Christie looked at him, all six foot two of him, and remarked quietly, 'Well, sir, that's surely what soldiers have always been for, they always carry the can.' And he went and did the job.

That was a fine professional stand.

Yes, it was marvellous. And he did carry the can. Also Monty Stopford who came after him. You see, the Dutch in The Hague really made it impossible for the British Government not to recall Christison. They tried hard to get me recalled too but did not succeed.

When Stopford arrived, I met him at the airport and brought him up-to-date on the way in to Batavia giving him all the latest details. He listened and said, 'Young Laurie,' – they all called me that after 'Christie' started it – 'it looks to me as if there's never been a job more neatly designed to get a general the sack than this one!'

He had no illusions about his fate from the very beginning?

No! He only lasted two months, poor man. It really was difficult. But then finally, when our troops pulled out, the Indonesian Prime Minister, Soeten Sjahrir, gave a party for the British troops. He thanked them and said, 'It is perhaps rare in the history of the occupation of a foreign country that the inhabitants should thank a force of invasion. But I, in the name of the people of Java, would like to thank you for the way in which you've discharged your very difficult charge in this country. By your example you have introduced us to aspects of Western civilization we did not know existed!'

He went on like this, and the Dutch Governor-General was furious. He said to the Prime Minister, 'What do you mean? You have insulted us!' And Soetan told me he replied, 'Dr van Mook, when you withdraw your forces from Java I'll give an even bigger party for them and I'll say even nicer things about them!'

Did you remain close to Mountbatten all his life, until he was assassinated by the IRA?

I did not see very much of him after the war. I feel that I saw him then at his best. The way he ran the South-East Asian Command after the war was magnificent – it was an incredible job. And it was always a mystery to me why the British Government, almost overnight after the surrender, accepted the whole of South-East Asia from the Americans as their responsibility and dumped it all in Mountbatten's lap, who in any case never had the resources he needed for his 14th Army and Burmese theatre of war. Yet he took it over without complaint and ran it superbly.

Then much later we worked together on his dispatches of our operations in South-East Asia. The Foreign Office would not let him do it at once. It was not until twenty-five years afterwards that he and I sat down briefly to work on them. It's just a colourless synopsis of events; not the real dispatches they could and should have been.

Have they been published?

Yes, but in such an innocuous way, designed not to give offence to the Dutch at any cost. I found it all rather sad because there was a great story to tell, full of lessons for the future. The British had, after all, done a remarkable job in Java. When we took over from the Japanese, belatedly, the killing and fighting were widespread and we managed to avert more with very little bloodshed.

———

Was your first contact with Wavell when you reported to him in Java?

No, I had already met him in Cairo and served under him. He was Commander-in-Chief in North Africa when the war broke out. I think he did astonishing work there because, like any British commander at the beginning of any war, the country found him totally unprepared. Wavell started under impossible conditions with small scattered forces, ill-equipped, but he took all this on without complaint or loss of nerve and worked wonders. He was an extraordinary, many-sided man, with a great interest in writing. His anthology, *Other Men's Flowers*, is probably one of the most successful anthologies of poetry ever produced in England. He wrote a significant biography of Allenby – a great cavalry commander. Wavell served with Allenby and had the insight and gift to write this remarkable book.

One of the things he praised Allenby for was the fact that when Allenby arrived to take over from a man called General Murray in North Africa in the 1914–18 war, he was amazed to find that General Murray had made his headquarters in the Grand Hotel in Cairo, and that the officers there, the staff, were leading a life of great luxury. Allenby could not stand this. Immediately, he closed down the headquarters in the Grand Hotel, and moved it nearer to the front, which was in the direction of Jerusalem. Now, Wavell quotes this as a sign of the greatness, and of the tremendous driving force of Allenby.

Well, having read this, I was amazed when I found on my arrival in Cairo that Wavell had established himself, his headquarters, in the Continental Hotel in Cairo. I wondered how the two things added up; whether this was really a blindness of all commanders-in-chief, or whether it made sense. Of course, when one realized how very complicated modern warfare had become, it was perhaps not so nonsensical after all. Communications are so much more complex and play so much more of a role, and the staff work has become so intricate and convoluted. It was a thing that horrified me about armies, how bureaucratic and how trade-unionized they had become. I think of the great commanders in the past, men like Lee, the great American general who fought in the Civil War: he had two staff officers and a notebook, and that is what his staff consisted of.

Of course, they were fighting more a guerrilla war than a classical type of war with a front, and large-scale battles.

Yes and no. The great battles of the Civil War were so vast and horrendous, events of subtle and profound moment – that this, astonished me in a way about Wavell. But I think that for Wavell, who has been criticized for repeating a mistake that he had condemned himself, really it was not an oversight. He felt that modern warfare needed that kind of communication and he could not get it in any other way. But when I met him, the more I saw of him the more I admired him. He was not very articulate, he was more of an introverted soldier. He had suffered a great deal and had lost one eye. And it was interesting and

258

saddening that many of the officers on his staff who had been in his regiment, the Black Watch, also had only one eye.

It was through them that I got my first job in Africa early on in the war, which was to go in behind the Italian lines in Abyssinia. I joined the few British officers already there to help to organize the revolt against the Italians. Now Wavell was convinced from the start that the Italians were going to come in to the war against us. He knew that we hardly had any troops in northern Africa. But he had foresight – and an immense grasp of detail. He sent for an ex-gunner, a man called Brigadier Sandford, who had lived in Abyssinia ever since the First World War and had an enormous coffee business there. He knew it and the people well, and only left the country when the Emperor was forced out by the Italians. So Wavell briefed Sandford personally and sent him to do a wide reconnaissance behind the Italian lines and verify rumours that there was still resistance. Sandford quickly found out exactly what sort of a resistance it was. He found that in the west, in the Blue Nile area, the Gojjam, there were some of the leading aristocrats still holding out against the Italians. He found some who had Italian prisoners. These prisoners had not been badly treated by this Abyssinian aristocracy in the traditional way by castrating them, proved by the fact that two of them had venereal disease. When Sandford returned with this report, Wavell was already heavily outnumbered by the Italians on many far-flung fronts on the Western Desert, in Somaliland and in the Sudan, even Kenya. But I was one of the officers he sent to Abyssinia to organize a revolt. And it was really through that connection that I ultimately went to the Far East; because when he took over in South-East Asia he sent for me to come, in the hope that we might repeat the Ethiopian pattern. He saw again that we were going to be heavily outnumbered by the Japanese. He saw it as a repetition of a scenario he knew only too well. And that's how I ultimately became a prisoner of the Japanese.

Did you see him again after the Japanese capitulation?

No, alas, I did not, because he had already vanished from the scene when I returned from this other war in South-East Asia. I had indirect contact with him through my first general after the war, General Christison, and that confirmed what I have told you about the man and his extraordinary quality. His was a life of great service, and the service was his only reward. The world of his day quickly passed him by, and it was even as if it had determined to obliterate the memory of his achievement and its continuation through his own family and son. I had a very sad last meeting with his son when I came back, in my home in London, the night before the son left for Kenya where, within a few weeks, he was to be killed in a skirmish with Mau Mau – killed in another eruption of the forces that European empires had released in the world but failed to control and to guide creatively when the logical challenge to their power from life presented itself.

I wish I could tell you all that I knew of Wavell because in many ways Wavell, who with another of the so-called 'failed generals', Auchinleck, was, alas, so unfairly misjudged and unappreciated by Churchill, had a certain Arthurian and Round Table purity of spirit very few men I have met possess. I think in their respective armies, Wavell in the British and Auchinleck in the Indian army, they served as if in a knighthood. There were many others, of course, who did likewise, from private soldiers and subalterns to field-marshals; thousands who belie the caricature of the serviceman commonly seen on television and held in the minds of contemporary generations. Even E. M. Forster, who did not like soldiers and was so critical of the British presence in India, told me that the last time he was in India, on the journey which inspired *A Passage to India*, one of the most sensitive and outstanding people of all the races he had met was a young staff major called Auchinleck. And I mention Auchinleck in connection with Wavell because neither of them, of all the great war leaders, ever wrote their autobiographies. They were content to leave what they had done to the judgement of life and creation.

Auchinleck was offered all sorts of awards and a peerage, which he declined, saying that he had only gone on serving so long in order to care for all the people under his command, and in the process, having been forced to participate in the dismantling of one of the finest military orders the world had ever seen, he could not in honour accept any reward for participation in so misguided a deed. Wavell never complained, and from Indonesia he went on to be Viceroy of India, where in the most difficult circumstances he did exceedingly well. But because of his misgivings, in particular over the emancipation of India at the cost of partition, he was dismissed by the Attlee Government after the war.

The manner of his dismissal could not have been more humiliating. It took place at a meeting of the War Cabinet where he was told that he had to go and that Mountbatten would take his place. He took the news calmly and with great dignity and as he was about to turn and leave the room for the last time, Attlee just said to him, 'Thank you, Field-Marshal. That will be all.'

I am certain Attlee did not mean that unkindly but it was singularly graceless and hurting nonetheless, uttered in that crisp, Major Attlee matter-of-fact manner which he had when he was caught up in important things, and anxious to move on. But it was too much for someone else in the room. As Wavell opened the door to go out, a great voice bellowed out behind him: 'For Christ's sake, Clem, you can't let him go like that. He is a great man after all. Can't you even thank him properly?'

It was the voice of Ernie Bevin, who was Foreign Secretary at the time and for whom I had a very great admiration based on the dealings I had with him. And Attlee immediately responded and called Wavell back to say, much more graciously: 'Field-Marshal, thank you very much for all that you have done, not only in India but in the war. Perhaps you would like to leave some words of advice for your successor?'

And Wavell replied, 'Well, I am afraid, sir, that the only advice I could leave my successor is the advice you have so consistently rejected in the last six months. I do not really think there is any point in that. Goodbye, sir', and he turned about and walked out of the room and out of the popular reckoning.

Courageous man!

Yes, he was as brave as he was honourable, and that really was his exit from history as it is nowadays written. My own general, General Christison, to whom I was devoted, heard the story from Wavell himself.

And Bevin, you said you had a high opinion of him?

Yes, an explanation of Ernie Bevin's intervention, and of the man himself, is also required. I find it important because it shows the immense gap which was to open up between the classic, the original

Labour Party and the shambled, scrambled and superficial, historically absent-minded collection of mere power-seeking politicians it has become. It was something which arose out of that mission which Lord Mountbatten gave me to report to the War Cabinet in London, and which ultimately led me to report to the Dutch Prime Minister and his Cabinet in The Hague, and to address the people of Holland on the radio.

On the night before I had to return to my post in Java, Bevin sent for me and I saw him in his room in the Foreign Office, sitting almost invisible among the piles of urgent dispatches on his desk. After thanking me, he asked me if it was true that I was of Boer origin. I was quite startled by the word 'Boer', because it seemed to have vanished from the English vocabulary in which it had once been so popular, except in that of Churchill and a few men like him.

When I said, 'Yes', Bevin elaborated. He said that that war, which Britain had fought against my people, made an enormous impression on him and had a great influence on the way he came to look on Britain's role in the empire and the world. He summarized it for me in a story he had heard as a young man from Tom Shaw, who was one of the great pioneer Labour leaders. He told me that after the defeated Boer leaders had come to Great Britain to plead with Campbell-Bannerman for self-government, the moment it was over, Campbell-Bannerman sent for Shaw to give him an account of the meeting. Campbell-Bannerman told Tom Shaw that, when confronted with this request, he looked at the Boer delegation and said, 'Is that all you want from me, gentlemen? I am really disappointed in you.'

At that, Abraham Fischer, who was perhaps the most articulate in the delegation – and incidentally the grandfather of my great friend 'Bram Fischer, who became a communist when he was at New College in Oxford in the Thirties and ended up with a sentence of life imprisonment ironically in an Afrikaner gaol because of his way of fighting apartheid – asked in a puzzled tone, 'I do not understand, sir. Surely we have only asked for what is natural?'

Campbell-Bannerman replied, 'Mr Fischer, I am disappointed because you have not asked for enough. I am prepared to give you so much more. I would like to give you the Union of South Africa.'

262

And after a pause, Bevin added, 'It is a story you might like to tell the Dutch when you get back to Java, because often it is wise to give more than you are asked for.'

I often think of the story, because the failure of the Dutch in Java was due to the fact that they were not prepared really to give anything; but also because it showed how alive a sense of history still was in public life in Britain and how it still played a creative role in the affairs of Parliament, instead of being cast out into the outer darkness of the minds of politicians today.

That night I had another experience of how this sense of history survived. I went straight from the Foreign Office to the War Office to see the Deputy Chief-of-Staff, Archie Nye. My meeting with the Dutch Cabinet in The Hague and the Prime Minister, Professor Schermerhorn and his Minister of Colonies, Professor Logemann, both of a natural liberal spirit, had, despite some misgivings, given me cause for some hope that we could resolve, without much more fighting, the differences between the Dutch and the Indonesians. I reported fully on how I thought our military political administration could contribute to this end. Archie Nye was another of the thousands of British soldiers who contradict the caricature of the British soldier common in intellectual attitudes today, and became a distinguished High Commissioner in Canada. When I finished my report he looked away and, after a moment of deep thought, said that he hoped I was right but history had taught him that men gave too little and gave too late, and he feared this would happen again. He concluded with a smile and expression of acceptance of the inevitable, but added nevertheless, 'However, do not let my reservations prevent you from having a damned good try.'

How and when did you meet Winston Churchill for the first time?

I did not meet him until after the war, and when we did meet we talked mostly about southern Africa and in particular about Botha and Smuts. Like so many people of his generation he had a very great love of southern Africa and of the Afrikaner people against whom he had fought. Among these, of course, his love of General Botha and particularly of Smuts was very real and very great – but it has been amply recorded in his own writing and the history of two world wars, so that I really have nothing to add to it, except that when I told him that my own father had fought with Botha and Smuts in the Boer War and had been a consistent ally of theirs in Parliament leading up to the great Act of Union, he showed me a regard and gave me an attention I would not otherwise have received.

But what struck me at the time as we talked was the enormous magnanimity of the person that came through to me. We all know now that he was full of all the human qualities to an extreme degree and therefore vulnerable to all the human fallibilities. But there was never anything ignoble or mean in the man, and when we had finished I went away profoundly impressed with the fact that none of that nobility, none of that courage and none of that magnanimity could have been possible if, consciously or unconsciously in the depths of his spirit, he had not been motivated by a great love, all the greater because he never experienced it in childhood from his parents. He was never soured or embittered by that, but reacted positively to its absence in the realization that this was the most important element in life. As a result, the whole of his life was a form of seeking and service of what he himself had been denied, and he set an example of the importance of seeking in this manner which, judged in the context of the values of his time, was of the highest universal significance and order. I believe there was not a gene in the man that was not heraldic, and not an atom of his spirit that was not chivalrous; and there was a sort of transcendent logic in the fact that he asked for no honour of his country, except that of knighthood. I remember, looking back on my own experience of war, how in many small ways one was aware everywhere of his presence and influence and his immense humanity, which was never perverted by the horrors of war and circumstance he had to endure or initiate in the defence of what he loved.

Finally, I also remember the moving impression made on me by his physical appearance. It was totally undisguised and without fear or shame of what life had done to it. It had the same kind of truth about it, even in its less shapely facets, that I seem to find in that last self-portrait of Rembrandt as an old man and which I think is the greatest portrait, self-portrait or otherwise, ever painted. To the last, Churchill had allowed life to paint its own self-portrait on him without restraint or inhibition and all in total acceptance of his utter subjection to its objective seeking.

While we are talking about leadership and great leaders, could you give your opinion on the Emperor of Japan, Hirohito? Do you think, as certain books written about him imply, that he is really a war criminal, and that he could have controlled the whole plot from the very beginning?

No, that is nonsense. I know one of the books you are referring to, Bergamini's book, isn't it?

Yes.

To me it is absurd to think that one man could have engineered all that. The Emperor was born to a destiny of being a great symbol for his people, and from the little I know of it he has kept that symbol as pure as is possible in both war and peace. He has remained a centre for them, something lasting, round which the best could rally again after the storm. If he had really been a conspirator and a villain he could not have played the role which he is playing today. I feel the Japanese were singularly blessed in having certainty at that level and, in a period of profound revolutionary change in the life of their country, the continuity which he represents. I remember when his father died, he became Emperor in the coldest of all winters in Japan towards the end of 1926, and he has been there ever since. That is sixty years: it is a blessed thing indeed for a nation to have such a living symbol of continuity on the highest symbolic level. I do not think he has compromised that continuity; it is a very great achievement.

But for Western minds it is rather difficult to understand how the Emperor, who is a very peaceful man and a biologist and a disciple of Bergson and therefore so respectful of life in all its forms, could have been brought to war and followed his generals. Could he not have imposed his will?

He did at the end when he had the opportunity to interfere. I always think of that *haiku* he wrote which to me is a very haunting one. He sent it to his generals when they were contemplating declaring war, which said in effect:

> 'They tell me that all men are brothers.
> Why then are the wind and the waves so restless?'

That is the traditional Japanese way — indirect, suggestive, symbolic. It seems that the Emperor could not, or dare not, speak out openly.

Yes. But there is a sort of awareness of dealing with forces which were beyond even his control.

You are a story-teller and therefore, I think, you believe not only in the written word but also in the spoken word. We have touched on it before but I feel there is much more to be said.

I have told you a little of my youth in the interior of Africa, when we always had a family service after dinner where the great, state Bible was put on the table and opened, like a gate into a palace. And I remember the first time I heard the key passage from St John: 'In the beginning was the Word, and the Word was with God, and the Word was God', leading on to, 'And the Word was made flesh and dwelt among us (and we beheld his glory, the glory as of the only begotten of the Father), full of grace and truth.' And my blood ran singing through me, I do not know why, but it seemed to me that that was one of the greatest statements I had ever heard, because for me the word represented meaning; the meaning and the word were one and together in the beginning. All this made a profound impact on me.

Moreover, I lived among a people for whom the word was the main means of communication. They did not write much and could barely read. Everything really depended on the word, the living word, the spoken word, not the artificial, the hacked-out word, but the word meant to be for ever. The sign of a well-brought-up person among my native countrymen was a person who spoke well. You were really not thought much of among the black and coloured people I grew up with, unless you were well-spoken. That did not just mean that you could talk fluently – they were too quick at picking up mere rhetoric or braggarts or boasters – but that you could use the word in a way that moved people, that changed people. It was always wonderful to me, in the evenings sitting and listening to them talking, to observe how they found the right words for the occasion, and how, when the only possible word was found, there came the smack of satisfaction, the joy that it had been spoken, and it instantly became an achievement for everybody sitting there.

My life has since taken me far away from such moments but not before they had made their point. So I have been uneasily aware, particularly since the war and the arrival of television and the new kinds of newspapers, that the importance of the living word, the right, the only word, is overlooked. The word is, consciously or unconsciously, under attack and in decline. Yet nothing else can replace it.

Just think of the word, the depth of the word: it goes back over the horizon of our beginnings, and God alone knows where it comes from. Even the animals have forms of sound that are their word. It is the earliest form of conscious communication in life. 'The Word was made flesh' means it was made conscious, and to live and be lived. This kind of word is what life is about.

And it is not just a rational thing, as the logical positivists try to make it out to be. It is a very complex, seed thing. With every good word some of it is rational, some of it non-rational, full of its own, independent associations, feelings, meanings and a very complex context like a seed that grows when the rain falls on it: it is received and the reception is its rain. Part of it is obvious: you see it logically and recognize its use at once. But there is a strong non-logical content in it, so great that the word is more than it expresses. One can listen to words, poetry above all, and one is aware of this immense, almost magical evocation of meaning, of ancient meaning that just comes along with the words as part of the package. So one cannot just define all words rationally and use them purely rationally. All the dimensions of meaning tend to have a part in their impact. And the right word will not only touch you rationally, it will also touch your heart, it will touch you emotionally. Your eyes, your ears, your sense of smell, your intuition, everything comes into the greatest word. Altogether words form a system of communication which is as profound, subtle, proven and experienced as life itself. And in a sense it is life and gives life. Without it, life as we have known it is inconceivable.

Living with people who have no other means of recording things, no other means of art except the word, as I did in primitive Africa, makes one suddenly realize what a tremendous debt the human spirit owes to the word. And really without the word, without this very complex, inner structure of the word to contain the spirit, it would die away. This structure does not stand still but is always growing. I think that is why, for instance, I have always had a very nasty feeling when I have written anything. I have always felt elated when I have finished a book, have felt

268

lighter, but very soon a feeling of dismay takes its place as I become aware of how much I have left out. I feel that even by doing my best for the written word I may have caused some damage somewhere, and that the living word would have served better after all.

And, of course, the Word that was meaning was not only the human word. When you heard thunder, which above all was the Word, speaking from the battlements of cloud, our Hottentots would say, *'Heitsé,* brothers, silence. The Old Master speaks.' Then the wind of spring wrote it on the greening grass and scribbled it on the water, and its hieroglyphic lines were etched on the face of sheltered cliffs, and there was nothing in nature that was not authenticated with its signature.

One of the greatest word-alchemists or word-magicians was certainly Shakespeare. You told me once that you loved his nursery rhymes, which are pure music and non-rational.

They are an essential part of the mystery of the word, when the word itself was young and still in the nursery of time, so that in a sense nursery is speaking directly to nursery, and like all mysteries they have tremendous power, tapped at the very source of the word where it emerges spring-like, packed with non-rational meaning and associations of a world before consciousness. They stir one and one cannot tell or know why. Try any nursery rhyme you like – I do not know why I am thinking of this one now:

> 'Ride a cock-horse to Banbury Cross
> To see a fine lady upon a white horse.
> With rings on her fingers and bells on her toes,
> She shall have music wherever she goes.'

Now that is just a snatch, but what a lovely thing it is to set flowing through the imagination.

And I think of one of Shakespeare's most evocative and haunting rhymes:

> 'When that I was and a little tiny boy,
> With hey, ho, the wind and the rain;
> A foolish thing was but a toy,
> For the rain it raineth every day.

But when I came to man's estate,
With hey, ho, the wind and the rain;
'Gainst knaves and thieves men shut their gates,
For the rain it raineth every day.

But when I came, alas! to wive,
With hey, ho, the wind and the rain;
By swaggering could I never thrive,
For the rain it raineth every day.

But when I came unto my beds,
With hey, ho, the wind and the rain;
With toss-pots still had drunken heads,
For the rain it raineth every day.

A great while ago the world begun,
With hey, ho, the wind and the rain;
But that's all one, our play is done,
And we'll strive to please you every day.'

It has got all the basic elements in it: colour, sense, nonsense, music, and is not only now but also before and after.

Finally, think how a true word raises the human spirit. The right word, the true word at the right time is the most dynamic thing in life.

Coming back to St John and his utterance, 'In the beginning was the Word', how did he know? Do you think those words were inspired by God, or was it intuition?

A very remarkable book* has just been published on this subject. According to the author of that book, St John was the only direct witness of what happened to Jesus Christ. Therefore he was at the source; St John knew, as we should all know, that the word is the subtlest instrument for increasing consciousness. And that is what life is about, we were talking about it before, about making life more conscious of itself: making the human being more conscious of what he is, of his possibilities, and everything else. And the word is the great instrument

* *The Priority of John* by John Robinson, Bishop of Woolwich.

for awareness because it cannot be absent without causing a loss of meaning.

And above all, it appears in our dreams, where it conveys the strangest and perhaps the most important of messages to us, where it speaks from out of the crucible, out of the fire in which the Word was forged and speaks of the fire itself, and its existence. I have been thinking a great deal about it, because much of my life has been occupied with the written word, but also with the spoken word. And I have had a feeling, coming towards the end of my life; I have been deeply disturbed because I have not been able to write more. I have had to talk more, which I do not enjoy. And I have begun to think that perhaps this is wrong of me and that I must realize there is a moment when only the living word will do, the unpremeditated word, the word which speaks also for the words which have not yet been formed, the word which has really some connection with this unexpressed not-yet world of infinite meaning, which is clamouring for flesh and blood to live it. And that, particularly in moments of world crisis, the clearly spoken, controlled living word is far more important than the written word.

Just before Socrates took hemlock and committed suicide, he said to one of his pupils, 'You know what is wrong with the spirit of Greece today? There are too many books.' Almost as if he were saying the books were impeding the forward movement of the human spirit. I remember one night in a tent in the rain in Abyssinia at a moment when our military plight was not too bright. I was with the Emperor and also a very unusual, famous and tragic soldier called Orde Wingate, who was saying to the Emperor, or 'Jan-Hoy' as we called him by his ancient title, 'Jan-Hoy, you will have to talk to your people.' He went on to say how military history was his study and, as far as he could go back, he knew of no great military leader who in the course of his career would not have been defeated and crushed if he had not been able to find the right words to say to his troops at the right moment. Perhaps the only one who was an exception, he said, was Marlborough, because there is nothing in history to suggest that he ever addressed his troops. But then something rang in my mind and I asked him if he really felt he was right. Because I remembered there was a critical occasion when he did use the right words. It was not a great speech, but it was absolutely the right message

271

and it had been all that was necessary. I thought it was at the Battle of Malplaquet but I was not certain. Marlborough was going up to the front lines when he met his officers coming away, fast. He drew himself up and looked at them and said, with all the irony of history on his tongue, 'Gentlemen, I think you are mistaken. The enemy is over there!' Without a word they turned about and went back towards the battle.

And that set me on to Frederick the Great and the Battle of Rosbach, where the Austrian artillery were getting the better of the battle against him. And he had to push his army, raw recruits, across this ridge at which all the enemy guns were firing – and the Austrian artillery was the best in Europe. As they came out on top of the ridge the recruits wavered, but Frederick came riding up on his white horse, and looked them over steadily before saying, with a very little smile '*Was, Kerls, wollen Sie nicht sterben?*' – Do you mean, chaps, you do not want to die? Little as it was, it was enough and they went forward, to win.

We talked like this with the heavy rain falling outside, and the next morning the Emperor did just that and talked to his rag-and-tatter followers, and the effect was marvellous.

All this shows how history is part of the living spirit with immense energies at its unique disposal, and only asks to be invoked. I cannot tell you how often I myself have been helped by reminding myself of our great Henry of Navarre's address to his knees. He was about to go into his first battle at the age of fourteen and was much distressed by the way his knees trembled. So he looked at them sternly and said, 'That's right, tremble! tremble! You would tremble a good deal more if you knew where I was taking you!'

So I have often asked myself how many times in history, when life seemed at a dead end, the word has come along and made people put another foot forward, try out another idea, or just say 'Sorry', and life moved on again.

Words are used so badly at the moment. People everywhere appear to have become more and more inarticulate. They are so increasingly visually oriented in their television world; they read less, speak less, and the word is not only under attack but undefended. And what about the living word, and I really mean the living word? It is a word that you have not deliberately thought out and through. When I have to talk to people in public I take hardly any notes and do not write anything out. I remember my daughter asked me, 'But how do you manage to speak like that, without any notes?' and I said, 'Well, I have prepared myself in my imagination as well as I can, but I stand there and I do not know how I am going to begin. And I sort of beat about the bush inside myself until a phrase like a bird comes up, an immense feeling of relief comes over me, and I just follow the flight of the bird. But the terror of it is that you might beat about the bush for all you are worth and no bird will come out. But that has never happened yet.'

South Africa is one country among many that needs to invoke that living spirit of which you spoke a moment ago; the guiding voice to help it find the right way forward.

In this terrible crisis which is going on in South Africa, one of the most frightening aspects of it is that no one seems capable of finding the living word that is needed. It is, of course, a failure of the world generally. That is why we are all so startled when one person speaks the word or phrase we need. Solzhenitsyn was such a one at the Nobel Peace Prize ceremony with his acceptance lecture in which he emphasized the importance of 'one word of truth'. That one word of truth was enough to change both us and Russia. It may not show all that much yet, but change has sprouted from it and nothing can be the same again. Leaders and people are deprived of the word because they no longer speak with meaning but use words as counterfeit to impress people, to prove a point, to deceive or extract an advantage. And that is not what the living word is for.

I felt it very deeply when I had to speak recently about events in Africa. And I said, what is so terrible is that the words that should be said are so simple, and they cannot say them, because the words know they will not live, not be made flesh. For the word breathes and lives only by honest and truthful intent. If the right words were spoken now I believe they could still have a redeeming effect. That is why I spoke on four occasions recently in South Africa, in an effort to find our word of truth, and the effect was most heartening. And I relied entirely on the living word.

That you should have been allowed on South African public television is surely good news. Haven't you been barred from it, for years now?

On the whole, yes. But what is terrible is that the words are there, waiting and not being used. We know the words if we make friends with them and seek them out, and they will come if we have the courage to summon them. So in many ways I think for me at this moment the living word, the spoken word, is the one most needed. What is so significant about the life of Christ is that though he was a scholar, a bright one, though he knew how to read and write, he never put anything down in writing himself. He entrusted himself and his message to the living word. He told stories, he told parables.

Planting seeds?

Yes, every living word and every parable has the seeds of new being in them. Nobody can take them into his imagination without being changed in the process. And I think this, in a smaller way, is also what sustains one as a writer: the feeling that if you use even the written word as truly as you can, nobody can receive it and remain the same. That is perhaps why we go on plodding away at this exacting job.

Do you think, at this point, words alone are enough to stop the fire and hate spreading in South Africa? Are you for or against sanctions? They are proposed by a great number of individuals and nations, who sometimes do not have the slightest knowledge of South Africa and her problems. Can sanctions have some impact and change policies and minds and hearts?

I find nothing about sanctions constructive, nothing whatsoever. To me it is a bankrupt approach, typical of the bankruptcy of the modern spirit, that they think that by using instruments of destruction, they can create something positive. I think it all goes back to this terrible concept and creed of revolution, that by violent overthrow, by doing something violent – by hurting the thing which is in the wrong – you can create something good out of it. And I think that the idea of applying sanctions is morally obscene, irreligious in the extreme.

And these are sanctions that nobody thinks of applying to other countries who continuously violate human rights, or who practise genocide – and the list of those countries is very long.

Well, this is the other thing. To single out one country which is by no means the worst, and to apply the worst form of punishment to it, is mad. There is something sick in people who want to make a sick society sicker still. And I always start with these considerations because I think it is extremely important to ask first, 'Is this good in itself? Is this morally defensible? Is this what life demands of us, that we should destroy and hurt and maim a country for its good?' And the destroyers, are they not people who should not throw the stones, because they are so wrong themselves?

I remember many years ago when talk of sanctions first arose. It was raised in my house by a priest who was fanatically pro-sanctions, and I asked, 'Have you ever thought about the moral implicit in the story of Sodom and Gomorrah?' And he looked startled, as if he were suddenly seeing me as a right-wing Jewish fundamentalist. 'The angels of God came to Abraham's nephew, Lot, at nightfall and told him they had been ordered to destroy the cities in the plain, but would take Lot and his wife and children away before it happened, since they knew they were not evil people. And then Abraham thought and said to the Lord, "But there might be fifty righteous people in the cities! Would it be right for you in your justice to destroy the good and the bad simultaneously? Surely, if there were fifty people who were innocent, you would spare the cities!" And the Lord said, "Yes. If there were fifty such people I would spare the cities." And then Abraham thought, "Well, they are very wicked places. Suppose there are only forty good people?" And so he went on, forty, thirty, twenty, ten. And the Lord said, "If there are only ten, I will spare the cities."'

And I thought, there is a tremendous moral in that, because it shows that it is built into life, already there in the Old Testament, that God does not wish to treat innocent and guilty alike. You do not treat the good and the bad all in the same way. And what sanctions would do is to harm not ten innocent but close on thirty million people who are politically innocent in South Africa. And why? To damage and show abhorrence of something that a government is doing to them all. For you must never forget it is not the people but a government, a government that polled less than three-quarters of a million votes in the last election, that is our common enemy; a government, moreover, opposed by thousands of white people as well, whose numbers are daily growing. You simply cannot inflict a vast, blanket punishment like that, not on moral, religious or even sensible practical grounds. You cannot achieve the right end with the wrong means. History shows how fatal it is. And this is precisely what the world, a sick world, all of a sudden wants to do.

They are urging us to do something immoral, with priests in the lead!

But let us put all that on one side. Suppose we apply sanctions and make them work. If they work, you are going to impoverish the country. Millions of people are already living on the breadline. There are millions of black people unemployed already. In the last few years there has been a terrible drought in southern Africa too, the same drought that has made millions die of starvation in northern Africa. The same drought; but the people did not die, because the country was big enough and just rich enough to import and buy the food to keep them alive. But if you impose sanctions now and they take effect, who is going to feed these people in the future? Because we get these droughts every three or four years in Africa. Who is going to feed the unemployed people who now have barely enough to eat? Who is ever going to find work for them again, these people who have done no wrong?

That is one aspect; there is another. The economy which has been expanding in Africa, particularly the foreign business end of it, has raised the black and coloured people into levels of skills and employment which would stagger their grandfathers, and indeed shame the rest of Africa. Their grandfathers would never have dreamt of such material well-being. And in the process, all the time they are acquiring a power and an education through an expanding economy, learning what it is to be a member of a technological community, doing disciplined and skilled work and how to use power, industrial power, responsibly. And they have already become so powerful that if they could unite at this moment, they could use their economic power to acquire their political ends. They need not destroy. If they would apply their own form of sanctions from within, by withholding their own labour, they would achieve their political ends and we would know that they were doing it of their own free will, and not having it imposed on them by a number of power-seeking intellectuals and ideologists. Moreover, until they can unite and use responsibly the great power they already possess, they will not be capable of exercising it responsibly in politics.

No, if you destroy the economy through sanctions you take this power away from them and arrest an evolution which is full of promise.

Another point about the economy that is important: foreign businesses, through the example they are increasingly setting, are changing the nature of industrial relationships in Africa. There is one international mining company, for instance, much criticized by environmentalists, which has mines in South Africa. Now most mines in South Africa recruit labour from all of Africa: men are taken away for nine months or a year from their homes – rather like indentured labour from Turkey, Yugoslavia and Italy in Europe. They are taken away and live in compounds, away from their wives and children, and after nine months or so sent home. The destructive consequences of such an unnatural arrangement must be obvious. So this particular mining company thought this was dangerous nonsense and in their mines started recruiting on a married basis. They have set up compounds where the wives and the children and families live as well. They provide work for the wives and schools for the children. The result is they have come to the point where they have to recruit now only when people die. They have humanized mining. I have been to these places and they do one's heart good. They have set a wonderful example which is beginning to revolutionize the whole of mining. Your thin-lipped sanctioneers want to ruin a company like that and destroy it? Why, and what do you gain?

In another place in Namibia, the same company has schools that are better than any schools you find in South Africa, both training people technically and for general education. They invest much of their profits in people and education. What is the sense of destroying that with sanctions? It is the madness of a mad, mad world and is a symptom of the increasingly pathological spirit of our time, a product of hate, malice, envy and projection of a rage against self-failure in our own systems – and is a reminder of the classic quarrel about the mote in our neighbour's eye and the beam in our own.

So the way you see it is that there are two levels on which it can be worked out. From the inside, the impulse should come from the South Africans, black or white. And from the outside, to work through friendly channels of communication. So we need perhaps – and you will be useful in telling us how – we need better knowledge of the character of the South Africans. Who are they exactly? What are they up to? How should we deal with them?

First of all, we should recognize that South Africa is already changing. There are thousands of white Africans who want to abolish apartheid. And apartheid itself is changing. I do not want to be thought apologetic for apartheid. It is an evil thing. I was one of the first, sixty years ago, to see it as evil and denounce it accordingly. What I want us to see is the total objective truth: the situation is so serious that in all our judgements we must see the whole, see it steadily and truthfully. Only the truth can save us and South Africa, and I say 'us' because we are in danger of betraying all that is decent in the European spirit, above all the 'Englishness', the precious English element in the British character, respect for the rule of law, fairness, justice, concern for the innocent and so on. All these basic civilizing and creative principles are involved and imperilled in the name of God and decency.

But concerning apartheid, to us who know South Africa from within, it is fantastic, the changes that have already been made. People dismiss these changes because they are not enough. But there are changes. After a generation of immobility, apartheid is moving and cracking. Take the South African law. There are very bad laws in South Africa but the dispensation of the law is incorruptible still, and even bad law is administered as decently as possible. And it is remarkable how the courts stand up against the political power in the country. There are so many good things, and good signs, and you do not want to destroy all this as if they were one. It would be evil parading as good.

In his novel Turbott Wolfe, *William Plomer discusses miscegenation as a possible solution to the colour problem? Do you agree with this opinion?*

No, I think to mix blood with the idea that this would be a solution is the wrong way to set about it. You should mix blood only for its own sake – not as a solution for anything. It would simply create problems of its own, as every union in life does. I would just like to feel that we are moving towards a world where the mixing of blood is not regarded as something wrong but as a good thing, as something which is potentially just as good. If people of different races love one another sufficiently despite all the obstacles, if they want to be together for the rest of their lives, then that is a bridge to the future. They're building great bridges.

What was the Bushmen's opinion on intermarriage?

Well, the point is that it was imposed upon them. They weren't asked whether they accepted it or not, and we have no record of what they felt about the matter because by the time I came on the scene, the Bushman culture had already vanished from my part of the world, except for one or two fragments like my nurse and little Bushmen on my grandfather's farm. But what we have, as a result of all this unplanned mingling and mixing of blood at the Cape of Good Hope in the beginning, before they had racial and colour prejudice, is a unique coloured people we call 'The Cape-coloured people'. They have Bushman, Bantu, Malayan, Javanese and European blood all mixed together. And they have produced a special type of their own, a culture of their own. Some of the loveliest things in the so-called Afrikaans culture came from the Cape-coloured people. They're full of music, full of humour, full of fun. They're creative, very gifted, dynamic, and full of temperament. They have lost their roots and insofar as they have an identity, they tend to identify with Europeans. But they are really something apart, something very precious, and until recently they were regarded as part of European Africa. They had the vote, they had Members of Parliament and so on, and it is only the present State which has removed them and put them back into a separate and somewhat inferior category. I know many, many poets and artists amongst them. And, for instance, when they have their carnival in the Cape, the whole place is transformed – music and singing and laughter and merriment. They're wonderful people. With them the Cape of Storms becomes the Cape of Good Hope.

Everywhere we say we must increase cultural flow between countries. We complain that we do not get enough cultural contacts with the Russians. But we want to cut the South Africans off. I said to someone, 'You know, the people who want sanctions remind me of a lot of missionaries, who are anchored off an island full of prancing savages and cannibals whom they say they want to convert, but refuse to disembark and go among them, shouting instead, "If you stop being cannibals, we will bring you the Bible!"' This is metaphorically what they are trying to do with sanctions in South Africa.

There is something an old Zulu said to me one day about sanctions which is worth a thought. He said, 'These people are like the stupid man who would cut off the tail of his dog and give it to him for food.' I was thinking of this old Zulu's comment and wishing that we were as good at spotting stupidity, and seeing what a force for evil it is in life, as my black countryman. And I was thinking how, not long after Sharpeville, I was back at home. It was in the days when I was shadowed by the secret police constantly, when my mail to my sisters and friends was opened and on occasions extracts, without acknowledgement of course, were read out in Parliament, and I always asked my lawyer to meet my plane and to see me off. It was again a lonely time, not unlike Java, and I had been all over my mother's farm – the one she left to me but I still think of it as hers – and one of our oldest servants, who had known me as a boy, had gone with me everywhere. It was getting late; we were very tired, and he looked exhausted. Very reluctantly I said to him, 'Old Father, please forgive me, there is still one more thing I have to do. I have to go to my father's grave. I have not been to see it for a long time. I am sorry because I know it is a long way and you have not eaten all day.'

He looked at me and without hesitation said, 'Little master, go. The hunger that takes you there is greater than any hunger I could feel.'

And somewhere within me there was a passion of rebellion against a government and a world who could not see what a unique quality of humanity, of all races, we had in my country, a quality of people potentially among the finest in the world, and already finer than anywhere else in Africa. I thanked him, nearly in tears, and said, 'Please, Old Father, never despair. There are now thousands like me who are against this terrible government and its evil system. We shall not rest until we have changed it. Please try to be patient a while longer.'

And he said, 'Little master, we can be patient. It is not the apartheid we mind so much, life is always full of prejudice; it is not even the unfairness we mind, life is never fair. But what is almost unbearable is the stupidity of it all. What do you do with such stupid people?'

However, to return to sanctions, for me the major sanctions issue may be in its moral aspect: how does it stand in the court of law and order which are a civilization's keep against chaos and night? There is a history which expresses itself in external events, the history of kings and queens and wars and treaties and so on – that is one kind of history. But there is something else; there is a history within a history – a history of which these external things are only surface externalizations and rationalizations. There is a meaning trying to achieve itself through history. We achieve it partially and we achieve it badly, but there is a thrust underneath which is trying to make life more complete, to take this immense diversity of life and make it integrated and make it into a greater and more creative whole: not a union of conformities, which is a source of weakness and is the collective, totalitarian idea, but a union of diversities, which is strength and is based on the classic concept of the individual.

This kind of history, and this sense of morality – a kind of cosmic conscience, which is built into life and the human being – is concerned also with things like sanctions. So the question whether things are morally right or wrong at any given moment is supreme and decisive and of the most urgent practical importance; because in the rightness or wrongness of our being and our seeking, our thinking and feeling, is the potential wholeness, the holiness, the saintliness, the sanity of things. At the back of it all is this overwhelming longing for a life that is right rather than wrong, a choice of truth rather than error, the meaningful rather than the meaningless; so I have often thought that the most important issue of our time is not racial prejudice or colour prejudice or anything else. It is this question of how we overcome evil without becoming another form of evil in the process.

I know I am repeating myself, but who are the South Africans, and how can we best deal with them?

One of the key factors certainly, when we are talking about the white South Africans who are in power at the moment and call themselves the Afrikaners, is their history which still has a half-Nelson hold on them and will not let go. They are not, as people tend to think, basically of Dutch origin. The core, the heart, the spirit of the Afrikaner is Huguenot, the extreme Huguenot of the right. The Dutch East Indies Company never had any intention of starting a colony in South Africa. All they intended was to have a kitchen-garden to grow food for their scurvy-ridden ships on their way to the East. But in 1685, when Louis XIV revoked the Edict of Nantes, and the persecutions of the Huguenots started again in the most brutal manner, they fled: they fled to England, to Holland, and the Dutch allowed them to come to South Africa. Practically all the best-known South African names are French Huguenot names.

Apart from a few retired and minor company officials who were scratching a living out of the soil there, and some tolerated deserters and mercenaries in the garrison who had taken discharge and been given a piece of land, there was no real settlement of people at the Cape. Then suddenly came this great influx of Huguenots. They became the core of the Afrikaner people. They had no alternative but to make Africa their home. They had nowhere else to go in the world and, what is more, they were extremely badly treated by the Dutch. The Dutch gave them land in Africa but would not allow them to speak their native French in their schools. They would not allow them religious services in French, and made it clear it was to be Dutch, and Dutch customs throughout, or else. So they were, in essence, rejected again. They were rejected where it hurt most, in their culture and in their Frenchness, and no wonder they came out of this with a great inborn sense of injury and deception, and never wanted to have anything to do with Europe again, saying in their hearts, 'From now on we are African and nothing but African. We shall make this our home and be our own people.' And the less they were Huguenot and French in their customs, the more they became so in their spirit. Their spirit, always extreme, became more extreme still. So the key to the Afrikaner ethos is their own rejection, and their rejection in return of Europe, as well as their extreme, Huguenot stubbornness. Henceforth all was a matter of the Huguenot spirit and a growing, two-dimensional isolation, one geographical and the other, most important, psychological.

But how does it happen that, by recognizing themselves as Africans and no longer as Europeans, they still do not meet on the same level with other Africans? Of course some have done it, and have a good and mature relationship with the Africans or coloured people, but they are not the majority, and above all they are not the ones in a position of power.

We are now going into the nuances. The meeting of cultures is immensely eventful. Neither culture can be the same again and pretend nothing has happened. I think an enormous amount of the spirit of Africa has entered the Afrikaners by the back door. Unconsciously they love Africa with a passion that nobody else can understand. Their attachment to the land is really very deep because they are born of it and have suffered and sacrificed for it. They are white Africans, but they are Africans. To call them Europeans is a misnomer. You just have to compare them with the English-speaking South Africans who came there much later and remained in contact with Britain. In fact, when I was a boy, all English-speaking South Africans talked of Britain as 'home' – they never called it Britain – which used to annoy the hell out of the Afrikaners. They complained angrily, saying, 'They talk of it as home, but this is home!' It really was a very sore point with them, and is a measure of the distance between the two psychologies.

I think that, given time, the Afrikaners and the coloured and the black people, not without great suffering and sacrifice . . .

Will come to terms?

There is a kind of fear which separates them at this moment but there is also a great potential love. If you watched them grow up in my day and their way with their servants – it might be feudalistic but there was a great love in it within the family. I know it is dismissed as 'paternalism', but it came out of an area of love which has to be discovered and can be discovered in a modern way. And countries who now try to tell them how they should live are doing great damage because they know nothing of these things, these hidden potentials which are all part of the problem and its solutions. They do not know and they do not understand these things. How can they? And how arrogant to assume they do! You would have thought that after Brixton and Birmingham, Tottenham and Toxteth, and Northern Ireland, English people would have some humility in telling others how to set about these problems.

The French have their Basque problem, their Breton problem, their Corsican or Occitan problems, their émigré problem. And they are not the only country in trouble: what about the Americans, the Russians, the Chinese, the Arabs, the Israelis or the Indians? Everyone, everywhere, seems to be in trouble.

Yes, and this is one of the interesting things in the modern scene – that in practically every country and every society there is a sort of 'Afrikaner psychology'. By that I mean people who are trying to preserve an identity which they see imperilled and which is their greatest value. They are fanatic about it. There is no great distance in psychology between Afrikaner and Québécois, particularly if you remember their common French origin. And there are other enigmatic variations on the same theme: the Basques, the Bretons, the Irish, even the Welsh or Scots, all still have hankerings, a great nostalgia for their ancient identities, their ancient psychologies and their ancient ways. Once you think of life today along these lines, you think of it in terms of what used to be called the 'soul of a nation'. Then what the Afrikaners fear, and battle for as they see it, does not seem so unnatural. It only seems unnatural because they are small in number. But if you think of the intensity and the reality of what they try to defend, and also that these little diversities are enormously precious to life, one does not want to see them wiped out. One just wants to see them in proportion and one wants to see them defended in a decent way – and apartheid is certainly not a decent way, or even a way that could succeed. In fact it is a certain way of crushing the Afrikaner for ever. The only way any identity or spirit can survive is on its merit to life.

Only by its quality and texture and pursuit of its inner creativeness and truth can any spirit survive. That is why I stressed earlier the importance of the Jewish, not the Israeli, example in history. Or take the Greeks who, though vanished, still live and give, give to our hungry, partial modern selves all the time. If only the world would look at the South African problem in some such way and instead of bashing it on the head, putting it as an untouchable in an untouchables' economic and cultural Coventry, would say it will support all that is valid and fair for it, and all other races, and see that they have time to grow out of their problem, and admit that it is more than a political problem but a great human problem that needs time to be lived and outgrown. For ultimately that is the only way problems are solved: they are lived first and then in the process outgrow themselves. Politics by itself does not initiate the vision needed, which is apolitical. There is no instant political solution to the problem of South Africa. The solution will have to be lived and grown, and will in the process acquire political expression. But you cannot put the political cart before so dark a horse.

I am doing no more than sketch the problem swiftly and in simple terms but only in that sort of spirit will it be solved. There is time for that, but there is no time to let it be artificially expanded into a vast world issue. Problems have their own size and place and time, and only the people who have to live them ultimately have the power and the right to solve them decently. When I think how people have changed in my lifetime, I believe that South Africans of all races and colours, left to themselves can redeem themselves and surprise a world itself in need of redemption.

And although apartheid is completely and utterly wrong, the world is piling another wrong on wrong by its grossly selective standard. There is, for instance, Russia. Think of Russia – with millions of people in concentration camps or in lunatic asylums, not for the colour of their skins but for the colour of their ideas. That a fellow human being should be declared mad or criminal because he looks at life in a different way seems to me a far more dangerous and retrogressive development in the European spirit than racial prejudice, abhorrent as this is.

Think of the precious diversity in life – that there are no two leaves even on a tree alike. Why should we want to obliterate it? And where does this thrust towards conformity go? It is something very archaic and very dangerous, and is the essense of all cancers, the proliferation indefinitely of a single cell at the expense of the rest. Every age seems to be accompanied by a sickness so peculiarly its own as to make one wonder if it is not merely a physical manifestation of the inner aberration of the time itself: and cancer certainly, within and without, is our very own.

Now much light has been shed by Jung and his analytical psychology on good and evil and their relationship. For the first time mankind has a conscious weapon which can help him in this abiding problem. To overcome it is not the goal: to aim at transcending it is the ideal, to contain these opposites with all the awareness we have and, when necessary, to choose truly and to stand fast. This is the way, the chosen way, the way Jung called 'individuation' and which, from the point of view of creation, was the incarnation of God in Christ. The whole of western culture was founded on the creation of an individual so whole and integrated that he will take upon himself the problems of world and universe and live them out in the focus of his own being and doing; in other words, would make the universal specific, the collective individual, the unconscious conscious, and through himself enrich the meaning of life for his community and enable it to renew itself. And, of course, here we are back with the problem of good and evil and their containment and transcendence.

Now for the first time we have got this way open in front of us, yet the sickening thing about the modern world is that this uniquely modern weapon, analytical psychology, with its immense healing potential, is ignored. Psychology is closely related to the great modern science of physics, with its penetration into the heart of the atom: analytical psychology penetrates the deeps of the soul of the atom that is the individual. Suddenly, pragmatically, within and without by way of the natural sciences, there is two-way proof of the great, intuitive scientific and religious assumptions of all time. For instance, when Christ says, 'Know the truth and the truth shall make you free', He is uttering a great psychological and scientific truth – because the more man knows the truth about himself, the greater his awesome freedom to choose between truth and error, good and evil. Take again Christ's reproof, 'Why do you behold the mote in your neighbour's eye and do not consider the beam in your own?' It is a great psychological truth because it is the precise way that what psychologists call 'projection' works. It is projecting the fault that one has in oneself but of which one is unaware, onto one's neighbours. This is where evil comes in. This is where the shadow of man enters. This is one of the most sinister and most common forces at work in mankind and bedevils human relationships, and is one of the most common sources of conflict and confusion on the political scene. One politician projects on to another. One party projects on to another, and the other projects back. It is like a series of negative mirrors reflecting one another's reflections indefinitely; and so we go on evading our own moral shortcomings by blaming them on our neighbours. Nations do it even more than individuals; we are all sooner or later caught in this black spider's web. And the outstanding collective projection, of course, is onto South Africa.

The whole world projects a darkness, its own darkness of which it is unaware, onto the South African darkness. The darkness is there, of course; apartheid is a thing of darkness. But it is there as on a stage where this ancient drama which takes place in the heart of every man, the characters dressed up in the classical colours of fate – black and white – is produced in its most dramatic and theatrical form. So it has a hypnotic attraction, and people do not see the problem for what it is so much as for this unconscious aspect in themselves which is projected onto it. They rob the problem there of its own identity and blacken it all over with their own dark, dishonoured selves. And you are only free to see it for yourself when you have confronted your own darkness projected and recognized it as your own. This becomes possible only by the hard, exacting, humbling way of individuation and unflinching self-knowledge. But its reward is the freedom of truth where at last you can pull back what is yours and leave behind intact what is your neighbour's.

But short of that, this is where evil thrives and negation and destruction arise. Trying to live your goodness not in your own life but in somebody else's life is a classical projection ploy and evasion, and is played off on South Africa in an enormous way just now. People want to feel good by proxy, not their own, but at the expense of the South Africans. One of the most terrible consequences of this form of interference, which comes out of national projections, is that you prevent other people from living their own problems. Now the problems of life, the problems of the universe, the problems of man, are our most precious possessions because they are the raw materials of our redemption. As I said earlier, no problem – no redemption. No problem – no meaning. They are the raw material of our increase. When you take another man's problem away from him, or another country's problem from it, you rob them of all opportunity of redeeming themselves, of getting to know themselves. This is one of the evil consequences of living other people's lives for them, telling people how to live a life of which you know nothing and of which you will not have to endure the consequences.

I know we started on this topic by discussing sanctions, but I can give you many, many other examples from all over the world. Wherever people find villains, wherever they are haunted by villains, it is a sign that they are projecting the villains in themselves of which they are frightened. That is why the concept of villains has such a power over them. The Russians are notorious for the fact that every country is in the wrong except Russia. They project and feel themselves besieged by enemies.

But this is in truth just a plea: a plea to observe the sanctity of our problems. And if you can come to a point where you can accept your problem as your own, begin to have reverence for it as a problem child of life, not condemn or reject but try to think of it perhaps as the raw material of your own increase, of greater new being, you will find it one day in the heart of what you love most, and know it, because the trumpets will sound that creation has been enlarged and enriched.

I sometimes feel very deeply that life seems to us so problematical all the time, because its problems are cosmic too. Life is our creator's way, God's way, the universe's way of solving a cosmic problem. Once that problem has been solved, life will become something else, will have done its work. We are here to share a problem of creation, so, as A. E. Housman said:

> 'The troubles of our proud and angry dust
> Are from eternity, and shall not fail.'

Our problems come from the highest source, they come of God himself. He has problems of his creation too and once we see this sanctity of problems, once we discover the love of this thing which is deep in us, this love that was preached on the Cross, we are out of our problem and into divine partnership.

I'm talking in a very simplified manner, but these are the kinds of things that ought to concern us. These are the kinds of things above all which should be the concern of the churches. And do they bother? No. I said the other day in a television interview – and I was very much berated for it, you should have seen my mail – that organized Christianity in trying to make politics Christian has only made Christianity political. And this ancient urge of religion, which was to keep man on track, on course within life, growing solutions, growing out of his problems, growing into a greater manifestation, increasing his awareness – all these things, I think, are terribly imperilled in our time because the institutions like the churches, designed to promote those things and to protect them, have failed and even subvert them, and no longer uphold the functions which were the justification for their creation.

━━━━━

Laurens, I would like to hear that story you promised to me, about the frogs and all that came out of their singing.

Well, as always, that story is part of another story. It started when I was

288

invited to come and open a new wilderness reserve in Africa. I immediately said 'yes', because I believe, as you know, that the conservation of the natural world and our reverence for the earth, plants and the natural things are the most urgent priorities of our time. If we go on as we are at the moment, neglecting that, and fighting and killing one another, there will not be any world left to quarrel about. And for that reason I am very much involved in it and I am a trustee of the World Wilderness Foundation.

So I agreed to open this wilderness, which is in a lovely part of South Africa, where there had been a severe drought. It is deep in the bush, and happily the rains had broken at last and there was a great sense of fulfilment round about. You could hear the earth singing about the rains. At the opening ceremony I gave a talk which was broadcast and televised to the whole of southern Africa, so that everybody knew what had happened there that day: and this fact had a role in what followed.

When it was all over, I wanted to get away from the people and be alone with my closest friend, who had come to the opening with me, and we went deep into the bush and ended up following a leopard around. When darkness came we had to leave it and returned in the Land-rover towards the main camp. We came into a large clearing on our way: there were immense thunderclouds all the way round, but above us there was a great open pool of stars. Suddenly, in the lights of the Land-rover, I saw a strange shape coming at us, and we braked instantly. It was a giraffe, which just missed the headlights and swerved past us: but in stopping so suddenly we had stalled the engine, and all was quiet.

Then I heard one of the most beautiful sounds I have ever heard: the frogs singing all around me. There were five distinct kinds of voices of frogs taking part in this chorus and their chorale was rising to a tremendous crescendo. It was a hymn of thanksgiving. It was as if the frogs were thanking God for creation, thanking creation for life, thanking creation for frogs, thanking and re-thanking in the night for us, and all living things. Every single frog was singing, and I thought immediately that for the first time now I knew why Aristophanes had fastened on the frogs for that great play he wrote, about the crisis which was facing the Greece he loved. I could have sat there all night, their ancient Hallelujahs and Hosannas were so beautiful. I had listened to frogs all my life but I had never heard anything like this before. There is no symphony, nothing I have ever heard, which could surpass the ecstasy, the thanksgiving, the sheer utterness of the music going on that night.

When I arrived back at the camp, I found there was a message for me. Someone who had seen me on television had telephoned to ask if I would start a series of Smuts Memorial Lectures, with an inaugural lecture on the life and work of Field-Marshal Smuts. Well now, I had promised myself I would never speak in public again, because I am not a public speaker; I do not really like it, I am frightened of it. But something stopped me saying 'no' outright. I sent a message asking if I could wait before deciding. They said that it would be quite all right to let them know in three or four months' time.

I came back to my home in London with the memory of the song of the frogs like an ache in my heart, and I felt at once that I must have a look at Aristophanes' *Frogs* again. I started reading it and I realized first of all why *The Frogs* was such an important play to me, because the world of Aristophanes' day, the Greek world, was very much facing the kind of problem our world is facing today. It was crumbling from within and there were enemy forces without. It was in peril in all sorts of ways, but particularly Aristophanes was concerned with the inner situation of Athens against Sparta, the Athenians against themselves, the slaves having been freed and having a voice in public affairs, lowering the level of dialogue and debate. It was very much like the kind of inner upheavals that are going on in Europe again at this moment, where there is a tendency for the uneducated voices to dominate the educated ones, using 'educated' in the classical sense of the word.

So I came to the moment in *The Frogs* where Aristophanes' people decide that the only thing that can save them is to summon back a great voice of history to rally them. Therefore they send a messenger to the underworld, to Hades, to Pluto, to bring back one great, historic voice to speak to the Athenians so that the meaning of their history could once again be evoked, live in them and unite them and put them on their true course. They accordingly chose Dionysos to go to the underworld, which was his own dimension, to see Pluto. There they decide to arrange a debate between Euripides and Aeschylus, because they know that the voice needed could only be one of those two, and that only a debate could reveal which was the more appropriate for rousing Athens out of a sleep of spirit.

At first they think perhaps Euripides is the one who will win the dialogue, because he is better in debate than Aeschylus: he is more adroit, he is witty, he is trendy, he is modern, with-it, and funny but also profound. He seems to combine all the qualities to make him popular; whereas old Aeschylus is more wordy, he is more solemn and writes almost as if his pen were the instrument of fate, and all in him appears dark, gloomy and out of date. Indeed, in the course of this debate it looks often as if Euripides is going to win, but in the end they chose old Aeschylus for one reason only – he has done something which Euripides has not: he fought at Marathon.

I can think of a number of remarkable artists of my own generation who not only did not fight at the Marathon of our civilization but deliberately avoided doing so, and so I understand the difference.

I put *The Frogs* down, unbearably sad, knowing how deprived the education of the world was today, because none of the children today would be taught their history, to feel about Marathon as we did, and I do still. Long ago as it was fought, it was fought also for us, and its echo in our souls oblige us in all decency of history to listen and know about it.

However, that roughly was the message that came through to me from the African frogs. And I thought it very strange because what those people had asked me to do the night after I listened to the frogs was to bring a great voice of South African history back to my native country, which was ruled by inferior men who had forgotten the meaning of history and the pattern of spirit that had made them leave Europe. Smuts and Botha are completely forgotten now. In fact, they have been murdered by historians in South Africa. People do not talk about them, they do not write about them, although what there are of sound foundations in the country they owe to them. As the Zulus say, 'Their praise names are forgotten; people do not speak of them any more.'

And suddenly it seemed as if something out of life had arranged it all: the opening of the reserve, the coming of the rain, the breaking of the drought and the Hallelujah of the frogs, all to coincide and to make me realize that I should be this kind of messenger to fetch a great voice of our history back. And when I realized this, I cabled and said 'yes', I would give the lecture. This is what I meant by living as if following the flight of a bird.

———

From the little I know of Smuts, he was certainly a great, international figure.
I think so, and what was so amazing is that he started with this tremendous sense which people born of the earth of Africa tend to have, of 'belonging' to it in almost a cosmic sense for a cosmogonic cause. Smuts was born in the Cape, and his family had been there for about 100 years. Although he was of Dutch parentage and his education was Dutch, he was an intense reader of English. One of the great influences on his life was Walt Whitman, who was the first great American poet of nature, the voice of nature in a way, whose first book of poems was called *Leaves of Grass*, the Whitman whom Chesterton hailed for his 'barbaric yawp', claiming that it put to shame all the effete, green-carnation period at the end of the Victorian era. Yet already there was in the young Smuts this recognition of a new poet and voice of nature, who was really recognized properly in England only after the 1914–18 war. Yet he was already a god to Smuts at school and university – the Smuts who loved plants and grass and nature and the mountains. He was already obsessed with seeing life in nature's way.

Smuts did very well in all his studies and then was sent to England to Cambridge, to study law, where he did something which had never been done before. He took his examinations in two years instead of three, and he did them so well that he got a brilliant Double First. This period in England made a great impression upon him because he came across the non-imperialistic side of Great Britain. He had known the officials, the governors, the administrators and those sorts of people abroad, but this was the abiding kind of England that he came in contact with, which was not the one necessarily identified with the empire. It made a profound impression on him.

Then he came out and began practising law in Johannesburg. Very soon he was asked to be Kruger's chief law minister, that is, the Attorney General. From then on he played a great part in the fate of South Africa.

He conducted the negotiations with the English and that steely Lord Milner, whom Harold Macmillan once described to me as the coldest fish he had ever met. When that failed and the Anglo-Boer War became inevitable, he helped to plan the military strategy. He was tremendously vigorous and hard-working. In the midst of all this he wrote a book on his beloved Whitman. When finally the war broke out, he went off to fight with copies of Whitman, and Kant's *Critique of Pure Reason* in his saddlebags.

He was a great soldier. He led one of the most romantic and far-reaching campaigns during the Boer War that followed. He led his armies right into the Cape to almost within shooting distance of Cape Town. His commandos in fact shot at a British cruiser off Port Nolloth for the fun of claiming they had fought the war's only naval battle, though just armed with rifles. He conducted a brilliant guerrilla campaign and, although great armies hunted him, they never caught him.

When the war ended he immediately started working for something that would redeem the war for both the British and his own people, by restoring self-government. That done, he began on his vision of the Union of South Africa. In 1910 the Union was accomplished, and it was an incredible achievement. If the South African constitution bore the stamp of one mind, it was the stamp of Smuts. In all this he acknowledged his leader, General Botha, who was probably one of the most magnanimous and noble men Africa has ever seen, because although he had fought to the bitter end he, like Smuts, believed in conciliation, building a new and greater nation.

In the 1914–18 war they brought South Africa in on the side of Britain and France against the Kaiser's Germany, although it meant that they had a rebellion and civil war in their country which they had to put down. Then Smuts was given command of the British Army in stalemate in East Africa against von Lettow-Vorbeck's forces in Tanganyika. Once that was well in hand he was appointed a member of Lloyd George's War Cabinet. As such he was a major force in founding the Royal Flying Corps. He and Botha were both at Versailles. While he was there he was one of the prime movers for the creation of the League of Nations and drafted its first constitution. With Smuts there was always this feeling of building, integrating, making whole, healing what was divided and apart, and in the midst of doing all this, not surprisingly, writing a long essay on what he called 'Holism', the seeking of creation for greater wholeness and the integration of a universal meaning in the individual human being, who was the carrier and promoter of new meaning and life in his societies. The essay is a much greater contribution than was realized, and it was unfairly rejected in its own day. Yet the perceptive, like the historian Toynbee, were immensely influenced by it – Toynbee quotes from it over and over again in his great *Study of History* – and in fact it was a staggering effort by an intuitive and brilliant mind, anticipating Jung. If only Smuts had possessed access to Jung, Heaven alone knows what he may not have contributed to our time.

If, thanks to his insight, he was able to foresee trouble in the Far East, did he also foresee trouble in Europe after the Treaty of Versailles?

He was very disillusioned by the peace treaty at Versailles. He and Botha had started out at Versailles in a different mood from the rest. Botha had sent him a little note across the table in which he had written, in Dutch, to the effect, 'I cannot help thinking back today to 1902 when you and I were in exactly the same position at Vereeniging in which the Germans and the Austrians find themselves today, and I can only pray that we shall be as magnanimous now as the British were to us then.'

That is the mood they started off in. Smuts himself thought they should fill all the British warships with wheat for the starving people of Europe. He worked very hard to get what he called 'a constructive peace treaty'. One of his firm allies was the great economist Maynard Keynes, whose influence lives on. He wrote that devastating book *The Economic Consequences of the Peace*. Maynard Keynes, one evening I had with him and Lopokova in Bloomsbury, gave me his own version, which was very much the Smuts version, of the gloom they shared so intimately at Versailles. Both he and Smuts were intensely dispirited by the way the conference went. Then Smuts was sent off to deal with Bela Kun in Hungary, came back and was so depressed by the treaty he said he was not going to sign it. He and Keynes were both sitting in Smuts's room in despair, and suddenly Smuts said, 'You know, Keynes, the only thing left is to pray, and to pray in the Hottentot way.' And they prayed the Hottentot prayer, which I know well because it comes from where I was

294

born, and it translates roughly as follows: 'Dear Lord, your children are in grave danger. Dear God in Heaven, please come quickly and save your children. Dear God, if you do not come and save your children now they will most certainly perish. But please take note: it is so serious this time that you must not send your Son, you have just got to come yourself!'

But why were men of such stature as Smuts and Botha, the real founders of South Africa, so quickly forgotten? Why was their thinking trivialized, their writing ignored and the examples they set totally rejected? Particularly Smuts's resistance against the Afrikaner Nationalists before the war, when they wanted to legalize colour bars in industrial relations?

Well, it started immediately after the 1914–18 war. Botha died, that was a great loss, and Smuts became what he never wanted to be, Prime Minister, and he had to cope with this vicious problem of psychological isolation in Afrikanerdom. The problem of South Africa all through her history is a problem of increasing psychological isolation from Europe. The country came about against the will of Europe, against the will of the Dutch, against the will of the English. But still the Afrikaners insisted on going into the interior and making a country for themselves. They were always isolated geographically, and politically, and as it were morally. As a result they developed this singular psychology of isolation and thinking that they had a divine right to preserve their identity at any cost. A strong section resented the presence of the English in South Africa because they felt that it endangered their national identity, that the English would take away their language and their institutions and their religion and everything else. And because of the isolation of the country, they made such headway that in the 1920s already Smuts was defeated, and Hertzog, another sort of man whom my family knew to their cost, became Prime Minister.

But Hertzog was a comparatively mild phenomenon compared to the Nationalists of today. He had really done little more than devise a wedge in the political system for introducing the segregation that was to become apartheid, but for the rest only emphasized what Smuts had already accomplished. Smuts made his peace with Hertzog and agreed to serve under him. It was one of the greatest, most magnanimous things he ever did. Smuts served under him until the outbreak of the war in 1939 and prevented him from doing the greater harm potential in his political philosophy.

Then in 1939 Hertzog wanted to stay neutral, emerging again in the colours which already before 1914–18 had made my father quit politics, and Smuts said, 'We cannot stay neutral at a time like this.' And Smuts took charge and defeated Hertzog and brought South Africa into the war.

Then after the war, he was more than ever engaged outside South Africa. In the meantime the opposition against him was nurtured by very clever propaganda, and in the first election after the war, when Smuts was really worn out and very tired, there came the fateful election. There was still a lot of discontent, as there is after a war. Business was in a terrible state. There was not employment for all the soldiers who came back, and all sorts of things had been neglected in wartime – it was all blamed on him. Above all, the people feared that Smuts was going to emancipate the black people, and they conducted the election on that issue, saying, 'If you elect Smuts, you will get a black South Africa' – and they defeated him. Not long after the election he died.

But in everything up to that point in South Africa, if one man had succeeded, it was Smuts, who fashioned and built South Africa into a united, modern scientific, technological state. This one man did it, with an immense idealistic vision. He was a man of science, a man of law, a man of letters and a very great statesman.

And so what was the message you gave in your lecture on Smuts?

Well, there is talk now in South Africa about reform, giving the coloured people their common citizenship. But I said that, when Smuts left, they already had this, and their right to it was entrenched in the Act of Union. This so-called 'reform' is no more than the Government beginning to try to repair the damage which it has itself inflicted on the country. I said that what they were giving back to the coloured people, even now, is not as much as they took away from them by one of the most fraudulent devices in Parliament. I was not saying that they should not repair the damage which they have inflicted. But do not let them pretend that any of their reform is real change.

I said, you must re-examine the claims made for the new agreement aimed at establishing new relations with the states in the interior of

Africa and improving their relationships with their black neighbours. You will note that then the relationships which Smuts had with the black states of Africa were much better. For instance, Smuts – not Britain – was asked by the East African states to reform their civil services for them after the war. And actually he sent up a brother-in-law of mine to establish a commission for the reform of the administrative services there. Southern Rhodesia, or Zimbabwe as it is called now, did exactly the same thing. Moreover, in Smuts's day none of the British Africans sent their students to study in England, they were all sending them south to study in the Union of Africa. I said that was the situation then; they have not even come near that now. I said there is no initiative, no spirit of great change in them, and if you look at Smuts's life in this light you will see how far we have got to go in order to pick up our genuine historical destiny, which is where Smuts left off; and continue from there to wipe out this disastrous period of apartheid as soon as possible. Already in 1924, when they were introducing a colour bar in industrial legislation, Smuts said, 'If you pass this law you will surround South Africa with a ring of hatred.' And that is precisely what they have done, I said.

Smuts after the war was thinking about a pan-Africa, and had great programmes ready to pursue if re-elected. He realized that now really the moment had come when the British and, as he thought, the Afrikaners were truly integrated by the war and united. The armies that came back from the north were marvellous: they had eliminated all the barriers of race wherever they had fought. It was a new, young South Africa and capable of immense new growth. I saw something of it myself, still alive and growing, although demobilized and in civilian clothes, and I was not surprised that Smuts, who had fore-suffered and came to foresee how the politically unrecognized millions of black South Africans would have to be integrated and welded into a single nation, said 'Now is the time to take on this burden.' I quoted from Smuts where he talked of the 'great mystery' at the end of the road; despite all our blunders this 'great mystery' was the birth of the soul of a nation which confronted us. I said the nation for him was not six and a half million white people but the thirty million people of all races and colours who constitute the people of South Africa. That was the soul and that was the nation of which he spoke, and this is what we have to aim to create as fast as we possibly can.

We should follow Smuts's way, which is the traditional, historical way, when confronted with a crisis of these proportions. We should call a national convention of all races and colours, and we should sit down and say, 'Look, we have all made terrible mistakes. We have hurt one another. We have called this conference to wipe out the mistakes of the past and we have got to create a concept of citizenship in South Africa with which everybody can identify, not rationally but emotionally, with the heart as well as with the mind. And we, the white people, who had the power, must accept responsibility for inflicting the greatest injury, apologize for it, be grateful for the patience of their subject countrymen, coloured and black, and in consultation with them move forward.' Unless we can do that we shall become irrelevant and lose our already diminishing power to shape the future.

It is not only a political, social and economic revolution that you are asking for, but also a spiritual revolution. Do you really think it is possible in the present situation?

I think one has to begin first of all by putting the idea into people's imaginations. From the reception I got that evening of the Memorial Lecture, it was quite clear to me that it was a message which was sympathetically heard and already planted in the hearts of the eight hundred people who listened to me. I was passing on something for which they were ready: the spirit of history within them was hungry and ready. I do not mean the record of external events we call history, but another kind of history, the meaning of history which is inscribed in a people's spirit and comes singularly alive and alert in moments of profound crisis, as this most immediate challenge to change is today, in the life of all South Africa.

If Smuts did have this vision, why did he not do something about it sooner?

It is a common error of present-day judgements to condemn their predecessors in terms of values and insights their age did not possess. The great and most immediate problems in Smuts's day were the consequences of the history of British-Afrikaner confrontation. The problem of creating an integrated, multiracial society was still only a vast but dormant potential, and kinetic only among the few. Roy Campbell and William Plomer and I already were acutely aware of what was to come, said so and attacked Smuts, especially in 1926, in a way I think today was unfair to him. But we were a lone, maligned phenomenon, so much so that Campbell and Plomer left South Africa never to return. It was only at the end of the Second World War that the long-dormant volcano began to awake, rumble and then erupt as it has now. But Smuts was aware of its first stirrings in its sleep and ready to act, and that readiness cost him that awful election.

What do you think Smuts would do if he were in power today?

South Africa would never have been allowed to be expelled from the Commonwealth. That was one of the most short-sighted and destructive results ever to come out of a Commonwealth Conference, because it deprived the opponents of the new Nationalists of one of their greatest sources of support and confidence. Then Smuts would long since have addressed both Houses of Congress and enlisted their help and understanding, spoken to both Houses of Parliament in Britain to ask them to do likewise, and possibly redrafted the Constitution of a United Nations which has violated its own Charter and broken both the law and spirit of its own creation.

He would never have allowed the country to fall into such an abysmal mess, and certainly would not have inflicted the damage, both political and human, that these terrible inferior little men who deprived him of power have done.

I said all this and more in that first lecture, and have since gone on to speak out far more drastically to even larger audiences in South Africa as the crisis accelerates and deepens. But this is enough to show you what the frogs, with their singing, had done. And I should perhaps add just one more stroke of the brush to complete this quick sketch of Smuts and tell you of our last meeting. I was on my way back from South-East Asia to report to the War Office in London, and I went to see him early one morning in the Prime Minister's official office in the Union Buildings in Pretoria. I was still in uniform and I was somewhat surprised to find that he was too. And I think of that little thing often, as a sign perhaps that his great heart knew that the war, though vanished from the battlefields, was far from over and was raging on in the spirit of men in a far more subtle and potentially lethal way. I remembered how almost all his adult life he had been at war: the Anglo-Boer War, the First World War and a civil war in his native country; a revolt on the Rand in the Twenties, as well as a Hottentot rebellion in South-West Africa; the first serious black riot at Port Elizabeth; the tragic religious riot at Bullhoek and another world war, with his own country seething with subversion and another potential rebellion. Yet there was no sign of a flagging of spirit or hope about him, and I was immensely moved by how much more resolved and calm and inwardly still he seemed to have become since our last meeting, eleven years before.

He examined me closely about South-East Asia and was obviously deeply concerned and thought, as I did, that the way the Dutch and Indonesians resolved this conflict would have profound implications for the whole of the post-imperial world, particularly Africa. About India, which was always written large on his heart in the future's most enigmatic code, he shook his head and murmured almost as if it were a biblical incantation, 'I pray they will know in time what they are doing and cease to know not, as I fear they do at present.'

We talked about Palestine, where he foresaw the creation of an independent Jewish state. He said he would welcome it and not hesitate to recognize it. This alarmed me, and I protested, saying, 'Please, Oom Jannie, that cannot be done without committing another monstrous act of injustice on people who have never harmed the Jews. We could easily be planting the seeds of another world war there if we did.'

He dismissed that and said there were already seeds far more fertile with war to worry about. He went on to talk about South Africa, ending with this prophetic conclusion, 'You know, outsiders have never understood that our politics have always essentially been a struggle between Afrikaner and Afrikaner about what role the British should have in our future. From now on, no one will understand us unless they realize it is going to be more and more a mortal battle between Afrikaner and Afrikaner as to the role the coloured and black peoples are to have in our country.'

And for the first and only time in his life, from my childhood onwards, he looked to me sad if not sick at heart, because all his life he had been engaged in the battle of one kind of Afrikaner against another, and it was as if he saw no end to it, even in his long-distance sight.

———

You say that if Smuts had been returned to power and lived on, one of his foremost aims would have been to promote his pan-African vision. It is interesting how many of the Europeans who went to Africa were instantly seized in their various ways by a vision of an Africa united in some way or other. The British had their Cecil Rhodes and his Cape-to-Cairo dream. I gather Smuts's vision was not imperialistic but indigenous. Was that not something which, in the far North of Africa, was also a vision of Haile Selassie, the Emperor of Ethiopia?

I would like to answer your question by beginning in Ethiopia itself, at a place in the Blue Nile Province when we first had news that the Emperor was joining the patriot forces we were assembling. Incidentally, the way the news reached us is yet one more illustration of the rare imagination with which Wavell and his staff prepared this campaign against the Italians. The news came to us at nightfall on the sound of drums, which was not only totally unexpected but could not have been more appropriate because it came on the one instrument which is of the heartbeat of Africa itself and made it a pronouncement of living history more than a signal in the present. And what happened was that among the aristocratic families who accompanied the Emperor in the British cruiser *Enterprise* when they had to be evacuated from Ethiopia after Mussolini's shameful conquest, a group brought the Emperor's own war drums with them and kept them safely in Palestine where they took refuge until they were summoned to join the Emperor in battle again.

Wavell and the War Office, through Sandford of course, knew of all this, and they had the imagination to put George Steer in charge of a sort of psychological warfare unit to be used against the Italians. George Steer, who most sadly was killed in Burma, was a remarkable human being of great resource, energy, imagination, courage and conviction. He had already made his name as a correspondent of *The Times* in the war against Franco. It was he who discovered that the Franco blockade of the Basque port of Bilbao was being broken by an ad hoc fleet of

British cargo ships commanded by some formidable Welsh skippers who all belonged to the great and distinguished clan of the Joneses. He did not know their Christian names and yet wanted to see that recognition of their valour went to the right address, so he called them after their favourite breakfast foods. As a result British readers of *The Times* every morning at breakfast were able to read of the latest exploits of 'Potato Jones', 'Ham and Egg Jones', 'Scrambled Egg Jones', 'Bubble and Squeak Jones', 'Sausage and Mash Jones', and so on. They all in due course became national heroes.

Hard on that, Steer came to report the war in Abyssinia with great distinction, and distinguished himself further by marrying a French woman correspondent as the city of Addis Ababa was falling to the Italians. George Steer, who was a countryman of mine and one I knew well, accordingly had his whole heart and imagination bound in a determination to do all he could to confuse and defeat fascism, and Wavell could not have made a better choice.

For instance, the moment George arrived in the Sudan he had the Emperor's war drums taken right up to the front lines of where our scanty forces were holding back the Italian divisions. Every night he picked the most adept of the young Abyssinian aristocrats with him to beat out the Emperor's own mobilization call. The sound of the drum penetrated far into the interior, was picked up by other drums and relayed throughout the vast hinterland of Ethiopia. I still remember the excitement that went through our rag-and-tattered patriots and how, on the first morning after the first drumbeats, their eyes shone and they uttered again and again, 'Jan-Hoy is coming! Already he is near!' And the effect on the Italians was singularly depressing and their morale visibly diminished.

I did not see the Emperor myself until some weeks later. I was sent to a place called Shaba at the railway on the banks of the Nile just outside Khartoum – the Shaba which is supposed to be a corruption of the Sheba from where came the beautiful Queen with whom Solomon the Wise, according to vivid myth and legend, fathered an ancestor of the Emperor. I had gone there to collect men consisting mostly of warrant officers and specialists in small arms and machine guns, who would accompany me behind the Italian lines to arm and train the patriot forces. I think we numbered some 120 in all, and the day before we had to leave by train I gave them permission to go into Khartoum for the last time. To my dismay at evening, when the first straggles of the party were starting to trickle back, in high spirits and obviously in various degrees of intoxication, I got a message that the Emperor and George Steer had just arrived in Khartoum, had heard of my impending departure, and the Emperor had at once decided it was his duty to come and inspect the first of his forces he could contact.

By nine in the evening I had the whole of my party drawn up for parade in the dim railway-siding light: the most sober in the front rank and the least sober in the last rank, which seemed to consist mostly of the taller men drawn from the Guards regiments in the Middle East at the time. Once drawn up on parade, habit seemed to me to remove a great deal from their appearance of over-indulgence and I hoped that I would have to offer none of the excuses to the Emperor which were already queueing up in my mind. When he arrived at last, a small, rather forlorn figure, he was covered with a cape which he wore elegantly but which trailed rather poignantly to the ground, so that as he started to walk down the first rank a slight sort of swish of the garment accompanied him. At one moment a kind of mutter of astonishment from the ranks silenced the sounds of our footsteps, and I began to fear that I had been over-optimistic. But happily it passed away because, I discovered afterwards, it had merely been a gasp of amazement at finding this great Emperor of history, for whom the men were going to fight, so small and frail in person. The same reaction reached its climax when he passed down the line of Guards and I heard plainly from behind me a Guardsman mutter, 'He calls himself the Lion of Judah, does he, Bill? He looks more like Tiger Tim to me.' And from that moment on the Emperor was known affectionately to our troops as Tiger Tim. This nickname, bestowed in affectionate fun, had some element of truth in it because the Emperor had something of both the tiger and the lion in him.

No stature ever belied the strength of character, the deep convictions, the courage and sense of royal mission, the dignity of the oldest and only royalty quintessentially of Africa, so much as the Emperor's did. Not only was there the myth of Sheba and Solomon to indicate the antiquity of his line but there was also the fact that the Book of Acts in the Bible clearly establishes how Ethiopia was ruled at that time by a Queen Candace, and that a negro plenipotentiary of hers who saw the stoning of the first Christian martyrs, converted Ethiopia to Christianity and so made it the first Christian kingdom in the world. All that had been involved in the evolution of a royal line over so vast a space of time always seemed to me to be active in the climate of the Emperor's personality, without enfeebling the bridgehead of spirit he had so painfully established in the present. This in itself seemed to me an immense achievement. We ourselves always spoke of Ethiopia as a Plantagenet country, and I only wish I had time to describe some of the Ethiopian Plantagenet ways that I encountered.

So what it was really like when the Emperor, as Ras Tafari and Duke of Harar, was a boy, defeats my imagination. But I had some glimpse of it when he told me once, sheltering from the rains in his tent, that as a young man of seventeen he had to fight a duel to the death with an opponent, and ended it by cutting off the head of his opponent.

Wilfred Thesiger, who was one of the first to go into Abyssinia, had been born there and of course was one of the most distinguished of our little band. In his book, *Arabian Sands*, there is a marvellous opening chapter about the turmoil and danger of the world in which the Emperor made his way to the crown that anyone who wishes to understand his background must read. I never ceased to marvel how, in those early, precarious days, he became a kind of hymnal to his people that was both ancient and modern, with neither the ancient nor the modern ever quarrelling with each other.

I have never forgotten how, at Debra Markos, one of the greatest of his barons, Ras Hailu, who had defected to the Italians and really deserved a sentence of death by almost any code, not only the Ethiopian medieval code, was publicly pardoned. For some eight or nine hours Ras Hailu's followers in their thousands passed by the Emperor, who sat there silent and immovable, as they reswore allegiance to him, and in the process recited to him all the acts of valour their swords, which they flourished in the sun, had performed on behalf of the throne in the course of being passed down from father to son, from generation to generation. It was probably the last truly Homeric parade to be seen on earth, and I could not help thinking at the time of the Homeric epics of Greece and the fact that Ethiopia already had contacts with Greece in the time of Homer, because the *Iliad* begins with the statement that when the trouble which led to the Trojan war broke out on Olympus, Zeus unfortunately was away in Ethiopia, 'a country famous for its system of justice'.

And what was humanly, perhaps, most impressive was that this frail person had the memory to match the occasion and give the right acknowledgement and responses to these endless recitals of war and battle, at the precise places, so that this vast procession never lost its impulse or motion but flowed on uninterrupted like a river.

Later I had a similar but nonetheless disconcerting experience of this incredible royal memory. I had with me W. E. Allen, the historian who ran away from Eton as a boy to fight with the white Russians and wrote what I still think is the best history of Georgia. He had come to me as a volunteer from the Blues, and was not attached to any particular group, so I mounted him on the only mule we possessed and used him to scout ahead of the vast train of camels, loaded with guns and supplies, which I was leading through sleeping-sickness country between the Sudan border and the escarpment of Ethiopia. It shows how full of a sense of history we already were that I had christened the mule 'Prester John', after the legendary King of Africa and ruler of the Monomotapo for whom the Portuguese sought so long in vain.

Bill Allen had, for a brief while, been a follower of Mosley and a supporter of Mussolini and been elected to Parliament on a Mosley ticket. All this was behind him and he was happily looking forward to getting a senior post in the Emperor's new civil service. When I introduced him to the Emperor, the Emperor said to him: 'Captain Allen, I am very interested in your name. I seem to remember that there was a Captain Allen who was elected as a member of the Mosley Party and represented Belfast in Parliament. Did you know him by any chance?'

Poor Bill blushed scarlet and said, '*Majesté, c'était moi.*' And that, of course, was the end of all Bill's hopes of advancement in the Emperor's service.

But from that moment at Debra Markos on, the Emperor's forces

305

joined in what became more and more a rout of the Italian army and he was restored to his throne in comparatively quick time. I have already told you in what mood he went towards his restoration, but I did not see him very much during that period because I was almost immediately recalled to the Western Desert. I can only remember that when I went to say goodbye to him, he said, 'I am so distressed, I do not know what is happening now, because they are taking all my own English officers from me.'

But I did see him a great deal after the war. I never travelled from Britain to southern Africa without stopping at Addis Ababa to be with him and see him, and always I was amazed at how much of work and resources he was putting into bringing his country out of its ancient ways and turning it into a truly modern African state. There was no way in which anybody could have done it faster, no matter what the people who murdered him say, no matter what the ideologies demanded as interpreted by the hundreds of students he had sent to Europe for their education and who came back to create the climate which led to his assassination. And, here is the parallel to Smuts you asked about, his vision was not confined just to his own country, but to the world, particularly to the African world. He inspired the first Organisation of African Unity and gave it a home in Addis Ababa. The African leaders for years met there annually and I think they gained enormously by it, because every year, in their renewed contact with him, something of the royal example, Africa's only royal example, brushed off onto them and influenced their ways. And his influence was all the greater because it was not exerted through a sense of expediency, but had a certain ancient royal integrity to determine its values.

For instance, when Rhodesia declared UDI there was an enormous popular outcry that the names in the streets of Addis Ababa should be changed because many of them were named after the British and South African soldiers who had emancipated his country. He resolutely refused, saying simply, 'These names are part of our history, whether we like it or not. It would be dishonest and dishonourable to remove them.'

What was fascinating, too, was how he balanced within himself a sense of imperial power in the medieval idiom and the responsibilities of a modern monarch. Because he had to be both all the time he could only grow slowly into something more advanced and contemporary – there was no instant way, and I can recall many fascinating glimpses of the imperial aspect of his office. At the twenty-fifth anniversary of his restoration, for instance, a small group of us who had been in his army, the only ones, alas, left alive, were asked to attend. And on the morning before the main celebrations began he invited the whole diplomatic corps, which was vast and included Russians, Chinese, Americans and all, to witness a reception he was giving for us. We had all been warned meticulously as to what we were to wear, and arrived at Court in full morning dress. But one of our officers had arrived late and lost his baggage on the way. We had great difficulty in insisting he should come with us dressed as he was in his flannel bags and rather faded blue blazer. We marched him off, much embarrassed, to the palace and there we were lined up in a row before this very special and rather glittering audience. One by one we were presented to the Emperor, bowed our heads when the moment came, and were decorated, after which we turned about and marched back to the main body in the hall.

But when it came to this officer's turn he stood very bravely to attention in front of the Emperor, and, calling him by the title we always used, said, 'Jan-Hoy, I am ashamed to appear before you like this, but all my baggage was lost on the way here.' The Emperor gave just a hint of a smile and his eyes warmed and glowed and he raised the index finger of his right hand and said, 'Captain, I have heard.'

That evening we had to go to a vast reception and ball at the palace, and, coming back from a visit to the royal stables to our hotel, were amazed to see a whole convoy of Mercedes cars coming slowly up the hill towards the hotel. I may add that we had each had a colonel and a Mercedes allotted to us, and so we thought, 'They are really calling for us much too early.' But it was not that at all. As the Mercedes drew up, out of each one jumped smiling, beaming colonels, with large cardboard boxes under their arms. They summoned us to the lounge of the hotel. Then out of these boxes there came everything and more that the bereft officer had lost on his journey. Frock-coats and trousers, dress-suits, tails, dinner-jackets, lounge-suits, shirts, ties, socks, shoes and boots, all combining to make him by far the best dressed man in our midst. What had happened was that from the moment the Emperor 'heard', he had set some two hundred Italian tailors to work and by nightfall they had created a complete outfit for this officer.

Two impressions in connection with the Emperor stay with me. The first is derived from the city of Harar, which is the capital of the Province from which he came. It is a legendary city and always had a close connection with the Middle East and the Ethiopian's semitic kinsmen in Palestine. I saw it first when Orde Wingate and I came into it in an old Italian Fiat truck by night. As we came down the gulleys between the hills which surround the city, our headlights suddenly caught the great mud-coloured walls and wherever we looked there were hundreds of hyenas in a fever of hunger and fear jumping over the walls into the city, and more hyenas jumping over their heads out of the city. In that light it had a very strange and powerful Goya-esque impact, as if we were entering the capital of the carrion kingdom. I got to know it well because I went all over it to find if there were still people who remembered a French poet who had a great influence on me, the young poet Rimbaud, who carried on a mysterious business there for years – gun-running reputedly not the least of them. Technically, it should have been possible to find lots of people who had known him because it was barely fifty years since he had contracted in Harar the disease that killed him. But I asked everywhere, all the old scribes and wisest-looking traders we could find, but it was as if neither men nor stone remembered him and all had cast him out for ever.

But a by-product of this search was that I got an insight into how remote from our reckoning were the kinds of historical elements and forces which the Emperor still had to transform, and at the same time how well he was doing it, how well he was setting his country on a process of growing out of this past – which is the only way that real change can come to men and their societies, not by these instant ideologies and European impositions that lead ultimately only to murder of mind and man.

The other impression is of the last banquet I attended at his palace. He served the best French food and French wines there for foreigners who liked it, but matched it also with a menu of Abyssinian dishes and Abyssinian mead, the antique 'tedj' of honey and its bouquet of wild African flowers. He had always had mead and Abyssinian food, and I

308

myself much preferred it, for such a reunion. But at the end of the meal he would make a sign with that slight hand of his, and his guests, one by one, would rise and leave, and he would remain sitting there, just as I had seen him sit that long day at Debra Markos when he was dealing with the revulsion of treason in himself and the compulsion to transform the treason alchemically into a new form of loyalty of his people. He had exactly the same air of stillness, of a kind of acceptance in him and indifference to past wrong and frustration, an objective sense of their irrelevance which inevitably amounts to forgiveness and I remember that when I stood at the end of the queue in the great doorway, the last to leave, he was still there, silent, unchanged and at one with himself and the occasion. We would come and go, but he, or rather the symbol he represented, remained for ever.

Not long after that the new missionaries of progress, who had learned the new religion of materialism at our universities, murdered him in the mindless way of the thousands in the world today who cut down great and ancient trees of man without even a sapling to replace them. It is one of the many things that have been allowed to happen, in a time of so-called peace after war, that makes the men who fought the war against what they thought was evil feel betrayed, and wonder how long men will still take to awake and realize that wars have their origin deep in the nature and character of the peace and so-called peace-makers, and not in some special, split-off area of aggression in the much-battered soul and spirit of individual man.

━━━

How much of you is still South African? You told me you recently sold your family farm in the interior.

I am what I have always been. I think property and physical location in the here and now are just like suits of clothes – you may change them, but the body is still the same. I was born a British subject at a time when there was a British Commonwealth. It was a very great reality and I am still that person: I still see the world in those fundamental terms. I feel it is very misleading in one way to talk of white South Africa as European. In the process we are leaving out of our reckoning the impact on us of three centuries of Africa. We are something new. I think I am, to put it symbolically, a white black man, and my black countrymen more and more are black white men. This is where we will find our new dynamic.

You put all your trust and all your hope in the individual man. He is the only one who can take care of the little flame which some day will make a big fire. But problems, crises, conflicts, wars continue to worsen and grow all over the world. They require urgent solutions. How can the individual man or woman have a say and contribute to solutions?

There always remains, of course, the immediate tactical dimension of life where we are compelled to act as best we can through our existing institutions, but in the clear knowledge of the profound change which the wider plan of life, and also the underground plan which is fundamental, demand and which are coming over the whole world. A great deal of what is unreal in the past is slowly being shed, very painfully with a lot of suffering, and I think nations are being compelled more and more to look within themselves. And for the first time in history the whole of the world is, by the day, producing more and more people looking in their own way to make a better world in a present that is pregnant with the future and speeding to the birth of a new world.

Is that why, at the end of your book Yet Being Someone Other, *you said you felt there was a 'Pentecostal spirit' blowing throughout the world?*

Yes, it is one of the signs, and like all fateful signs is apocalyptic as well as redemptive. I think you never get a thrust into the human spirit which is not also accompanied by a thrust into the world without. This introverted thrust of nations and people I am talking about is accompanied by this extrovert thrust into outer space. And as we go farther into space and look down onto the earth, we will see it whole, not fragmented as it appears from here. We have now a universal goal both within and without in which everybody can participate and unite. This, I feel, in the end, will contribute decisively to a united view of human diversities designed not for conflict and fragmentation on earth but to enrich our meaning in a common preparation for our journey to the stars.

━━━━━

I was struck by your remark that if only Smuts had discovered Jung his stature and impact on world affairs would have been immeasurably increased. There was also the point you made about Smuts's essay on 'Holism', and his conclusion that it was the human personality which carried the real charge of creation and change in life; and I remember you stressing how much this impressed Toynbee, the historian, and influenced his Study of History. It seems to me that there are great parallels in your own instinctive approaches, not so much to Smuts but to Jung, in these dimensions. Did it never occur to you that an analysis with Jung would have been a natural consequence of what you are and what you were trying to do? Did you ever discuss this with Jung? Because I get the impression that without analysis one cannot really know what Jungian psychiatry is about.

Yes, of course, I did talk to Jung about it. It was not so much that I felt I had a profound psychological problem myself and did not know how to resolve it, but I had a general feeling that if an analysis could add to my capacity for understanding and coping not only with myself but with the life of my time, it would be criminal not to do so. So I asked Jung one day if he would, as it were, take me on. To my amazement he looked truly taken aback and paused before he asked, 'Why would you want to do an analysis?' I told him at greater length what I have just told you, and said that already there was so much meaning for me in the work he had done that if I could add to my understanding of it and learn more about myself and life, it would be an immense privilege to do an analysis with him.

'But you have your own work to do,' he replied. 'Do you really feel that your work has failed you? Do you really feel that you are in the fire?'

I said that my work, fortunately, had not failed me and that, on the contrary, I had a feeling of re-beginning at last at the real beginning after the war, and that there was nothing specific, like a feeling of being more in the fire than normal, that prompted my request. He looked at me firmly, rather than sternly, and said, 'If ever you feel that your work has failed you come to me and we shall talk about it again.'

That really was the end of the matter. Looking back on the episode, normal as such a request must have been to Jung in the course of a day's work, I think he was glad that I had asked, glad I thought that I had not taken myself for granted, as something not a part of the community of the searching and suffering people who came to him. I think our relationship crossed not a slight impediment so much as a frontier after the question was asked, and our friendship deepened as a result.

But all this brings me to a very important aspect of Jung's character, an aspect that has seemed to me to become clearer as I have grown older. One of the most significant things about Jung is that those of us who knew him fairly intimately have one experience in common: although he died many years ago, and during all that time Jung's great chair has stood empty in the room the years in between have made for us, Jung himself does not recede but becomes nearer and clearer. One of the characteristics that stands out most of all is the lack of doctrine, dogma and preconceived attitudes in his approach to people and life.

It is true that analysis as he practised it had a method, but it was rather the 'method of the rose', which is simply that which enables it to grow and bloom. Freudian analysis has very rigid, inflexible rules. For instance, in Freudian analysis, an umbrella appearing in a dream has only one meaning, and it does not matter what the so-called patient thinks it means to him, the Freudian analyst tells the patient what it has got to mean – or else! In Jungian analysis most important of all are the associations of analysands with the symbols and images that come to them in their dreams. Their dreams are their own most precious possessions and Jung would have thought it sacrilege to lay hands on them and level them to any concept or dogma. He never laid down laws for people to observe, but he created certain everyday rules and a method which provided signposts leading to a climate in which the solution of the patient's problem was more rather than less likely.

And there were very many patients with severe problems to whom Jung never applied his own analytical method. The method in any case for him was less important than the integrity, the insight and the understanding of the analyst and physician: 'Only the wounded physician heals', he would say. Only the physician who went down deep into the patient's suffering and, in a sense, found that area of suffering in himself, succeeded in healing. 'I learned from early on in my work at the Burghölzli Asylum,' he told me once, 'that I could not, and indeed no one could, take his patient further than he had taken himself.' The physician was far more important than the method and, as he was fond of saying, even the right man using the right method at the wrong time produces disastrous results. He had at heart an immense sense of the importance of time in all these things and I think that Hamlet's great cry when he discovered that his time was out of joint, 'The readiness is all!', was at the heart of Jung's seeking, seeking always to be aware of a readiness in things as well as people.

I know many examples of his refusal to use analysis. Most of them are easy to understand, such as the time he recognized that the patient was assailed so seriously by the contents of his own collective unconscious that he could not take any more without a total blackout of what he had of consciousness – the last thing needed was to stir up his unconscious with analysis.

And then there were many people who, without being threatened with total alienation, were just not fit subjects for analysis. He told me, for instance, that the people he found most difficult and often incapable of benefiting from analysis were 'habitual liars and intellectuals'. He said this with a laugh, but without doubt of its application as a general truth.

And then there were many simple people with very little education who came to him in desperate trouble, not because of any intrinsic problem of their own but because what they were and what they had learned of life in their natural context, was rejected by the time in which they lived. I am thinking in particular of a simple peasant girl who everybody thought was going mad. A doctor in some remote valley in the mountains where she lived had heard of Jung and sent her to him. After talking to her for a while Jung realized that analysis would not do for her at all, and yet what else could he do? He watched this nice, plump, simple peasant girl, totally at a loss, and as he watched her, from far far away in his past he heard his mother singing a cradle song. He immediately saw what the girl needed, took her on his lap, cradled her and hummed his mother's song to her – and at once he felt all the tension going out of her, and at the end seated her on the chair again and got her to tell him all about her childhood. In the process they danced some nursery dances together and sang some songs together and played some children's games. At the end of that day he sent her back to her mountains, and did not hear of her again until twenty-five years later at some medical conference. There he met the doctor who had sent the girl to him, and the doctor said to him, 'I have always wanted to ask you what you did to effect that miraculous cure on that unhappy girl I sent to you.' And Jung told me he was most embarrassed because he knew the conventional Swiss doctor would never understand if he told him. But he said, 'All I did was to sing my mother's cradle song to her, play with her a little, dance with her a little, recite some nursery rhymes and listen to some stories, and that was all she needed to recover the honour with herself of which our kind of life had deprived her.'

I remember other similar stories of simple, half-educated Swiss women who came to him and he would ask how they knew of him and they would reply that they had read his books. 'You really mean to say you read those books of mine?' he would ask. And one old lady, who presumably spoke for many, said, 'But of course, Doctor. They are not really books, they are bread.'

When I first went to Zürich I met a very beautiful, slight, frail young girl who was doing an analysis with Jung, who was close on his seventies then. She is still alive, a happy, resolved and distinguished woman today, and only the other day she said to me, 'Looking back on that period I cannot tell you how moved I am still that not for a minute in the three years I worked with Jung did he take me out of my depth or into an area where I could not follow. Not once did he impose himself on me but always was there behind me and my dreams, as it were, in close support.'

I know another very distinguished person who went to Jung for six months and just sat in his presence, totally dumb, not knowing what to say or why she was there. He just talked to her about life and things in general in a way that interested her more and more, and one day the gate opened and she entered, as she said, a totally new world with Jung.

I hope this gives you some understanding of the enormous range and profound humanity of the man and his love, his great objective love of our problematical nature. For me, in this almost total extent to which he achieved a condition of wholeness and objective love, he was one of the greatest religious phenomena of all time. I find myself all day long being aware of him and this nearness which I have mentioned to you. I have hardly ever dreamt about him, perhaps three times in all since he died, and I think it is because I have no need to dream of him. This nearness of which I am speaking is for me almost an objective fact because it manifests itself in so many ways in such extraordinary coincidences, or what he called synchronicities. The last one was only a few weeks ago. I had agreed to do a series of talks at the Jung Institute in Zürich on my experience of primitive psychology. Driving from Zürich in the twilight to the Institute at Küssnacht, which is almost next door to Jung's home, there was a remarkably pure and beautiful afterglow from the sunset. I found myself thinking back without forewarning to Jung's first conscious experience, when he was lying in his pram at nightfall in the garden of his father's vicarage at Laufen within sound and sight of the falls in the great mythological River Rhine. And from somewhere behind him a voice, I think the voice of an aunt, said: 'Oh! Look at the Alps, how lovely the snow . . .' And he had his first experience of those great waves of mountains losing their white in the red and then the black of the night. And from this my imagination went full circle to almost the last conscious thing he did before he died, close to where I was watching the sunset. He was in bed, apparently asleep, and his son was in the room with him because Ruth Bailey, who looked after him with such dedication and care ever since Emma died, had gone out to take the air. Suddenly his son was startled to see he was awake and throwing off his blankets and saying: 'Quick! Help me to the window so that I can see the mountains before Ruth gets back, because she will not allow it!' And so, briefly, he circled the entire vast range of his vision of the earth and came home to where it consciously began. After that he went to bed and never left it alive again.

I had just told my friends in the car this story when we came to the end of our journey, almost at the back of the garden of Jung's old house. As we stepped out of the car in what was now the brown of evening, from one of the great trees between us and the lake suddenly an owl hooted. Everyone was startled and said they had never heard an owl there before. I was more startled perhaps than most, because one of the things I wanted to tell the students was a story of the Bushmen and an owl. It was the story told me by Dorothea Bleek, the daughter of the great Bushman scholar, W. H. Bleek, to whom we owe so much. The day he died the little colony of Bushmen he had established around his house, so that he could study their language and write down their stories, were heartbroken. So were his children, and at sunset they all gathered in his great African kitchen to find comfort in one another's company. Suddenly an owl appeared, fluttering at the kitchen window, and hooted loudly. Bleek's children were all terrified, but the Bushmen started dancing and clapping their hands, singing, 'He has arrived! He has arrived!'

As we walked to the Institute building the owl followed us from treetop to treetop, and for the two and a half hours of my talk continued to hoot so loudly at regular intervals that its voice mingles with my own on the tape-recording. For me there is great comfort and reassurance in this little happening and, above all, its timing, and the certainty which never left me that Jung has arrived at the true destination not only of himself but for us all and all time.

Looking back to your past and putting things in perspective, what are your feelings, your conclusions?

I have no final conclusion I could come to. I think my feelings tend to be what you call religious feelings, without a church, because I do not belong to a church. I could not honestly ever join a church although I believe in churches. I also believe in temples and shrines. Whenever I go to foreign countries, I go and pay my respects to their temples, just as I do in Africa at those little heaps of stones which are the shrines of the Hottentots and the Bushmen. They move me very much, and I will add a stone to them as my contribution. The Hottentots put up these little stone piles to their god, '*Heitsé Eibib*', the god who fights the forces of darkness. This god, they say, goes and fights for the power of light against the forces of the dark, and they say you can see him coming back from battle, bleeding in the red of the dawn, and you hear his voice in the rustling of the wind in the leaves of the trees. Wherever they crossed a river or stream they put down a stone in honour of the god and everybody who came by added a stone to it. The Hottentots have vanished, but these stone piles remain and these Hottentot churches, as I call them, in a strange way move me more than the great cathedrals have done.

And in this feeling memory rounds, and I return to where the first sunset I remember is a rainbow sparkle in a blue bead of a heavy necklace round a slender smooth apricot throat which rises to meet the pointed chin of an oval face, with high cheek-bones and those dark, antique eyes of my beloved Klara, who was the last of her kind who had once been the first in our vast land; and this bead, necklace and face, illuminated with the dawn of human life, are going down with the sun into the dream that was the unconscious of the child I was then, on the rim of sleep. And clasped as with gold to this first recollection, so near – though it was on another evening – that it shared the same mother-of-pearl shell of deep sea meaning, there was the sound of one of the dear Griqua Hottentot voices of the number who were part of my home, and the voice was imperative with a power that was not its own but plenipotentiary because the thunder had just spoken and rumbled across the earth like a *drum*, and it commanded, '*Heitsé*, brothers! Listen! The Old Master speaks!'

And ever since, I believe, I have tried to listen.

INDEX

Abdul Kadir Widjoyoatmodjo, Raden,
    244, 253–4
Abyssinia *see* Ethiopia
Addis Ababa, 127, 306
Adenauer, Konrad, 101
Aeschylus, 291
Afghanistan, 111
Africa: L. van der P.'s attachment to, 6, 8,
    16, 149; and Japan, 8–10; sun in, 10;
    Jung on, 33–4, 120–2; political
    problems, 87–9; colonial inheritance,
    118–19; reaction to L. van der P.'s
    books, 124; stories in, 173; and the
    word, 267–9; pan-Africanism, 301,
    306; *see also* South Africa
African Medical Foundation, 122
Afrikaners, 281–4, 295, 300–1
alchemy, 42–3
Allen, W. E. D., 305
Allenby, Field-Marshal Edmund Henry
    Hynman, 1st Viscount, 258
Ama-Xhosa tribe, 14
Amin, Idi, 111
Amirsjarifoedin *see* Sjharifuddin, Amir S.
animals: L. van der P.'s feeling for,
    13–15, 24; in old age, 15–16; sense of
    smell, 18; Jung on, 25, 33
apartheid, 4, 199–200, 277–8, 280,
    284–6; *see also* South Africa
Apollinaire, Guillaume, 64
Argentina, 52, 96
Ariadne, 75
Aristophanes: *The Frogs*, 289–91
Arthur, King, 171–2
Ashcroft, Dame Peggy, 227
astrology, 43
atheism, 78
Attlee, Clement (*later* 1st Earl), 95,
    244–5, 253; dismisses Wavell, 261
Auchinleck, Field-Marshal Sir Claude,
    260
Auden, W. H., 227
Augustine, St, 71
awareness (consciousness), 144–5

Bailey, Ruth, 315

Barnard, Lady Anne (*née* Lindsay), 233
Baudelaire, Charles: 'Les Phares', 39
Bellinger, Paul, 150n
Ben (guide), 20–2
Bennett, Arnold, 194
Bergamini, David Howland, 265
Bevin, Ernest, 249, 253, 261–3
Biancheri, Boris, xix
Bible, Holy, 8, 171
Bilbao (Spain), 301
Blake, William, 81
Bleek, Dorothea, 315
Bleek, W. H., 315–16
Bloomsbury group, 224–5, 240
Boer, War, 262, 264, 293, 300; *see also*
    Afrikaners; South Africa
Botha, General Louis, 263–4, 293, 295
Botswana (Bechuanaland), 28
Bowes Lyon, Francis, 233
Bowes Lyon, Lilian: friendship with L.
    van der P., 230, 233–7, 240; poetry,
    235–8; death, 239; *The White Hare and
    Other Poems*, 234
Britain: political situation in, 88–96,
    99–100; third party in, 93–4; and
    India, 116–17; reform in, 117; and
    colonization, 118; kinship with Japan,
    145
Britten, Benjamin, 198, 204, 210; *The
    Burning Fiery Furnace*, 212; *Curlew River*
    212; *Gloriana*, 210–11; *The Prodigal
    Son*, 212
Browning, General Sir Frederick Arthur
    Montague ('Boy'), 243
Buddhism, 116, 129
Bullhock (South Africa), 300
Burckhardt, Jacob, 36
Bushmen, 3–5; L. van der P. opposes
    destruction of, 26–9, 31, 159; art, 27;
    in Kalahari, 27, 158; mythology, 30;
    sense of belonging, 30–1; L. van der
    P.'s TV film on, 150; mimicry, 151; and
    intermarriage, 278–9; and owl,
    315–16; stone shrines, 317; *see also*
    Hottentots
Butts, Anthony, 200, 204–7, 232

Italy: in Abyssinian campaign, 259, 302, 306

Jacob's ladder, 76, 79, 83
Jahrr, Soetan S., 135
James, Henry, 173
James, William, 152–3
Janin, General M., 231–2
Janin, René, 197, 199–201, 204–5, 227; described, 230–3; sent to Costa Rica, 237
Japan and Japanese: L. van der P.'s understanding of, 8–9, 56–9, 61–4; and war's end, 50; prison camps, 53–60, 216; cruelty, 61–2; and character of East, 115–16; Christian converts in, 133; in Indonesia, 134–6; surrender, 136–7; and nature, 145; Plomer in, 197–9; Western attitude to, 215–18; and death, 216–17
Java, 53, 55, 57–8, 133–6, 243, 245, 247–9, 256–7
Jesus Christ: Jung and, 43–4, 46; coming of, 81–3; as modern man, 85; on following nature, 141; as artist, 148; and wholeness, 219; on seeing evil, 286
Jews, 169–70
Jinnah, Mohammed Ali, 248
Job, Book of, 66, 80
John, St, 54, 267, 270
John of the Cross, St, 183, 189
John, Augustus, 185
Jonker, Ingrid, 208
Journey into Russia (L. van der P.), 61n
Jung and the Story of Our Time (L. van der P.), 84, 160
Jung, Carl Gustav: friendship with L. van der P., xiii–xv, 37–9, 239, 311–16; L. van der P. speaks on in USA, 4; on 'I' and 'thou', 7, 35; and L. van der P.'s lion nightmare, 22; on plants and animals, 25; on participation mystique, 26; and religion, 29; interest in Africa, 33–5, 120–2; and 'collective unconscious', 34–6; vision, 35; described, and ideas, 37–47, 68, 155, 312–13; and Ingaret, 37, 39, 160–2, 165; death of wife, 38, 154; and Freud, 40–1; on drugs, 41–2; on evil, 45–7; on love, 65–8; and pragmatism and the spiritual, 77; on God, 84; and India, 120–1; on other self, 143; and

paranormal experience, 152–4; and old age and death, 154–5; Swiss background, 167; and 'wholeness', 220; on Russia, 221; and individual, 222–3; on understanding people, 241; on good and evil, 285; declines to analyse L. van der P., 311; analytical approach, 312–14; *Memories, Dreams, Reflections*, 33, 43, 65; *Modern Man in Search of a Soul*, 78
Jung, Emma (C. G.'s wife), 38, 48, 154, 315

Kadir, Abdul *see* Abdul Kadir Widjoyoatmodjo, Raden
Kalahari Desert, 19, 27, 157–9; *see also* Bushmen
Kanchenjunga (mountain), 129
Kaspersen, Thor, 20
Keats, John, 155
Kennedy, John F., 104
Keynes, John Maynard, Baron: *The Economic Consequences of the Peace*, 294
Khama the Great, 14
Kilvert, Rev. Francis, 207
Kipling, Rudyard, 115
Klara (Bushman nurse), 3, 5, 8, 26, 124, 317
Korean War, 51
Kruger, Paul, 292
Kun, Bela, 294

Labour Party (British), 99–100, 261–2
Lambarene, 122–3
Lang, Andrew, 180
language *see* word, the
Laszlo, Philip Alexius de, 232
Lawrence, D. H., xvii, 174–8
Lawrence, Frieda, 175
Lawrence, T. E., 103
League of Nations, 109–10, 293
Lee, General Robert E., 258
Lehmann, Rosamond, 130, 227
Leonardo da Vinci, 75
Lettow-Vorbeck, General Paul von, 293
Lezard, Julian, 240
life after death, 143, 152–4
Lindsay, Lady Jane, 236
lions, 12, 15, 21–2
Logemann, J. H. A., 263
London Magazine, 197
Louis XIV, King of France, 281

322

Steer, George, 301–3
Stelios (restaurateur), 206
Stevenson, Robert Louis, 130
Stirling, David, 113
Stopford, General Sir Montagu George North, 248, 256
Sukarno, Ahmed, 119, 135, 246
Switzerland, xiii–xv, 106, 167–8
synchronicities, 315

Taylor, Jane, 150n
Tennyson, Alfred, Lord, 13
Testament to the Bushmen (L. van der P.: book and TV film), 150n
Texas, 4
Thatcher, Margaret: character and administration, 88–90, 92–3, 95, 98–9; and Falklands war, 96–7; hostility to, 97
Thesiger, Wilfred: Arabian Sands, 304
Thompson, Francis: 'The Hound of Heaven', 145
Thucydides, 108
Tibet, 126–31
time, 125–6
totems, 14
towns see cities and towns
Toynbee, Sir Arnold: Study of History, 294, 311
trade unions, 90, 92
Tyrol, 106

Uganda, 111
United Nations, 28, 109–11, 138–40
United States of America, 104
Upanishads, 116
Urquhart, Brian, 111

van der Post, Emma (L.'s sister), 224
van der Post, Ingaret (L.'s wife): in London, xiv; and Jung, 37, 39, 160–1, 165; and intuition, 126–7; practises psychology, 160–2; poems, 162–5; war work, 165; and Eliots, 182–3; and Britten operas, 210–12; reads to Leonard Woolf, 227
van der Post, Laurens: Pottiez meets, xx–xxi; lion nightmare, 22–3; as prisoner-of-war, 53–60, 133–4, 144, 216, 222; learns and teaches Japanese, 57–8; roots, 143; other (inner) self, 143–4; and future, 149; on writing

books, 149–50, 157; isolation, 156–7; on sense of home, 166–7; reading, 171–3; on Cape Times, 176, 178, 188, 199–200; joins Voorslag, 186; literary and artistic friends, 224–8; as frustrated poet, 235–6; 1945 mission to London, 244, 262; in Abyssinian campaign, 259, 301–2, 305; and the word, 267–70, 273; sense of identity, 309–10; Jung declines to analyse, 311
Venture to the Interior (L. van der P.), 166, 238
Versailles, Treaty of, 294
Voltaire, 29, 182
Voorslag (magazine), 186–7, 197

Waley, Arthur, 224–5
Walpole, Sir Hugh, 200
war, 51–2, 202, 309
Wavell, Field-Marshal Sir Archibald, 133–4, 248, 257–60, 301–2; dismissed, 261; Other Men's Flowers, 257
whales, 20, 25
'White Justice' (newspaper article), 178, 188
White Victor, 41, 45
Whitman, Walt, 292–3
wildernesses, 139–42
Wilhelm I, Kaiser, 36
Wilhelmina, Queen of the Netherlands 203
Wilson, Harold, Baron, 138
Wingate, General Orde, 271, 308
Wolfe, Teddy, 193–4
women's lib, 221
Wood, Sir Michael and Sue, Lady, 122–3
Woolf, Leonard, 225–7; The Village in the Jungle, 226
Woolf, Virginia, 225–7, 240
word, the (language), 267–73
Wordsworth, William, 76–7
World Council of Churches, 119
World War I, 51–2
World War II, 49–52; effect on Plomer, 202–3
World Wilderness Foundation, 139, 289

Yet Being Someone Other (L. van der P.), 133, 187n, 197n, 214, 310
Yevtushenko, Yevgeniy, 147
yin and yang, 73, 76

DATE DUE

Demco, Inc. 38-293